# GROWING BEYOND EMOTIONAL PAIN

## Action Plans For Healing

# DR. JOHN PRESTON

*Impact* Publishers®

SAN LUIS OBISPO, CALIFORNIA 93406

*Library of Congress Cataloging-in-Publication Data*

Preston, John, 1950-
   Growing beyond emotional pain : action plans for healing / John
Preston.
      p.   cm.
   Includes bibliographical references and index.
   ISBN 0-915166-78-X
   1. Adjustment (Psychology)   2. Interpersonal conflict.
3. Conflict management.   4. Problem solving--Psychological aspects.
5. Psychotherapy.     I. Title.
BF335.P74     1993
152.4--dc20                                          93-3212
                                                        CIP

Cover design and illustrations by Sharon Schnare, San Luis Obispo, California
Printed in the United States of America

Published by ***Impact Publishers***®
                POST OFFICE BOX 1094
          SAN LUIS OBISPO, CALIFORNIA 93406

# CONTENTS

# PART III: ACTION PLANS FOR HEALING

# APPENDICES:

# *Acknowledgements*

This is typically the part of a book rarely noticed by most readers, but for those whose names appear below — my heartfelt thanks. I hope the messages in this book may touch the lives of many people; each of you in various ways has helped make this possible.

First I should like to thank the following friends, colleagues and teachers. Your ideas, your support, your criticisms and your compassion have had a tremendous impact on the development of my thinking about emotional healing: Drs. Dennis McCracken, Mac Sterling, John O'Neal, John Kohls, Douglas Hooker, Rev. Larry George and psychotherapist and fiddler, Jim Doak.

One of the greatest blessings I have received is to join with my psychotherapy clients in helping them to discover, to heal and to grow. The most important lessons I've learned regarding emotional healing have come from you.

I want to give special thanks to two friends who agreed to read the manuscript: Sandy Duveneck and Dr. Cliff Straehley. Your ideas were tremendously helpful and you had the remarkable gift of honesty in giving me much needed feedback. To the Wet Ink women who all contributed in the preparation of the manuscript: Desiree Zweigle (!), Janice Rosenthal and Laurie Barrall — thanks! And as always, I want to acknowledge the support and guidance of my publisher/editor, Dr. Robert Alberti.

Finally, special thanks to two special women — my sister and a major support during the past years, Suzi Camferdam. And to my wife and best friend, Dr. Bonnie Preston... Bonnie, this really is your book too. Thanks for everything.

— J.P.
1993

## *Sooner or Later, Everybody Feels the Pain*

*T*he young woman had tears in her eyes when I took my seat next to her. I had just boarded an airliner bound for Little Rock, and my teenage seatmate was visibly upset. She eventually told me that she was on her way to college, 2000 miles away from home — and 2000 miles away from her boyfriend. With sadness in her voice, she said, "I don't know if I'll be able to stand it."

At that moment, I was thinking, "I don't think I'll be able to stand it, either." Listening to her, but mainly preoccupied with my own worries, I was on my way to visit my father, who was in the latter stages of his struggle with cancer. "I'm a fairly mature guy... I'm a therapist. I know how to handle these things," I thought to myself. But I also knew that this was the scariest, saddest event of my life. I could hardly stand to picture myself sitting beside my father feeling his fear and pain. At that moment, I honestly wondered if I could make it through this extremely difficult time. Knowing that others live through these events and survive did absolutely nothing to comfort me or quiet my pain.

Five years of graduate school, many classes in human emotions and behavior, even nineteen years as a psychotherapist hadn't fully prepared me. When faced with my own extremely difficult emotional crisis, I wondered, "Will I make it? I feel overwhelmed. What should I do?"

So many people think these same thoughts at times of great emotional stress. Wouldn't having some possible answers or solutions or a guide through these times be helpful? I wondered, "Does this young woman next to me know what to do with her sadness?" Here we were traveling on the same airliner and both in pain.

Like my teenage seatmate and me, every human being sooner or later will live through at least some times of great emotional distress. Different people manage this distress in very different ways. In many cultures across the eons, some people have turned to "experts" for help: physicians, holy men, gurus and therapists. In my lifetime, psychotherapy has evolved from a form of treatment for people who are "insane" with its negative stigma, to an acceptable — even popular — experience to which many people now turn for help. Yet the truth is that most people who go through very difficult times do not seek psychotherapy. They do their best on their own.

Many times people trying to do their best to live through difficult times actually experience multiple sources of emotional pain. Probably the most common experience shared by most of the people I've counseled during my two decades as a practicing psychotherapist is the perception that they shouldn't feel the way they do: "There is something terribly wrong with me... I feel crazy... I shouldn't feel this way... These feelings aren't normal." This human misery is often compounded by a perception that "I am utterly alone with this experience." The events of their lives are unique to them and isolate them. In addition, for a number of reasons, they're convinced that others do not understand. Some people encounter terribly painful events for which they blame themselves or for which they harbor a deep sense of shame. The mere thought of revealing the secret results in fears of condemnation, rejection or abandonment by others. They keep the truth of the painful events locked inside. Other people may have been directly or indirectly told to keep quiet.

(This is often times the case in instances of child sexual abuse.) To speak of the forbidden events may result in physical violence, shaming, or even the destruction of the family.

Most of us who have lived through an awful experience have heard "advice" from others who either can't truly relate to the experience, or who are strongly motivated to deny that there even is a problem: "Don't let it get to you," "Put it behind you," "You'll get over it," "Is it still bothering you?!" Most people, myself included, find little real comfort in these platitudes. Such comments may lead us to conclude that we are inadequate, weak, bad, or mentally ill. In the words of William Talley, M.D., lots of people begin to think that they are "sinners, wimps, or fools."

In general, people are motivated to deny the personal reality of many emotionally traumatic events. On one level, everyone acknowledges that people do die, get fired, go through divorces, contract cancer; that children are abused and atrocities are committed. But on another level, the inner belief is that "it happens to others; it will never happen to me." Getting away from awful experiences, or even the thoughts about such events, makes sense. It's a way to maintain a sense of "safety" in day-to-day life. But encountering a society or social network that denies the reality of our pain doesn't help when bad things happen to us. The result is an increased sense of alienation and aloneness. A concerned friend may say "I understand," and is trying to be sympathetic but without being truly understanding. Shallow or phony expressions of understanding can result in an increased sense of isolation. One woman I know who lost her son, said, "How can they know how I feel? They have their children! How can they really know how I feel? They've never really listened to me talk about my sadness... my loss... my boy."

All emotional pain is considerably more intense when it must be experienced alone. One of the really valuable healing experiences happening in the course of psychotherapy is the decreased isolation and estrangement that come from confiding in another human being. This change is often dramatic in group therapies or support groups when group members begin to share their experiences and start to learn that they are not alone. One of the tremendous benefits of the various self-help programs (e.g., Adult Children of Alcoholics, Emotions Anonymous, bereavement support groups, etc.) is this sharing of common human experiences. This sharing also happens naturally in the context of close, intimate friendships and in healthy families where people turn to one another and talk about their pain. The very first step to take in emotional healing is to become aware of and to acknowledge that, "This is human stuff... I sure don't have to like it, but it's real, it's normal and it matters." You are not alone in your pain.

Let's take a brief look at the lives of four people* who've gone through some very rough experiences.

### Sharon

Sharon described her early life in a word: "lonely." Her parents were very caught up in their work and rarely even noticed if she entered the room. She recalls sitting for hours alone in her room, reading or staring at the television set. Her dream throughout junior and senior high school was to fall in love and get married, to have children, and — most of all — to escape her sense of aloneness. She met Tim in college, fell in love, and got married at the age of twenty-two. Since then it's been hard for Sharon and Tim to spend much quality time together. At first it was law school that consumed Tim's time. Then it was studying for the bar exams, and now he's trying to make it in a law firm. They "might" have children once Tim is established, but in the meantime, it seems that one thing after another has "come up." Married for nine years now, Sharon is realizing that she's still alone... she's not happy... there's no end in sight. Lately she's gained weight, sleeps a lot and feels empty.

### Dale

Dale's wife Joyce died three months ago in an automobile accident. They had been married for twenty-three years. "She was my whole life," he exclaims. Every day he cries. At night he sometimes reaches for her in bed only to find that she's not there. Once recently

---

*Note: All people mentioned in this book in basic ways represent actual people, but names and details have been changed to maintain confidentiality.*

he thought he smelled her perfume in his home, only to have a moment of hopefulness give way to a wave of grief. His good friends tell him, "You look like you're doing o.k.," yet in the privacy of his thoughts he knows he's not doing well at all. He fakes enthusiasm at work, but his life seems meaningless, and he misses Joyce so much.

<u>Katherine</u>

Katherine would have told anyone that her childhood was "happy and normal" even though she didn't remember much about being a kid. During the past six months, things have changed. At thirty-six, Katherine has started to recall episodes of severe abuse and sexual molestation when she was 6 or 7 years old. For several months she was molested by a man in her neighborhood. Almost every day now her mind seems flooded with overwhelming, painful memories.

<u>Gary</u>

It's been three months since Gary's surgery for cancer of the bladder. The doctors told him they "got it all," but that it could recur. Everyone says, "Oh, you're so lucky... You should be so thankful." Gary doesn't feel thankful at all. Every day he is preoccupied with the fear that the cancer could return. "I feel as if I'm carrying around a time bomb inside of me." He is consumed by worries and recurring nightmares.

These are sad and difficult situations. The life experiences of Sharon, Dale, Katherine and Gary are quite different, yet each of them is plagued by some form of significant emotional despair. They can't just ignore it — their feelings are dominating their lives. These are not cases of mental illness, but examples of ordinary human beings living through painful times. Despite their differences, these four people fortunately all share one vitally important human quality: to a greater or lesser degree, all human beings have an inherent capacity to heal from deep emotional wounds.

Perhaps a metaphor more vividly captures certain aspects of the process of emotional healing: embarking on a journey. In pioneer days, before starting on a journey into uncharted territory, travelers knew they needed to take steps to assure their survival. Even though the hazards of the road ahead were unknown, the chances of success were increased if the pioneers knew something about the process. Loading up adequate supplies, planning a realistic pace of travel, and having strategies to handle unforeseen troubles increased the odds of survival and success. The pioneer travelers talked with scouts who had gone before and returned to describe the new territory. To avoid being caught completely by surprise, travelers learned all they could about potential difficulties likely to confront them.

In this book, I've attempted to give you that kind of "advance map of the territory" to help you prepare for the journey of growth beyond emotional pain. I've written this book to share some of what has been learned about human emotions and emotional healing, to separate fact from fiction. (There's a lot of fiction out there these days!) The material in this book comes from numerous sources but is drawn primarily from a large body of sound scientific research in psychology. I hope to help you more fully understand human emotional reactions and, perhaps more important, to look very specifically at ways to help yourself get through difficult times. And, along the way, we'll see how each of our four "example people" — like you, human beings with the capacity to heal — took action that helped them to deal with and grow beyond their emotional pain.

In Part I, we'll take a close look at an array of stressful and emotionally-trying life circumstances. Becoming acquainted with the complex nature of stressful events will give you a decided advantage in coping with difficult times.

In Part II, we'll examine the basics of human needs and emotions. This foundation helps set the stage for understanding how the human mind responds to stressful life events.

Part III will guide you on the growth journey itself. How do people make it through hard times? What approaches, action plans, and strategies will help you reduce risks, minimize disaster, and yet make progress toward your destination? These final chapters cover the nuts and bolts of emotional healing processes, including specific actions which have been found most helpful to people who have successfully navigated their ways through difficult times in life. These strategies and actions are neither specific prescriptions nor quick fixes, but they do represent general guidelines that can make a real difference.

Pioneers who move into new lands always encounter tremendous perils and obstacles, and yet somehow they persevere. Although the challenges of geographic frontiers have been conquered — even beyond the earth — most human beings will continue to confront times of painful emotional distress. By calling on natural, internal resources for emotional healing, by traveling in the company of supportive friends and/or family, and often by getting help from a guide (therapist), most of us can discover inner strengths and capacities not only to survive, but also to grow and to thrive on the journey.

As you read this book, you'll be learning much about the pathways already established with the help of ideas and guidance I'll share with you. But I want to acknowledge and honor the fact that you must find your own pace and create your own path — carve out your own way — as you make your journey. You will learn about people who are living through painful experiences that may be similar to your own. Parts of the book may be emotionally difficult to read. But there is realistic hope that you, like them, *can* make it through very difficult experiences.

Indeed, life is often hard. The task, as I see it, is not only to survive, but also to live through the hard times and emerge with the desire to continue living and growing. Let's begin the journey of *growing beyond emotional pain.*

# PART I:
# WHEN LIVING HURTS

## One

# What Is Emotional Distress, Anyway?

$Y$ou're stopped at a red light behind another car. The light turns green, and the man ahead of you doesn't move. You wait a few seconds, then honk your horn and think, "What's wrong with this guy?" You feel irritated and call him a jerk. Would your view of him be different if you knew he had just found out that his son has leukemia, and he is extremely worried and preoccupied? Of course it would. Knowing the context puts the situation in a different light. You may still feel irritated because he is inconveniencing you, but your experience of this man as a person would likely be vastly different. His behavior would begin to make sense to you because he's attending more to his own pain than to a traffic light. Now he's not a jerk, but a deeply worried man, and you'd feel compassion for him.

### Judging and Understanding

Your two perceptions of the man at the red light — one based on judgement, the other on understanding — show the two main ways people can look at a situation. "Judging" generally involves some sort of comparison; for instance, noting that one person weighs *more than* another person. Many, if not most times, judging also involves attaching value. Jim has a *better* job than Robert, and thus in some ways Jim is *better* (or at least better off). This valuing aspect has to do with opinions about what is right or wrong, good or bad, desirable or undesirable. The other major perspective is "understanding." This is a way of looking at the world in which a person gathers some facts and then draws conclusions, such as, "Well, this makes sense to me," or "This is understandable." The understanding perspective is less critical and less judgemental. It is a way of putting together facts or observations and making sense of an experience without making a judgement about good vs. bad.

I believe strongly that a good deal of emotional pain results from viewing ourselves and others through judging eyes: "That guy is really screwed up." "She's too sensitive." "He's so neurotic!" "What's the matter with her? Why is she taking things so personally?" These kinds of statements are more than mere observations; they are critical judgements of other people. Buried in each statement is a non-acceptance of the other. Such statements are common and may be seen as very human ways to react toward others. However, such ways of viewing others (or yourself) are simply not helpful.

A good deal of emotional suffering is made worse by people's sitting in judgement of others, sometimes simply because of limited information. And it is just as common for people to direct judgement toward *themselves,* (e.g., "What's wrong with me?! Why am I letting this get to me? I've gotta snap out of this."). This kind of self-damning almost never helps a person cope or heal emotionally. This is a point that we will come back to throughout this book. In fact, one of my major goals in writing this book is to help you understand the common human processes of emotional and psychological healing. A lack of understanding is the cause of untold stress in our lives, while developing a sense of compassion and understanding for yourself and others is at the heart of the healing process.

### How Much Does It Hurt?

The term "stressor" has been used widely to label an event that puts pressure on a person to cope, adapt or take action. Stressors are not necessarily negative events. Many times stressors can be seen as the ordinary demands of daily life: picking the kids up from school, cleaning the bathroom, depositing a check. Some stressors are actually positive experiences, such as getting a raise or falling in love, while others are clearly unpleasant, frustrating or painful.

Several factors are important in understanding how stressors can lead to emotional distress. The first has to do with how many sources of stress are there and the fact that stressors are cumulative and additive. The more stressors you encounter during any one period of time, the greater is the demand placed on you to cope. It is quite common to have a period of time, let's say a few months or a couple of years, in which you encounter an excessive number of stressors. Maybe generally you are a well-adjusted person. However, everyone has a certain limit to the number of stressors that are manageable at one time. With an overload of stressors, almost anyone can begin to feel overwhelmed. Your usual means of coping become taxed, and you may develop physical and/or emotional symptoms — e.g., fatigue, headaches, insomnia, irritability or tension, to mention a few.

### Stress and Distress

A second factor has to do with your perception of competence in managing the stressors. A person who is encountering a good deal of stress in life and yet solidly believes, "I'm handling this... I'm making a dent in it... " or "I can see the light at the end of the tunnel..." may feel pressured or stressed to a degree, but generally can cope well without developing marked stress-related symptoms. The perception of having control over stressors and of confidence in the ability to manage the demands in a potent way keeps people afloat. For such people, stressful events may even be seen as "challenges" or opportunities for new growth.

However, a lack of confidence or sense of powerlessness in the face of stressful events often can lead to tremendous emotional despair and ineffective coping. Some events are truly beyond a person's control (extreme poverty, physical handicaps, a child who is being severely abused). At times, people are simply bombarded by too many stressors at a given time. And finally, others may have grown up in a way in which they never learned effective coping skills. Psychologist Martin Seligman* has identified the concept of "learned helplessness," which demonstrates that a person who repeatedly experiences a highly stressful situation and is totally unable to reduce or escape the stress will, at some point, appear to collapse emotionally. The person will at first mount a number of attempts to cope with the stressors, but when all attempts repeatedly fail, will give up. She has learned, "No matter what I do, it won't help." The result is an ever-increasing state of hopelessness, withdrawal and depression.

### *Stressors + Lack of Confidence in One's Ability To Cope = Distress*

Not all events are equally intense. Many situations are stressful but ultimately manageable. Some events are extremely intense and are deemed "traumatic." Psychiatrist Lenore Terr defines trauma as "the mental results of one sudden external blow or a series of blows, rendering the... person temporarily helpless and breaking past ordinary coping and defensive operations." A time of *crisis* occurs when one encounters especially stressful events; such experiences can be called *trauma* when the person is rendered helpless or has the perception of extreme powerlessness. Here again, the key element — helplessness/powerlessness — is a crucial feature of situations that are experienced as "traumatic."

### *Overwhelming Stressors + Perception of Extreme Powerlessness = Trauma or Crisis*

Some traumatic events (or crises) occur during a limited period of time, while others, unfortunately, can be quite prolonged. The duration of very intense stress plays an important role in the emergence of stress-related symptoms and at times the evolution of long-lasting, maladaptive personality traits.

---

*The work of professionals referred to in the text may be found in the References on pages 275-282.

### How Long Does It Hurt?

There is an important relationship between the intensity of stressful events and their duration. This relationship is illustrated in Figure 1-A.

Figure 1-A

INTENSITY

| | | MILD | MODERATE | SEVERE |
|---|---|---|---|---|
| **D U R A T I O N** | BRIEF | a. | b. | c.<br>Single-blow Traumas |
| | PROLONGED | b. | c.<br>Pervasive Emotionally-toxic Experiences | d.<br>Recurring Traumas |

a. Not likely to create lasting problems.
b. May result in lasting emotional distress depending on the person's "stress-resistance" and social buffers (see below).
c. Probability of lasting emotional distress.
d. Very likely to cause lasting emotional distress.

One type of emotional crisis results from a single, sudden, unexpected traumatic event. Examples of this might include the death of a child, an industrial or automobile accident, a heart attack, being robbed or raped. Some "single-blow" traumas are brief and discrete events; although they can evoke tremendous emotional pain that lasts a long time, they are not repeated events. Recurring traumas, conversely, are "long-standing, repeated ordeals," such as repeated child abuse/molestation, on-going physical/emotional abuse by a spouse, confinement and torture in a concentration camp, on-going experiences of near-starvation such as those experienced by many impoverished and homeless people. In recurring traumas, the original emotional wound does not heal, in large part because of on-going repeated injuries and an ever present worry: "When will it happen again?"

Somewhere between single-blow and recurring traumas are those very painful events — the single blows — that leave more than emotional scars. Examples of this include disfiguring injuries; accidents or illnesses that result in significant, on-going pain; the loss of a parent, which results in the family subsequently collapsing into a state of poverty.

Pervasive emotionally-toxic experiences (P.E.T.) is a term I like to use to identify very prolonged, fairly serious emotionally damaging life experiences. These conditions would include, for example, living with a parent who is continuously belittling and very critical, or cold and non-loving, or living in a family where the father has died and the mother (although a loving person) is not emotionally available to her children because of severe depression. The differences between recurring trauma and P.E.T. have a lot to do with the severity of emotional injury and the presence or absence of positive social supports. Let's take a look at this last point in some detail.

The availability of *alternate social supports* — extended family, friends, neighborhood, school, church, community groups or agencies — is a very important factor which may serve as a sort of buffer to protect people during times of significant stress. Let's consider the example of a very difficult life experience: the loss of a parent. The emotional survival of a child who suffers the loss of a parent through death depends on many things. But possibly the most important asset is the presence of other loving and caring people to provide nurturance, support and protection. Children who live through extremely painful life experiences and yet go on to grow and thrive often have been blessed with the presence of at least one loving adult in their early lives. Extreme losses or trauma can be survived when they are balanced with lots of love and support.

A number of my friends and psychotherapy patients were exposed to God-awful events as children, and by all rights ought either to be psychotic or completely psychologically devastated, yet survived emotionally. They certainly bore the scars and pain of the events, but they were alive and capable of being in the world and loving others. How come? Most times it turns out that they had one person, perhaps a parent, a brother, a grandmother... someone to whom they turned, a person who was there for them and who cared

Strong connections with others can be a tremendously important resource in times of stress or tragedy during adult life also. Emotional healing and physical health have been shown to be enhanced by such meaningful connections. Mortality rates, suicides, and mental illness are all higher in groups of people who are loners or isolated, including those who are single, widowed or divorced. Communities with strong bonds and social networks (e.g., churches, support groups, etc.) show enhanced disease resistance and lower rates of depression. After devastating illnesses or injuries, such as severe brain injury, the quality of social supports may be more important to the patient's eventual outcome than other factors such as physical therapy or rehabilitation programs. Some people are fortunate enough to already have such social supports in their lives. Others find it tremendously helpful to seek out connection with others during stressful times (e.g., a support group, a church, or therapist).

The *time of life* during which stressful or traumatic events occur can be a crucial issue in understanding the impact of the event. A profound rejection of a young child by her parents can grossly interfere with her personality development. If such an event occurs when the child is only one year old, there might be life-long difficulties with intimacy and attachment. The girl may, as a young woman, find it tremendously difficult and scary to open up and form close relations with others. In contrast, significant rejection in a relationship can result in a good deal of sadness for a thirty-five-year-old man, yet it is *much* less likely to completely derail his desire to seek out other companions.

Finally, *emotional sensitivity* varies tremendously among individuals. People don't respond to stressful life events in the same ways. Their differing responses may be rooted in variations of human biology and most certainly are influenced by the effects of early psychological development. If nature, nurture and fate have been good to you, you may have the blessing of emotional strength and resiliency. If not, there is much you can do to heal and to grow (topics which will be addressed in Part III of this book).

As is apparent by now, a multitude of factors have great bearing on how people come to experience difficult aspects of living. As a therapist, I often wonder if it is really possible to truly know another person's pain. I can certainly appreciate how people react when they hear others superficially comment, "I understand how you feel." The complexity of human emotions makes the process of navigating a journey of emotional recovery more challenging. However, interwoven in that complexity are many potentials and strengths which can help vitalize the process of healing.

## Two

## *Childhood Pain: When It Hurts to Grow Up*

*G*rowing up can be hazardous — and painful.

The damaging effects of nature, nurture and fate affect countless thousands of children. At times, these result from conditions that are largely beyond the individual's control (e.g., the child with severe epilepsy or other disabilities, the loss of a parent in an automobile accident, homelessness, wide-spread famine and starvation). In other cases, emotional deprivation or neglect may be an outcome of severe social/economic problems, (e.g., poverty, racial discrimination, overpopulation). Abuse or neglect may stem from a parent's own problems, such as mental illness or drug addiction. And at times tremendous suffering is produced at the hands of people consumed by — no better way to say it — evil.

In 1989, estimates the National Association for Prevention of Child Abuse, 2.4 million children were referred to child protective service agencies in the United States (49% for neglect, 27% for physical abuse, 16% for sexual abuse, and 8% for emotional abuse). And the 2.4 million represent only those cases reported. Importantly, the available evidence suggests that false allegations of child abuse/neglect are infrequent — only 8% according to one major study. Clearly many, many children are abused and/or neglected and never come to the attention of the authorities. A number of studies estimate that as many as 33% of all women were sexually molested in some manner as children or adolescents, and one out of every six or seven men were victims of sexual abuse. Some authorities claim these staggering figures likely represent an under-estimate of the actual incidence of child abuse/neglect.

### How Harmful Is Childhood Trauma?

Emotionally damaging experiences take a heavy toll on a child. How heavy a toll depends on a number of conditions (some of which were addressed in Chapter 1). I would like to briefly highlight the most important of these conditions by posing the following five questions.

1. *Is the painful event a single blow or a recurring/pervasive experience?* Unless extremely severe, the single blow traumas generally do not change the course of a person's emotional life. In contrast, recurring or pervasive experiences gradually mold and give shape to a child's emerging personality. If the day-in, day-out experiences are negative, the painful effects can be deeply etched into a child's view of the world, her attitudes toward others, and enduring beliefs about herself.

2. *Does the painful event also undercut or destroy a child's primary support network?* For example, sexual molestation by a neighborhood boy, although quite traumatizing to a child, is probably less damaging than molestation by a parent. In the latter case, in addition to the severe emotional injury of the molestation, the child also is faced with a situation in which the primary giver of care and protection has now become a victimizer. The child's most natural source of safety and nurturance is no longer available and is indeed the *cause* of extreme emotional distress.

3. *How traumatic is the painful event?* It would be convenient to be able to rate severity of events in a clear, quantifiable manner such as is done in rating the intensity of earthquakes. However, what matters most is not the event per se, but how the child perceives the event, i.e., the particular meaning of the event to the child experiencing it. A 7.0 earthquake centered in downtown San Francisco is

infinitely more destructive than another 7.0 earthquake occurring in a remote wilderness area. To use an example offered by Psychiatrist James Garbarino, children seriously hurt in auto accidents or sporting events experience much less emotional trauma than if the same degree of physical injury were inflicted by an abusing parent.

When we look at types of emotional pain later in this chapter, in each instance we must bear in mind that there are varying degrees of severity associated with painful life events, and determining the severity is often incredibly hard to do. There are undoubtedly some rare children who live through hellish experiences and truly bear few scars. At the same time, some more sensitive kids will experience fairly mild levels of neglect as being overwhelmingly traumatic. The magnitude and meaning of emotional stress is *always* based on the child's perception.

4. *To what degree has the emotionally painful event resulted in rather massive personality changes?* The basic core of emotional pain is bad enough, but some events (especially if pervasive, long-lasting, and/or severe) can lead to marked changes in self-concept, negative perceptions about the world, and altered lifestyles. Generally speaking, the earlier in life one encounters pervasive or severe trauma, the more likely that the events may alter subsequent personality development.

5. *What resources does the child have to turn to in times of distress?* Intact families, open expression of feelings and nurturance, and appropriate role models of healthy emotional functioning can make a crucial difference as a child attempts to heal and recover following major stressful events.

### Traumas that Derail Human Attachment

Some types of emotional trauma have an impact on the natural human tendency to seek out connections with others. The desire to bond with others — to reach out for support, help and companionship — is part of our emotional hardware, our "psychological make-up." Psychoanalyst Karen Horney called it the tendency to "move toward others." It takes something powerful and devastating to extinguish this very human tendency. *Extremely* traumatic experiences early in life will sometimes derail the natural tendency for attachment. Horney described two outcomes of such painful experiences: the first is "moving away from others." There are people who, at a deep level, may want contact with others, but who are extremely afraid of intimacy, openness or attachment. Such people are discussed in the psychiatric literature as "avoidant personalities." Even more severely damaged people are "schizoid personalities" — people who may have had even the tiniest flicker of need for human connections totally extinguished.

Interestingly, some of the same kinds of horrible experiences early in life that lead to avoidant or schizoid lifestyles may, in some people, provoke the development of a style Horney calls "moving against." These people have decided at a deep level that "people are no good and can only serve one purpose: to meet my needs." Narcissistic individuals, as they are called, treat people like a can of beer: they suck them dry and without a second thought, cast them aside. Psychopaths are the even-more-malignant version of this style. These people thrive on creating pain. They derive enjoyment by hurting others. Such people, in relatively benign forms, are con-artists; in the extreme, they are people who commit violent rape, murder and sadistic torture. It should be noted that, although these types of personality disorders can develop as a result of extremely painful life experiences, some theorists also suggest that these behavior patterns may be due to inherent temperamental and/or biochemical factors.

Here is a final question to add to the list of five above: *To what extent have childhood traumas extinguished the desire to move toward others?* As we shall see, meaningful contact with another human being can be a major component of successful emotional healing. In a trusting and supportive human encounter — with a relative, a friend, a clergyperson, or a therapist — we can find our best chance of movement toward recovery. When the desire to connect has been totally lost, the prospects for emotional healing are extremely poor. Schizoid and psychopathic people rarely enter psychotherapy. But even if there is only a faint hint of desire for human connection, there is hope.

## Is It Abuse... or Not?

A variety of (unfortunately) common types of emotional pain can occur during childhood. As we move into this material, you need to know that the pages you read may touch on your own inner emotional pain. Sometimes it's helpful or necessary to face painful feelings, but "dosing" the exposure is an important way of taking care of yourself. When I've presented this material in workshops, it has clearly evoked strong feelings, and I want to suggest, if this is the case for you, that you please seek out someone you trust to talk with about what you are feeling.

A multitude of potentially damaging events befall children. A number of these are examples of "man's inhumanity to man." Distinctions among blatant child abuse, mental injuries and neglect are often blurry and ill-defined. Child protection agencies are many times at a loss to clearly identify cases of emotional abuse that leave invisible injuries to the heart and the spirit of a child, but no physical bruises. Garbarino and his colleagues have suggested the term "psychological maltreatment" to describe a wide array of experiences that damage children. Some types of psychological maltreatment are of an active nature, willful, intentional abuse of children. Others are more passive (e.g., a child is ignored) or quite unintentional (e.g., a child is emotionally neglected because her mother is bedridden with a severe illness or a major depression). This discussion will focus on the nature and meaning of the events, rather than attempting to blame or judge (although some types of abuse absolutely are the result of cruel, intentional brutality). It should be borne in mind that, while certain factors may play a role in contributing to child abuse (e.g., a parent's mental illness or alcoholism), and may be at least partial *explanations,* they do not in any way constitute *excuses* for such mistreatment of children.

The following section presents eleven categories of psychological maltreatment (the first five of which have been suggested by Garbarino and his colleagues). It is important to emphasize that in all families, even those considered to be healthy and growth-promoting, occasional emotional distress is the rule. Even the best of parents are, from time to time, preoccupied — ignoring their children's needs, stressed-out, irritable, and prone to making blunders in dealing with the difficult job of raising children. Occasional times of emotional upset absolutely do not constitute maltreatment or abuse. Children must grow up knowing that life is not always rosy. And learning how to live through stressful times is an essential experience as a child comes to develop coping skills and emotional resilience. Maltreatment occurs when one of two conditions are met. First, it is "a concerted attack by an adult on a child's development of self and social competence, a *pattern* of psychologically destructive behavior." The key word is "pattern." It is typically on-going mistreatment; if a "single blow," it is a tremendously intense or severe event. Second, there is a significant lack of essential nurturing, support, respect, guidance and protection provided by a parent.

### *Types of Psychological Maltreatment*

**Rejecting:** The child is actively shunned. "The parent refuses to acknowledge the child's worth and the legitimacy of the child's needs." Parents may refuse to touch or hold their children; they may exclude children from family activities or fail to acknowledge accomplishments. In more severe instances, there can be clear-cut emotional abandonment or a strong message given to the child: "I hate you."

Gretchen, a woman whom I treated, was at a loss to understand why she felt so terribly depressed throughout childhood. She searched her memories and was totally unable to recall any episodes of physical abuse, sexual molestation or severe loss. However, very gradually she realized that in her apparently normal, happy, conventional family, she had continuously felt left out. During the course of therapy, she gradually came to recall and understand that, in a very deep way, her parents hated her. They took no interest in her school work, they belittled her art, and they repeatedly told her she was "too sensitive," "too emotional." Gretchen developed a pervasive sense of worthlessness and unlovability. Until she put the pieces together, she could not understand the nature of her despair.

People often think they must be able to point toward very clear and concrete signs of abuse (e.g., physical bruises or sexual abuse) in order to believe it's legitimate to feel bad. Profound rejection, belittling and harsh criticism can be tremendously painful experiences for a young child. The poet Robert Bly has said "...verbal batterings are injuries. Blows that lacerate self-esteem, puncture our sense of grandeur, pollute enthusiasm, poison and desolate confidence, give the soul black-and-blue marks, undermining and degrading... these all make a defilement. They damage and do harm."

**Ignoring:** Rather than an active process, as is the case with rejecting, ignoring has more to do with unavailability; it is passive and neglectful. Ignoring can occur for a number of reasons. In some instances, a child may be temperamentally quiet, passive and non-demanding. Such kids have the same inner needs for love and closeness as do other children, but their needs are less evident — they are less inclined to demand attention. They may seem relatively content and thus can fairly easily fade into the background, becoming increasingly less a part of the parents' lives.

---

Sharon

"I keep remembering my mother say, "In a minute." I'd go to her, she'd wave me off... the minute never came. She was just so busy. I think sometimes she felt guilty. She'd say, "I'm sorry... I know I need to spend more time with you." But she didn't. I was just incredibly lonely.

I had a fantasy that there were these wonderful people who adopted me. And we spent evenings together sitting by the fire with my make-believe Dad reading to me. I know it sounds kind of silly, but now I understand why that daydream felt good, and why it sometimes made me cry."

---

### Parental Narcissism

All parents will, from time to time, become wrapped up in their own needs. Dealing with personal stresses, forced to work extra to make ends meet, being preoccupied with careers... all of these life events will almost inevitably take the parents' focus off their children and onto themselves. To a degree this is not only natural, but also necessary for parents and children alike. Kids need to realize that the world doesn't revolve around them and that others have needs, too. Parents need time for themselves. However, in some instances, the parents' own egocentric focus can come to dominate the experience of the young child. Egocentrism and self-centeredness taken to the extreme are sometimes referred to as *narcissism*. Day-in, day-out, children of narcissistic parents may re-experience the reality that in the hearts and minds of their parents, they hold little place of true value.

Narcissism can certainly contribute to the child's experience of being ignored and, in the extreme, can leave deep emotional scars on the developing child. The child's impression is "I'm not worth it." All kids want to feel that they matter. The words "I love you" have little power to undo the truth of always being left out; the *reality* of little genuine love or connection is what kids notice most. Sharon recalls that as early as the age of seven, her parents never gave her a birthday present; they would always give her money. They explained, "Oh, we want you to choose your own gift." Years later Sharon began to realize that buying a birthday gift would take her parents' time, effort and thoughtfulness. "It's like they gave me my token gift... but I didn't feel their involvement; I didn't feel special enough that once a year they could spend an hour shopping for my birthday."

In the most extreme, severe cases, a parent's narcissism can extend to a total obliviousness of a child's needs. The parent may use or exploit a child. Examples may be pushing a child into sports or music or other activities for which the child has absolutely no talent, interest or joy in pursuing. This extreme narcissism has been seen tragically in the lives of child movie stars, beauty contestants, and athletes. The parent's own need to derive fame, fortune and status completely dominates the scene. The child's own feelings, needs and self-expression are completely ignored.

Yet another version of narcissism occurs when the parent harshly discounts and degrades a child's emerging talent or interest. A friend of mine had dancing in his blood. There was a free spirit in him and when he'd dance, he felt alive. But growing up in the South, he was ridiculed (especially by his father). His dad often said, "You're just a God-damned fairy... I feel ashamed of you." This young man endured considerable shame and conflict in growing up, yet was still able to forge his own path. Dancing is still an important part of his life, as are the inner emotional scars of shaming at the hands of his father. Psychiatrist M. Scott Peck has written about the effects of profound narcissism. He believes that in the the extreme, narcissism constitutes evil:

> *Evil is also that which kills spirit... awareness, growth, autonomy, will.*
>
> *It is possible to kill or attempt to kill one of these attributes without actually destroying the body. Thus we may break a horse, or even a child, without harming a hair on its head.*

According to Dr. Peck, just as love enhances, nourishes and embraces the growth and autonomy of others, evil kills them. It is not my intention to point a finger of judgement, but simply to acknowledge that extreme forms of narcissism do exist (whether you choose to call it "evil" or not) and the effect is emotional damage to the growing child.

At times, significant physical or mental illness can result in a parent's being unavailable emotionally for prolonged periods of time. Some families are so stressed by life events (e.g., extreme poverty) that parents expend all their energy simply coping with day-to-day survival. Children are told to stay in their rooms or are left for hours sitting before a television set. Ignoring is also seen in homes where parents are primarily occupied with their careers or other life interests, making little time for their children. Children in these families often grow up feeling worthless, "worth less" than their parents' careers, according to therapist/author John Bradshaw.

Ignoring can also be evident if a parent simply fails to notice when a child needs help. The child may have academic problems, may be hurt or abused by a sibling, or may be in a state of depression — it all goes unnoticed. In many homes where a parent molests the child, the other parent may be either uninvolved or oblivious to the abuse and is unwilling to take a stand to stop it. At times, a sibling molests a brother or sister, unnoticed by parents. In this case, *two* children are being ignored: the molested child and the child doing the molesting. (These children often aren't simply "bad" or "perverted," but rather, kids with much emotional pain of their own. The sexual acting out is but one symptom of that youngster's psychological distress.) People who have experienced abuse or molestation as children often feel a good deal of inner anger and outrage not only toward the abusing parent or sibling, but also toward the parent who ignored the problem and did not provide protection.

Even in the absence of more active abuse, significant ignoring can transform the child's life into an emotional wasteland.

**Isolating:** "The adult cuts the child off from normal social experiences, prevents the child from forming friendships and makes the child believe that he or she is alone in the world." Isolating can lead to tremendous loneliness, and with time, the child fails to be a part of normal social life. He doesn't learn how to make friends or to develop normal social skills.

I once treated a family in which the parents strongly believed that the world was full of sin and that it was crucial that their children not be exposed to evil or temptation. They did not allow their children to play with other kids after school. The children were never allowed outside their home on weekends and were told to not socialize with fellow students while at school. My reason for seeing this family was that their teenage son — openly psychotic — had just attempted suicide. His thirteen-year-old sister had somehow escaped the tremendous emotional devastation experienced by her brother. One day, during an individual session, she said to me, "I just don't think it's right. My parents keep us at home all the time! My friends think my folks are crazy!" Her friends were probably right. Doing what they felt was right, her parents honestly did not intend to harm their children. But the results were tremendously damaging.

**Terrorizing:** This involves threatening a child in extreme ways. It can lead to a pervasive sense of fear. "In its 'mild' form," say Garbarino, et. al., "it suggests an arbitrariness and the use of scare tactics in discipline." Verbal threats, bullying, intimidation, brutal criticism and humiliation characterize this form of maltreatment. In the extreme, children are physically abused, sadistically tortured or subjected to horrific forms of brainwashing.

Joey was a profoundly shy, withdrawn man who reluctantly came to the mental health clinic for help. His presenting problems were low self-esteem and poor occupational functioning. Only after a full year of very gentle, supportive therapy did he cautiously tell me of his childhood. For no particular reason, out of the blue, his mother would hold his hand over the flame of a gas stove. If he complained or cried, she would call him foul names and slap him. Sustaining burns was bad enough, but the craziness of the situation, the totally unpredictable nature of the abuse at the hands of this most important person in his life, made this experience all the more bizarre and terrifying. Terrorizing abuse is often unpredictable, making it impossible for a child to anticipate when the abuse will occur or to take action to avoid the abuse. Such children are often plagued with a continuous sense of incredible fear.

In many cases of sexual molestation, threats often generate feelings of terror: "If you tell, I will kill you," or "If you tell, I will kill your mother," or "If your mother finds out, she will commit suicide."

Sometimes abusers will kill small animals in front of a child and say, "I'll do this to you if you tell." Children need a certain degree of safety in their world in order to feel secure and to grow. These early experiences of terrorism can plant seeds of tremendous fear and mistrust that can last a lifetime.

---

<u>Katherine</u>

"There are times, when I'm not concentrating on something or working, that feelings flood over me like a wave. My head spins and I feel swept into another world. It's like watching a movie of a little girl being molested. And the man said if I told, he'd hurt me. I keep seeing and hearing it in my mind over and over, and I can't make the movie stop. I feel like I'm going crazy. When it's really bad, I feel like I am almost not sure of where I am, and I feel pain or other sensations in my body as if I'm actually in the movie. During these times, it feels like a bad dream, like it can't be real — it's a nightmare: it couldn't have really happened. But I awaken finally, pull out of it, and look around, and I'm at home. I feel detached and nothing feels real — not the dream and not the present. This is something I've never thought or felt before but yet it feels vaguely familiar and true. What's happening to me? I don't know what is real anymore."

---

It should be noted that sometimes parents who genuinely love their children periodically become enraged (not just angry, but *enraged*). They lose control of their anger and explode. They may hit or shake their children, call them names, or say "I'm going to kill you," only to later experience a tremendous sense of guilt and regret. These parents may not intend to damage their children, but such episodic rages can be devastating to youngsters. This pattern of maltreatment is often seen in parents who are under tremendous stress, who have serious impulse control problems, and/or are abusing alcohol or drugs.

**Corrupting:** Some parents, intentionally or inadvertently, actually train their children in antisocial or deviant behaviors. Aggression, sexuality and substance abuse are common areas of such unfortunate misguided parenting. This broad category of maltreatment includes sexual abuse (in all of its subtle and blatant forms), encouraging the use of alcohol or other drugs of abuse, involving children in criminal acts or prostitution, modeling and reinforcing hostile, aggressive behavior and exposing children to pornography.

Sally was a lonely child whose mother was a tense and cold woman. She and Sally's father had divorced when Sally was two. Because there was very little open affection or nurturing in the family, Sally was emotionally starving to death. When Sally was six, her uncle Bob moved in with the family and spent a lot of time holding her on his lap. It felt warm and good. However, within a few weeks, Uncle Bob's hugs turned into sexualized caresses and eventually led to stimulation of Sally's genitals. He told her that he loved her, but if she told anybody about their "cuddling," he would leave her forever. Sally started to develop a facial tic, chew her fingernails and develop strong feelings of potential abandonment — all direct results of the sexual assault by her uncle.

These kinds of intense feelings and resulting strong emotional conflicts take a tremendous toll on children. To the extent that use of addictive drugs or illegal behaviors are encouraged, moral development can also get off track. The long-term consequences may be the development of severe personality disorders, repeated encounters with the law, and/or a lifetime of drug or alcohol abuse.

**Intrusiveness:** Although parents certainly must spend time with their children and provide oversight and guidance, children must also have some alone time, some privacy and some space to be on their own. At times, however, parents can become so over-involved with their children that they go beyond certain limits, and kids experience a sense of intrusion. In its milder form, this may involve over-monitoring of children's behavior. In more extreme cases, the child may have little or no sense of privacy. Janet, one of my psychotherapy clients, related to me that her mother told her not only never to close the door to her room, but also, "I can read your mind... I know everything you are thinking." Janet felt a profound sense of vulnerability. All people need times when they can be alone with their thoughts and feelings. These times give children the sense of a boundary between self and others and contribute to the development of a unique, individual identity separate from that of their parents.

**Overprotection:** Protecting a child from undue distress and danger is obviously an important part of parenting. Infants and young children are vulnerable and helpless. The urge to reach out and catch a toddler as he starts to fall feels etched in parental instincts. Yet in some families, protection is taken to inappropriate extremes. All children must be kept safe and at the same time gradually exposed to age-appropriate challenges. Parents must at some point back off and let a child explore the world. This is how children eventually begin to learn how to stand on their own two feet and deal with the demands of life. A child develops ever increasing skills that help her cope and master the tasks of growing up. When the exposure to new challenges happens in appropriate ways, the child not only acquires skills, she also develops an inner sense of mastery and competency. As most parents have observed, when a child first walks on his own or successfully stacks several blocks, a large grin comes to his face, as if he's saying, "Wow! Look at me! I did it!"

Overprotective parents usually have good intentions but may inadvertently stifle a child's development by "smothering" and "infantilizing." In the name of providing protection, they unfortunately also send the child a message: "I don't think you have what it takes to cope with the world." Most kids growing up under these circumstances do not develop a solid inner sense of esteem and competency.

Sometimes parents react with overprotection because they have come to see the world as a very dangerous place. Many of these adults encountered frightening situations when they were young and are now trying to weave a protective web around their own children. Their children may also begin to develop views of the world as being an especially dangerous place to live. This fear thus becomes a multigenerational problem. In other instances, parents may have felt little involvement from their own mothers and fathers. The current overprotective atmosphere is a sort of compensation; they are attempting to provide their children with what they missed as kids, but are overdoing it. Some parents feel very bad to have their babies grow up. Lots of parents, if not most, feel a sense of loss as babies become young kids and eventually teenagers. Holding and hugging your child feels good. But sooner or later, most kids pull away, and it is a loss. With growth and maturation, children naturally move toward increasing independence. All parents must come to terms with this change, but for some it is very difficult. The response may be to continue babying a child, hoping somehow that he will stay young and remain close. Yet, as Margaret Mahler has advised wisely and poetically, good parents must give their kids "roots *and* wings."

Children who have the good fortune to receive the right amounts of protection and encouragement to grow-up find leaving home and moving into adulthood easier. They can separate and individuate, yet retain a positive connection with their parents.

**Inappropriate Discipline:** Three broad types of faulty discipline can be seen: discipline that is *too harsh*, discipline that is *too lax*, and discipline that is *inconsistent*. What is considered to be "appropriate" discipline has been a very controversial issue for many years. Older notions of "spare the rod, spoil the child" gave way to ultra-permissive, lax approaches to child rearing. It is far beyond my own wisdom to know what is *the* right type and amount of discipline. While it is very hard to know what's "right," it is clear both from anecdotal findings and well-controlled research studies that *extreme harshness damages children and so does excessive permissiveness.*

*Very harsh discipline* (especially when combined with verbal attacks directed toward the worth of the child) scares children. It dampens or destroys spontaneity and aliveness. It can lead to an inner hatred of the punishing parent. It can provide a model for aggressive-critical behavior. And often it simply does not work (i.e., it is not a very effective method for *teaching* children). Children subjected to harsh punishment tend to develop in one of two directions: either as overly repressed, submissive, compliant and fearful or seriously aggressive. (Many delinquents and criminals were raised by exceedly harsh parents.)

*Overpermissiveness,* on the other hand, often results in children who are selfish, demanding, inconsiderate — in a word: "spoiled." These children, raised with little or no parental discipline, often fail to develop a true appreciation for social norms and are at high risk for entering into relationships where they exploit others. They grow up expecting others to cater to their whims — after all, Mom and Dad did!

Markedly *inconsistent* discipline can make it "difficult for the child to establish stable values for guiding behavior." These kids also often grow up feeling confused and afraid. Parents' behavior is hard to predict: one time they fly into a rage; another time they ignore the child. Unpredictability almost always leaves children with a sense of uncertainty and fear. Don't misunderstand here: *absolute* consistency in discipline is not possible. Parents often disagree with one another about certain disciplinary issues. And many times follow-through and consistency simply take a lot of energy. Mild levels of inconsistency don't damage children. But when the parent's reaction is *grossly* inconsistent or extreme, and/or highly unpredictable, the stage is set for developmental problems.

**Unrealistic Demands:** Some parents place excessive demands upon children to do things that they cannot reasonably do. I'm not talking here about appropriately encouraging or challenging the child, but instead demanding the child to perform in ways that are inappropriate for his age. Such demands are often unrelenting standards for accomplishment and perfection. "These parents," says psychologist Jeffrey Young, "place a higher priority on achievement than on happiness." Under such pressures, a child may be able to stretch himself and achieve at a high level, but often at great costs emotionally. These kids often feel incredibly tense and worried. They become adults at a very early age and sacrifice their sense of playfulness and aliveness. In many instances the demands take on an all-or-none quality: "You either get an A+, or you are a failure." From this perfectionist view, if the child falls 1% below the mark, he's worthless. So even if maintaining the 100% performance, the child feels an ever-present, impending sense of worthlessness should she not live up to expectations. Children growing up under these conditions incorporate the unrealistic, demanding parent into their own conscience, so that years after leaving home, they hear parental voices echoing in their minds: "You either do it perfectly, or you are a failure."

Unrealistic demands not only pertain to achievement, but also to moral issues. This emphasis can be seen in families that demand, "You are to *never* get angry in this family!" or where "All sexual feelings are sinful!" Personal opinions may not be allowed: "Children should be seen and not heard!" Such demands can lead to a severe constriction of normal human feelings, the development of excessively harsh or unrealistic guilt feelings, and the stifling of autonomy.

*Too few demands* can result in serious developmental problems, too. There is, of course, an important place for parental expectations. These are the only way we can help children internalize values and develop inner guides for appropriate behavior. But the key seems to be communicating reasonable expectations to children which probably can be characterized by the following: they are age-appropriate; they are not extreme or rigid; and they do not attack the basic worth of the child. All parents get irritated with their kids and have frustrating moments of disappointment. It's not only o.k., but also necessary to give children feedback on their behavior. But attacking the *person* of the child is damaging: "You are worthless," "You're a total failure," "You are just a good-for-nothing little shit." This kind of name-calling is maltreatment! If your kid blows it or really disappoints you, it is natural to feel upset, but *there are ways to discipline without attacking the child.* Transmitting reasonable expectations to a youngster might take this form: "I really want you to do well in school. I expect you to do your best. But you need to know you don't have to be 100% perfect, and even if you didn't do well, please know that I'll still love you."

Unrealistic demands often take the form of parental "injunctions" given to children. These messages are often transmitted as direct verbal communications, such as, "Don't talk with your mouth full." Others are non-verbal, or indirect, but nonetheless powerful messages transmitted by facial expressions of anger and disdain: a young boy begins to cry and his father shoots him a glance that says "I'm ashamed of you... don't be a wimp. Boys don't cry." Injunctions are parent-to-child communications generally repeated hundreds, if not thousands of times throughout childhood. Bit by bit, these messages start to sink into the child's mind, usually in two ways. The first takes the form of an interpersonal expectation. It is clear knowledge (although possibly registering only at an unconscious level) that "I shouldn't act, feel, or be a certain way, or else I'll be punished, shamed or rejected." In the second form, the message is gradually incorporated into the child's own conscience, so that an inner voice continues to be present even when parents are not around (even years later when parents are dead and gone): "*I* shouldn't cry. *I* should be ashamed of myself."

Some injunctions are reasonable, realistic and necessary. They form an important part of the child's evolving sense of self. They operate as an inner guide or "behavioral gyroscope" helping the child to behave and operate in the world in socially acceptable ways. However, in families where unrealistic demands dominate, the parental messages are often extremely rigid, unrealistic and lacking in compassion (See Figure 2-A). These powerful and unreasonable demands or inner voices are what Karen Horney has referred to as the "tyranny of the shoulds": "You *should* or *must* be a certain way!" Rather than guiding adaptive behavior, they are like a ruthless dictator, constricting aliveness, evoking unnecessary guilt, and cutting poeple off from their humanness.

---

### Figure 2-A
### Common Parental Injunctions

| | |
|---|---|
| Don't be emotional | Don't be so sensitive |
| Don't cry | Don't rock the boat |
| Don't get your hopes up | Don't be childish |
| Grow up! | Don't really trust people |
| Don't get too close | Don't ask for support |
| Don't trust your feelings | Be logical |
| Don't get mad | Be perfect |
| Don't accomplish more than Mom or Dad | Don't give up |
| Don't feel proud of yourself | Please others |
| Don't be selfish | Don't complain |

A very extreme injunction can be seen in parents who directly and indirectly give kids the message, "Don't be!" In such cases, parents cannot simply allow the child to be or to become who she uniquely is. The parent insists that the child become what the parent wants, at all costs. Such parents simply cannot allow, encourage or appreciate unique aspects of the growing child to emerge. When children encounter this message in the extreme, the result often is a stifling of the growth of the child's true self and the development of an inner belief that "I am basically defective. Who I really am is not appreciated, loved or allowed... and if I were to be true to my own inner self, I'd be either ashamed or abandoned." Such a belief is rarely made conscious in the mind of a child, but lurks as a constant undercurrent that can be carried forth into adult life. Psychologist Stephen Johnson (1987) puts it this way:

*If the environment can accept and nurture... love the wonders of an emerging person... the realness of the individual is bolstered, reinforced and actualized... When the environment lets her be, she is, and there is no disorder of the self. But when you are too much or too little, too energetic or not energetic enough... too independent or not independent enough..., you cannot freely realize yourself.*

**Faulty Communication:** In some homes children are raised by parents who have odd or irrational ways of thinking and communicating. Sometimes this takes the form of seriously inadequate communication. Withdrawn, aloof or preoccupied parents, for example, may simply not talk enough with their children. When children are not able to talk about their experiences, thoughts and feelings, they often are unable to come to a realistic understanding of the world (and especially the world of human interactions). I have known a number of people with this kind of background who, although intellectually competent, have poorly developed social skills and difficulty understanding and relating with others. By talking with our parents, we absorb a tremendous amount of information, and we also develop ways of thinking that are, at least, somewhat similar to others (e.g., learning how to think and communicate in logical ways or in ways that can be understood by others). An inability to think in common ways (to a mild or moderate degree) can result in patterns of thinking that appear to be peculiar, eccentric, or at times even creative or unique. However, in the extreme, uncommon thought processes leave a person unable to communicate with others. Such people often feel terribly alienated and estranged.

In homes where one or both parents are mentally ill*, there may be enough communication, but the kinds of thoughts expressed are crazy. Crazy talk does not provide a good model for clear thinking or for the development of effective interpersonal communications. These thoughts may be patently bizarre or apparently magical. A young woman I once treated told me how her mother would arrange dead flowers on the kitchen table. Somehow she was supposed to look at the configuration of flowers and tell what was on her mother's mind!

In other situations, the communication is filled with marked inconsistencies, mixed messages and "double binds." Henry spoke in psychotherapy of his experience in growing up with his father. His mother, other relatives and people in the community saw his dad as a "saint": an exceptionally kind humanitarian. His mother often said, "Your dad is a very good man, and you know he really loves you." Yet the truth of Henry's day-in, day-out experience was that his father was very critical of him, rarely affectionate and almost always unavailable. (He spent most of his time either working or involved in charitable events outside the home.) So Henry was faced with two powerful images of his father: the public image of a saint and his personal experience of a profoundly non-loving, non-involved parent. The lack of clarity generated by these kinds of circumstances can lead to tremendous amounts of confusion, uncertainty and insecurity for the youngster.

**Invalidation:** One woman told me that when she had her first menstrual period, she experienced tremendously painful cramping. She complained to her mother, who responded, "You are too young to have a period. Quit faking it and leave me alone." This is but one example of a very common type of maltreatment in childhood. The child is simply expressing the truth: an emotion, a physical sensation,

---

*Note: Especially the case where the diagnosis is one of Schizophrenia.*

an opinion or idea. The parent says that it should not or does not exist: "It doesn't hurt," "You aren't afraid," "We don't say that kind of thing in this family!"

What is a child to do in a situation such as this? Some kids fight back and insist it *is* true. But for many, if not most children, fighting back is very hard to do. Parents are seen as being extremely powerful. Most commonly children manage in some way or another to suppress the pain, ignore it, banish the thoughts from their minds or change the subject. Children also may start to *feel* crazy. Their natural experience (e.g., the menstrual pain) is directly denied and invalidated, one of the most devastating experiences a child can endure. The child not only fails to receive much needed support and caring, but is left doubting her own perceptions.

Invalidation is such a tremendously common experience that it deserves extra attention here. To explore this form of emotional maltreatment in childhood, I'd like to propose an analogy: the evolution and growth of an individual self is somewhat like the creation of fine pottery.

In the beginning stages of making pottery, the clay is molded and takes on its own very unique shape and form. However, once formed, it is crucial that the pot (bowl, plate, vase) be fired in a kiln for a particular period of time and at a certain temperature. The process of firing allows the piece to develop tremendous added strength and durability. Unfired, the clay either stays soft and very malleable, or it dries out, cracks and falls apart. The firing is necessary, but something already within the clay, the inherent make-up of the clay, allows the transformation into an object of greater solidity and strength.

Like clay, the stuff that is fashioned into an expression of the self is initially quite fragile. Certain experiences in life either can transform the emerging self into a more solid form or can cause it to fall apart. The real self is made up of the physical sensations, perceptions, emotions, thoughts, hunches, images, beliefs, values, needs and hopes that naturally arise out of a person's inner being. These experiences of the self can be registered only at an unconscious level and barred from conscious awareness; they may be noticed inwardly, but without outward expression; or can be revealed to others (e.g., expressing your feelings, stating an opinion, taking action).

The process of validation is one of the primary life experiences that can turn a *potential* personal quality into an *actual* one. It is like the heat that fires the pottery. When a child cuts her finger and cries, if her parent acknowledges her pain, the experience is validated. Validation does not mean passing judgement, such as *good, bad, right* or *wrong*. It simply involves a verbal or non-verbal message that conveys the thought, "You are hurt and I believe you." It is as if the parent shines a light on the reality of her daughter's feeling and says, "This is real... you *are* hurting and I accept that it's just the truth." The girl's expression of pain is a very brief demonstration of one part of herself. When someone else — particularly someone as powerful as a parent — recognizes and believes the feeling, that show of emotional support influences both the development of the child's self for the moment and in a more profound and lasting way.

An important message shines through when a parent validates a child: "You are worth listening to, and worth believing." Children need to know that they matter. This is the message that is registered in the heart of the child when an adult acknowledges her pain or other experience. In a powerful way the acknowledgement shows a deep sense of respect for the experiences of that child. And each time she expresses something, whether joy, pain or an idea, and it is treated with respect, the adult encourages further self-expression and strengthens the child's self.

Invalidation — that denial of the reality of the child's experience — can be very pronounced, but also can be incredibly subtle. Consider the scale illustrated in Figure 2-B. "A" represents a clear, outward acknowledgement of a child's feelings, thoughts, experiences. "B" is minimizing: "Well, I know you got hurt, but it's nothing... it's no big deal." "C" is the message, "You may feel that way but don't express it... keep it to yourself." "D" is "You shouldn't feel that way" or "You should be ashamed or yourself for saying that."

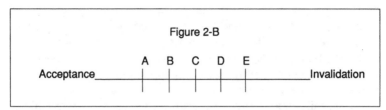

In examples A-D, there has been at least some acknowledgement of the child's inner experience, although increasing non-acceptance is the message. As we move toward the right end of the line, the invalidation becomes extreme and often results in a marked distortion of reality. "E" says "You *don't* feel (hurt, angry, etc.)!" or "The painful event *did not really happen.*"

Here are a couple of common examples of this extreme. In many families where there is spousal abuse, a battered wife may tell her children, "Oh, I just fell down and hurt myself," as a way to explain her injuries and to deny that her husband beat her up. The children very likely heard shouting, cursing, and slapping coming from the parents' bedroom, or actually witnessed their father hitting their mother, only later to be told, "It didn't happen." Another very common example is the comment that "Your mother is just sick," a dark version of a "white lie" told to children to hide the truth of their mother's drunken stupor.

> ### Katherine
> "I now remember one morning when I talked to my mother about bad dreams I was having... dreams of a man chasing me and hurting me and touching my private parts. She looked at me and said, 'Don't talk about such things. You should be ashamed of yourself... anyhow, it's only a dream.' I felt I was bad. I thought she was right. It was *my* fault... I couldn't dare tell her about the sexual abuse! I never mentioned it again."

Invalidation certainly can accompany childhood traumas; however, as we shall see later, invalidation is not unique to children. It frequently occurs as adults experience painful contemporary events or as they begin to remember and re-experience painful childhood memories. Many survivors of child abuse and molestation will attest that, as they begin to talk about their pasts, many friends, relatives, and even therapists may respond with denial and disbelief. This response reignites painful feelings of aloneness and the very common experience, "I must be crazy."

Some childhood traumas, unfortunately, may be unavoidable. If any child is emotionally hurt, to be with the child, hear the pain, and say, "I believe you" are probably the most important and compassionate things a person can do to help. This basic statement of belief in the child is like water for a young plant. It nourishes the growth of the self.

> *"I look around and I wonder*
> *How the years and I survived.*
> *I must have had a mother that sang to me,*
> *An honest lullaby..."*
> — Joan Baez (1979)

### The Experience of Loss During Childhood

I have not included this topic under "Psychological Maltreatment" because it is a type of very painful experience that may be better understood as a consequence of fate. Many children encounter significant losses from deaths and parental divorces. Human attachments, a sense of bonding and connection, provide us with our most important source of joy and aliveness. And it is in the greenhouse of human closeness that the self finds protection and nurturance. For many of us, the loss of a loved one may be the most painful experience we can ever encounter. Unfortunately, losses during childhood can often be even more devastating than those experienced as adults.

Almost all human beings go through predictable periods of grief and mourning following the death of a loved one. In addition to their feelings of anguish and grief, children commonly encounter other problems as a consequence of early losses. Let's look at a few.

Early losses often heighten sensitivity so that later losses hurt even more. Many people who suffer from severe recurring depressions as adults have a history of early losses. Often the times of depression are ushered in by current-day stressors; sometimes the triggering events *appear* to be rather minor. I have known people who became clinically depressed after rejections in fairly shallow, casual friendships or following the loss of a pet. The depression was due in part to that particular loss, but it also touched on deep unhealed wounds from childhood.

An early encounter with loss may leave a child in a perpetual state of fear — an inner belief that, "If I get close again, I'll lose that person, too." Such beliefs may be conscious, but more often they are not. The person grows into adolescence and adulthood with a tendency to maintain distance and avoid true intimacy or attachment. I must emphasize that these inner fears may be completely out of awareness. The person may have little or no memory for the early loss. (This is especially true for losses sustained prior to the age of three.) Margaret Mahler has called these very early losses "unrememberable, but unforgettable." Yet the unconscious fear can exert strong effects on the person now; silent, but powerful warnings and cautions signal potential danger in closeness. Such people may remain isolated or seek out only superficial relationships. Intimacy and commitment may be difficult to achieve. A person who has experienced such longstanding fears if she marries at all, might marry someone who is also emotionally distant.

In addition to the primary sense of grief, a child who loses a loved one may, from that point on, miss out on those very important experiences provided by that person. A child needs parents, siblings and friends to provide interaction, support, encouragement, companionship and a sense of belonging. Often the loss of a parent results in tremendous financial strain for a family, followed by a cascade of economic, social, and lifestyle changes. The loss of a sibling can result in such profound grief and despair that bereaved parents are unable to love and nurture the remaining children (who then have lost a sibling and, emotionally, lost their parents as well).

A final type of loss for children is the loss of capacities. Political idealism aside, all people are not created equal. Many children are born into the world with physical and mental disabilities which make the process of growing up even more difficult. Examples include children who suffer from illnesses that interfere with their ability to engage in normal childhood activities, such as cerebral palsy, severe asthma, birth defects or paralysis, mental retardation, learning disabilities or attention deficit disorders which lead to recurring academic failure, extreme over- or under-weight, ugliness or deformity. Painful consequences associated with many of these disabilities are social rejection and isolation. Most of these kids inwardly suffer from tremendous feelings of inadequacy and loneliness.

The more children can be encouraged to openly grieve losses when they are young, the less chance that they will continue to suffer from these deep wounds on into adult life. Fortunately, we are often given a second chance to heal from early losses when as adults our locked-away pain is re-opened by the experience of present day emotional stress and the continuing processes of growth.

## Three

# *Adult Pain I:*
## *Time Doesn't Heal All Wounds*

You're all grown up now. As an adult, you're supposed to be strong, independent, able to handle whatever life deals you, right? Then how come life events can hurt so much?

Most difficult events we encounter as adults will touch — directly or indirectly — on a few basic human needs: the need to feel loved by others; the need to feel a sense of self worth; the need to feel some degree of safety; the need to hold stress and stimulation at an optimal level. In this chapter we'll explore some all-too-common painful adult experiences, how they interfere with our needs, and why they hurt us so much.

### Interpersonal Losses

Losses stand out as a very common source of human suffering. The only people who do not experience loss are those who have never been able or willing to form attachments — those who have never truly felt love for another person.

Interpersonal losses occur in many contexts. The clearest example, of course, is the death of a loved one. Each year approximately eight million people in the United States experience the death of a close family member; there are over 800,000 new widows or widowers and more than 27,000 suicides annually. Among the many other causes of loss are the million divorces which are final each year, and the untold thousands who go through marital separations. Job transfers and geographic relocations account for many losses of close friends and social networks. Census studies suggest that every seven years approximately 25% of people in the United States make a *significant* geographic relocation. Children grow up and move away from home. Friendships may dissolve and marriages can grow cold and distant, even if the couple still choose to live together under one roof.

A tremendous sense of loss is experienced by couples struggling with infertility problems, as numerous attempts to get pregnant are followed by significant, repeated disappointments. It is very human to become quite attached to unborn children. Miscarriages and still-births can be devastating. (For some peculiar reason, many people seem to think that if you never actually give birth to a child, it's no big deal to lose it, as if it weren't a real baby. This is absolutely not the experience of those grieving mothers and fathers who must endure this kind of painful loss.)

In the aftermath of an abortion there may be a significant sense of loss, even if the mother were reasonably sure she wanted the abortion. The loss may be felt soon after the abortion, or not for years to come.

Another common interpersonal loss is seen when people experience some form of brain damage. This affects both the injured person and everyone in the person's life. The injured person is alive, but may become very different as the result of severe head injuries, brain infections (e.g., encephalitis), strokes, brain tumors, oxygen deprivation (caused by electric shock, heart attack, serious blood loss or near drowning), and various types of degenerative neurological illness (Alzheimer's disease and other types of dementia). At any one time, 6.5 million families in the United States are caring for a relative with an Alzheimers-type disease. In these situations, you lose the "person" you knew, even though he or she is still physically present.

- The mother of a teenager who sustained a serious head injury: "He was so bright... so alive... a wonderful kid, and now he's not the same. Of course I still love him, but I feel like I've lost my boy."

- The husband of an Alzheimers victim: "This is not the woman I married. She used to be so caring... so sensitive. Now she's just not there. I don't matter to her anymore. It's like each day I lose a piece of her... this woman is still living with me, but my wife has vanished."

About these experiences of loss, some people rationalize: "Well, losses are just a part of life." But this truth obscures and minimizes what for most of us are tremendous sources of emotional pain. People need people; we get attached and losses hurt.

### Existential Losses

All of us want to believe that our lives count for something, and that we have a certain amount of control over our own destinies. Life sometimes shakes those beliefs, however.

Robert had just heard that a co-worker died of a heart attack while playing golf. The friend was only forty-eight years old. When I spoke to Robert, he said, "What upset me most was that it could have been me. It made me think about my life. It made me wonder, am I really happy? Is my life meaningful?" Often such losses force us to face very difficult questions about the meaning of our lives, our mortality, our basic satisfaction with life. It may be that much of what is behind the so-called "middle-age crisis" is a sort of depression triggered by these kinds of issues of existence.

Sometimes life reminds us that, despite our sincere hopes and best efforts, our dreams are not going to come true. Most of us have hoped "to have a fulfilling marriage and family life," or "to find success in a career." But the reality of a relationship or job may not match what one longs for inwardly. It is not unusual to wake up one day and be struck with the painful awareness that, "I'm not happy with my life." The resulting sense of disillusionment or loss of a dream is an all-too-human experience.

To avoid a sense of personal failure, people often go to great lengths to maintain hope, even in the face of disappointing realities. Thirty-eight-year-old Pam told me: "It's been there for eleven years, every day. My husband doesn't care about me. He's treated me like trash, ignored me. Sometimes he's abusive. But I kept hoping he'd change. I kept saying that all we needed to do is to try a little harder. It's just now hitting me. He hasn't changed and he won't ever change. How could I have been so stupid?"

Pam wasn't stupid; she was hopeful. Hope can be a bridge that helps people get over painful or difficult times. It can also blind us. Pam was able to ward off more painful feelings of loss by maintaining hope, but at some point the bubble burst. The eventual awareness of her profound disappointment triggered a sense of loss and emptiness. Her dream of happiness in marriage was destroyed. This type of event is just as real and powerful as other losses, but often not fully appreciated. Pam's friends made comments such as, "I don't see how come you're so upset. You've known how he is for years." These remarks didn't help. Pam's friends may have good intentions, but their critical comments hurt. It doesn't matter how long she had lived with her husband's abuse. When her *illusion* of hope disappeared, she began to feel her loss.

A second major type of existential loss is the recognition of mortality, that "I won't live forever." A twenty-year-old college student knows that this statement is true, but probably doesn't think about it much. A forty-year-old person may look at this truth very differently. The death of parents or friends their age often has a powerful way of forcing people to face their own mortality. Rabbi Harold Kushner, author of the best-seller *When Bad Things Happen to Good People*, has said, "It is not the fear of death, of our lives ending, that haunts our sleep so much as the fear that our lives will not have mattered..." This acute awareness of "time running out" may provoke not only worries about the future, but also grief about a life that has been empty, disappointing, or lacking in meaning.

Society recognizes deaths and divorce as "legitimate" reasons for grief and depression. Existential issues, however, are often seen in a different light. Joan said to me after the death of her husband, "Oh, these things happen. It's just a part of growing old and you've got to accept it." She was trying to convince me (and herself) that "these things happen," and that she should be able to cope with the situation. The reality was that Joan was suffering tremendously from the loss of her life-mate. Her friends and family were sympathetic about her husband's death, but they did not openly understand or support her fears and sadness as she now faced the painful awareness of *her own* life coming to an end. Somehow, the death of her husband was a more acceptable loss; her existential crisis was minimized. As a result, Joan felt even more alone with her pain.

Existential losses must be understood as very real and powerful causes for human suffering.

### Losses Related to Careers and Future Plans

Painful as they are, interpersonal and existential losses are not the whole story. Many of us will encounter other life events that can be significant sources of despair.

**Unemployment:** Millions of Americans struggle through the agony of unemployment; sometimes briefly and sometimes for a period of many, many months. In addition to the obvious financial hardship unemployment brings, this difficult life event can hit people on many different levels.

Work is a fundamental life activity. Although seen by some as "just a job" or simply a way to "make a buck," for lots of us, our work helps provide structure in our lives. Work offers us identity, outlets for self-expression and meaningfulness; it is a major source of self-esteem. Even in jobs that seem routine and boring, when unemployment hits, people often start to realize in dramatic ways how working had given them a sense of worth as providers and members of the community. Short-term unemployment can create financial strain and a lowered sense of self-esteem. Longer periods of unemployment can be devastating. With chronic unemployment, initial worry and frantic searching for a job can eventually result in a collapse into despair, hopelessness, apathy and impotent rage. A sense of diminished self-worth may be intensified by uncaring comments from friends or relatives. If it lasts a long time, this life situation can deteriorate; a profound loss of identity and self-respect may be added to the anguish of increasing financial strain.

**Major disappointments:** We all have hopes and dreams. Often they provide the driving force behind years of hard work and devotion as people attempt to build a business, climb out of poverty, obtain an education or raise children. The "American Dream" is fashioned around a belief that people can succeed if only they try hard enough: hard work and perseverance lead to success. Sometimes.

Sometimes, the most well-thought-out business, built with integrity, sweat and tears, falls prey to the competition of a slick national franchise. Economic factors beyond one's control create massive shifts in the economy and wipe out a family's savings. Racism and bigotry create a hostile neighborhood and school environment for an otherwise successful family. Ruthless con-men steal from senior citizens. Children are persuaded by their peers to start using drugs. An uninsured house burns down. After fifteen years, a couple realizes that despite all their attempts, they are unable to have children.

People put their hearts into their plans for the future. Because they care deeply about such things as their careers, life missions, and people they're close to, these kinds of disappointments can be a source of considerable loss.

### Events that Lower Self-Esteem

Many life events may deal a blow to one's sense of esteem or self-worth. Personal failures (such as failing to receive a promotion), personal rejections and criticisms, and making mistakes are but a few of the many events that can lead to low self-esteem.

Andy accidentally set his kitchen on fire. His house was saved, but there was extensive damage to the kitchen. Even though his insurance paid for the repair costs, for many months this forty-three-year-old bookkeeper felt a terrible inner sense of self-loathing. "What was wrong with me? I was so stupid. I can't believe that I could have been so dumb." He suffered both the initial loss and the burden — for months afterward — of being unable to forgive himself for making a mistake.

Carl had worked for twenty-three years for a machine shop. The owner sold the business and, despite his excellent work history, Carl was not part of the deal. For two years, he was unable to find a job in his usual craft. He was also subject to ridicule and cruel jokes from a brother-in-law who took every opportunity to point out Carl's "chronic unemployment." These experiences caused Carl tremendous inner suffering and feelings of worthlessness.

Every human being has a need to feel a basic sense of self-worth; events such as these undermine that sense, often leading to despair and self-doubt.

### Physical Disease

Illnesses can create serious emotional distress. In some instances, a physical disease results in intense, daily pain, diminishing the quality of life and making it hard to experience moments of joy.

Some life-threatening and degenerative illnesses carry the frightening specter of increasing disability and possible death. One study (Duveneck, et al. 1986) compared the physical and emotional status of a group of patients who suffered from spinal cord injuries, and another group which had muscular dystrophy. In both groups the degree of current disability was similar. However, spinal cord injury is generally a static condition: it doesn't get worse. With muscular dystrophy, there is continual deterioration. The degree of depression in the muscular dystrophy group was significantly higher than that of the the spinal cord injury patients. It is human nature to look toward the future, and many diseases — like spinal cord injuries — unfortunately have a poor prognosis. It is understandable that such life stressors can be incredibly difficult to face.

Some illnesses can result in physical limitations that dramatically alter one's lifestyle. Cheryl is a thirty-four-year-old woman whose passion in life is modern dance. She used to work as a secretary, living for the end of the day when she could leave work and go to her dance classes. Two years ago, she developed severe, crippling rheumatoid arthritis and had to give up dancing completely. "My whole life has changed. It feels empty now." Physical illnesses not only result in pain and sometimes fear of an uncertain future, but also may change a person's life in dramatic ways.

> Gary
>   "Since getting cancer, my whole life has changed. I was told that the surgery was successful, and in the last few weeks I have absolutely no pain or discomfort. But I worry about it all the time. Will I be ok? Will it come back?... I almost never worried about my health; now it's like all my focus is on my body. Sometimes I hardly even notice if it's a nice day outside; I'm just so preoccupied. I hate it!"

One of the most agonizing situations for parents to endure is living with a seriously or chronically ill child. Thousands of parents live with the possiblity of death, disability or suffering of their ailing children. Not only must these mothers and fathers experience the pain of witnessing their children's suffering, they may miss out on one of the sustaining joys of parenthood: the hope and fulfillment of seeing a child blossom into adult life.

### Exposure to Extreme Danger

Every day newspapers and television programs confront us with tragedies occurring across the globe. Horrific things do happen to people; however, for most of us, direct exposure to extremely dangerous and terrifying events is unlikely. For most people, denial ("It can't happen to me.") and desensitization (e.g., having watched hundreds of accidents and murders on television shows and movies) create a sort of buffer — a protective blanket of emotional insulation. While extremely dangerous and terrifying events do happen to some people and have profound effects, those of us who are fortunate enough to avoid these hellish experiences have little true understanding of the emotional devastation such trauma can bring.

Many life experiences fall into this category: being assaulted or raped, being severely injured in an automobile accident, being sexually molested, witnessing a murder or a gruesome death (including casualties of war and street crime), being tortured, experiencing repeated spousal abuse, regaining partial consciousness during surgery, being exposed to war or starvation, living through a natural disaster such as an earthquake or a dangerous flood, witnessing the injury or death of your child, accidentally killing someone, contracting AIDS or some other of God-awful, terrifying illness.

These events are almost always experienced as traumatic because of their severe intensity and because of the tremendous sense of powerlessness that often occurs. Even if such events are "single blows," most people who live through them are haunted by extreme anxiety, nightmares, and memories for weeks (and many times for months or years) after the event itself. These symptoms seen together make up what is commonly called Post-Traumatic Stress Disorder. (Please see Appendix A for a more detailed description of this disorder.) Such tragedies profoundly affect a person's sense of safety in the world and can unleash tidal waves of existential anxiety (e.g., agonizing questions about the meaningfulness and fairness of life).

### Toxic Relationships

No important, on-going relationship is totally without friction. In all good families, marriages and friendships, some degree of conflict, disagreement and disappointment is the rule. One of the hallmarks of emotional maturity is to be willing and able to really stick with important others during difficult times. However, it is fair to say that some relationships are *toxic*. Regardless of attempts to work through problems, the friction and conflict are so severe that one or more people in the relationship continue to be hurt. The hurt may take the form of blatant physical or emotional abuse; it may show up as an undercutting of the growth and/or autonomy of one person; it may simply be lack of love and nurturing. Such a relationship leaves at least one person stranded in an emotional desert.

The awareness that a relationship may, in fact, be destructive can be obscured by blinders of hopefulness and denial. Most people do not want to see or believe that their parents, spouse, children or friends are harmful to them. This kind of denial may last a lifetime, or it may give way to an increasingly clear but painful awareness that the relationship is not healthy. This awareness may dawn on someone gradually, or it can become immediately apparent through an intense event or interaction. At first, simple *awareness* of the toxic nature of the relationship can be a major source of emotional shock or poignant disappointment. Partial denial, combined with partial awareness — "Oh my God... I can't believe this!" — is not uncommon. The initial painful awareness is sometimes followed by desperate attempts to fix things (i.e., to resolve the problem) or to slip back into denial.

When there is no fix, and the reality can no longer be denied, a second source of despair can set in: *loss.* It is both a loss of the other person(s) as a meaningful source of love or support, and the loss of an ideal. The ideal may be a highly valued belief or hope that parents can be loving, that a spouse can be faithful, or that a friend can be trusted. I believe that these hopes and ideals, when we can continue to believe them, serve as flotation devices, helping us keep emotionally afloat even in a sea of toxic interactions. Loss of an unhealthy relationship can puncture our ideals and hurt like hell.

Concerned friends may offer "supportive" statements such as, "Well, he wasn't good for you. It's better that you're no longer in that relationship." These observations may "objectively" be true, but that reality doesn't neutralize the pain of lost hope. Even a bush struggling in lousy soil can be damaged as it is being lovingly transplanted to a healthier spot. Its roots have found a home in the inadequate soil and can be damaged in the process of replanting. Just as the bush clings to its lousy soil, it's often incredibly difficult for us humans to give up even very toxic relationships.

Painful relationships develop for many reasons. Sadly, there are times when people hurt people out of meanness; they intentionally use, abuse and damage the other person. At the same time, many harmful, toxic interactions have nothing to do with the desire to cause pain. The troubles may be largely due to a person's own emotional woundedness, stressful lifestyle, mental illness or addictions to alcohol. Perpetrators of abuse in such instances may harbor deep regret when they see the results of their behavior.

I want to emphasize that toxic relationships need not imply that the people involved are bad. It may simply be that the chemistry just isn't right. Rather than a matter of people being good, bad, right or wrong, it's more often a matter of lack-of-fit. One person's style simply doesn't mesh with the other. Or maybe there *was* a good fit or "good chemistry" at some point, but with time, the people have grown and changed. The relationship isn't the same. This is not a crime. It's just one aspect of human nature and blaming has no helpful role, but it can be toxic all the same. Sometimes when there have been good times together and shared lives, the move away from what is now a toxic relationship can be especially difficult — fraught with guilt, loss and remorse.

### *Interpersonal Conflicts*

One of the most commonly encountered sources of emotional distress in adult life arises from significant conflicts in interpersonal relationships — marriage, family, friends and neighbors and co-workers. Such conflicts can center around themes of power, control, intimacy, disagreement, racial and sexual harrassment, unfair treatment, and a host of other problems.

Blatant cases of sexual and racial harrassment, for example, are coming into greater awareness in America, and rightly so. At the same time, a more subtle, covert level of prejudice permeates the lives of many cultural groups. This may be experienced and re-experienced thousands of times throughout a lifetime. Snide comments, jokes, unequal treatment, looks of disdain or disgust and subtle acts of racism darken daily life for many people. The long-term effect is often an erosion of basic feelings of self-worth.

Interpersonal conflicts may account for only minor frictions in daily life, or they may develop into more serious on-going problems — especially in intimate relationships. A complete discussion of this extremely broad area is well beyond the scope of this book; however, we will take another look at these issues in Part III. Your attention is also directed to the References.

### Facing Difficult Tasks

I once saw a cartoon of some Vikings who had obviously just pillaged and burned a castle. One Viking said to the other, "It's a dirty job, but somebody has to do it." It's no joke, however, when it's your turn to face very unpleasant experiences and carry out difficult tasks. One of the most awful things I have had to do was to fire someone. Though it was a part of my job, and I knew it was necessary and right, it was extremely hard to do. For days before the firing, I could hardly think of anything else. (After the firing, of course, the person I had fired confronted the *really* difficult task.)

Many life events fall into this category of "difficult tasks." Here are a few examples: hearing very bad news from a doctor; giving bad news to someone you care about; placing an ailing parent in a nursing home; telling a grown-up child that she must leave home; encountering a grim accident scene; standing by the side of a close friend whose spouse is dying. Emotionally difficult life tasks are a part of the job for many of us. Health care professionals, police, fire and rescue workers frequently must deliver bad news to relatives, and military personnel and police officers are expected to fire weapons intended to harm or kill enemies or fugitives. (Most police officers *throughout their careers*, never fire their guns in the line of duty, and when on occasion they do, the majority of officers are severely traumatized by the event.)

Again, it is tempting to rationalize, "Well, these things happen," but I do not believe for a minute that such rationalizations really quiet the inner fears, losses, resentment and despair that accompany these hard tasks.

Figure 3-A

**Common Sources of Emotional Distress In Adult Life**

| | |
|---|---|
| Interpersonal Loss | Major Personal Change |
| Existential Loss | Exposure to Extreme Danger |
| Major Disappointments | Toxic Relationships |
| Diseases/Chronic Pain | Interpersonal Conflicts |
| Discrimination/Racism | Economic Crises |
| Events that Lower Self-Esteem | Facing Difficult Tasks |

## *Time Doesn't Heal All Wounds — But Many Can Be Healed*

Personal losses, unfulfilled dreams, career disappointments, economic crises, racism, infertility, crime, lowered self-esteem, physical disease, exposure to extreme danger, toxic relationships, interpersonal conflicts, difficult tasks . . . the life events described in this chapter are painful even to *read* about. But they are all-too-real sources of emotional stress for many millions of people.

Before you go on to the next chapter — which discusses even more sources of pain for adults — I encourage you to take some time to reflect on your own painful experiences, to admit to yourself (even if to no one else) that your emotional pain is real, to recognize that countless others face similar circumstances, and to allow yourself some modest optimism that you may be able to grow beyond the pain. In later chapters, you'll find out how.

*Four*

---

*Adult Pain II:*
*When You Hurt But Don't Know Why*

$N$ow that we've examined emotional pain that is clearly related to childhood trauma or adult life experiences, let's take a look at those emotional hurts that are not easily traced to their specific origins.

Many times people encounter times in life when they experience noticeable emotional distress or other psychological symptoms, and yet they are at a complete loss to understand what has precipitated or caused the crisis. During my years as a psychotherapist, I have talked to a number of individuals who came to me with severe psychological symptoms but were unable to identify any precipitating stressful event in their lives to help them account for the presence of their emotional suffering.

In the face of obvious causes of psychological pain, people don't feel confused; they are able to see a connection between the life events and their current emotional distress. But what about those psychological problems or symptoms for which the person is unable to identify the source or the cause? In this chapter, we'll examine five of those confusing conditions: biochemical abnormalities, traumatic events earlier in life, current stressful circumstances, developmental changes leading to the emergence of one's "true self," and being "off time."

### Biochemical Abnormalities

New understanding about the functioning of the brain makes it clear that certain types of *medical, biochemical abnormalities* can cause significant psychiatric symptoms. These biological malfunctions can be set in motion by thyroid disease, fluctuations in hormone levels (for example, during menopause or childbirth), the use of certain drugs (prescription medications as well as recreational drugs), and biologically based forms of mental illness.

People experiencing such malfunctions will feel confused and perplexed about the origin of their difficulties because they are unable to pinpoint any particular stressful events, losses, tragedies or something to account for their despair.

When the primary cause is rooted in biology, medical and/or psychiatric treatment is indicated. Appendix A lists the major signs and symptoms of such psychiatric disorders; listed in Appendix B are certain medications, recreational drugs and medical illnesses that may result in emotional problems. If you are experiencing significant emotional distress and have absolutely no awareness of life stresses or environmental causes, please consult these appendices. Effective treatments are available for these particular types of major mental illnesses and medically induced emotional problems.

### Recall of Traumatic Events

Beginning to reexperience the effects of *traumatic earlier life events,* experiences many years in the past, is a second major cause of unexplained emotional stress. Many, if not most, adults who have lived through severely traumatic experiences as children may have little or no recollection of those events. The human mind blocks out these painful thoughts, feelings, and memories from conscious awareness. If it weren't for this process, children would go through most of their young lives experiencing overwhelming degrees of emotional suffering.

*For years I did not have to face the demonology of my youth. I made a simple choice not to and found solace in the gentle palmistry of forgetfulness. A refuge in the cold lordly glooms of the unconscious... I've pretended for so long that my childhood did not happen. I had to keep it tight — up near my chest. I could not let it out.*
— Pat Conroy
*The Prince of Tides*

For most people, the repression of painful childhood memories is not a conscious choice, it's an automatic process. Blocking out traumatic memories provides some degree of protection from tremendous emotional pain. But it's only a temporary solution. Just as the toxic waste buried in the Nevada deserts thirty or forty years ago has begun to seep toward the surface, so do traumatic childhood memories eventually seek conscious expression. People who have experienced recurring sexual or other physical or emotional abuse as children are often able to repress those memories until their twenties, or more often their thirties or forties. Automatically, for the first time in twenty or thirty years, the person catches glimpses of painful childhood experiences. The experience of having and raising children is often the key which unlocks the door to the past.

Largely unaware of what's really going on, the adult who was victimized as a child may begin to experience feelings of anxiety or panic, depression and despair, subtle feelings of uneasiness, insomnia, nightmares, tension headaches. These and other symptoms precede the emergence of actual memories and seem to come out of the blue. The survivor of early abuse often is only dimly aware that these problems may be emanating from events long ago.

Once the doors to the past begin to open — perhaps in the course of psychotherapy — healing is facilitated as she gradually becomes aware of the source of the pain. Intense memories and dreams may lead to the recall of the painful experiences themselves. The source of the painful symtoms becomes clearer and clearer. Talking to a therapist or trusted friend about the memories, feelings, and thoughts aids this process of recall. Working with a therapist over a period of weeks, months, or even years can help to uncover and ultimately heal the painful memories. Acceptance of painful realities is the beginning of healing.

### Stressful Current Events

The third category of unidentified pain is quite common. Many of us will experience primarily either the emotional or physical part of emotional stress without making clear connections between stressful current life events and the emergence of these particular symptoms. Here's an example from my own life. On a number of occasions I have come home after a full day of work feeling somewhat upset, discouraged, or anxious. When my wife asked, "How come?", I didn't have the faintest idea why I felt this way. A good person and a good therapist, she encouraged me to talk a little bit about what happened to me during the day. Oddly enough, as I recounted the events of the day, the source of my distress became clearer: an unpleasant encounter with a co-worker, some disappointing news, or what-have-you. In any case, I had not consciously connected certain stressful current life events to the resulting feelings. Making that connection takes the ability and willingness to start talking about what has happened. Simply putting feelings and experiences into words helps to illuminate and clarify connections between events and feelings. Initially, many people don't have a clear notion about why they feel bad, but the opportunity to talk openly about the stressful events enables them to make the connections more clearly. Sometimes this process is easy and quick to accomplish; sometimes, it requires a lot of talking and soul-searching. These connections could be made with the aid of a therapist, or by talking with a trusted friend, relative, family member or clergyperson.

### Developmental Changes: Emergence of the "True Self"

Your values, your beliefs, your inner emotional self, your skills and talents, your hopes and dreams. . . all of these are parts of what we define as "self." In fundamental ways, the self has continuity over time, and there are advantages to this internal consistency. An inner sense of self can serve as an anchor, a stabilizing internal "I."

Yet people do change. Sometimes this change is forced upon us as we are buffeted by stressful events. In the process of socialization by parents and teachers, for example, children feel pressure to act in certain ways. It is a gradual shaping process that sets the direction for development early in life. In this process, for better or for worse, parts of the natural, true self are blocked out of awareness. This accommodation may stay intact for a lifetime or may undergo changes during adulthood.

Sometimes adults start to change because they notice an inner voice, an awareness of some feeling, need or impulse that heretofore was unheard. Especially during middle age, many people start to discover something inside which may be the beginning emergence of a new "self"... a "truer self."

It's almost like living in a house. Early on you shut and lock the doors to several rooms and gradually forget that the rooms are even there. The house you live in — with its locked doors — is the house you know. Similarly, the *self* with parts blocked out seems and feels familiar. Then one day you start to hear something, some sound coming from behind one of the closed doors. Or possibly the door starts to open on its own. At first glance the contents of the room may be upsetting, scary, perplexing, or at least unfamiliar.

Many adults find a newly rediscovered "room" contains the capacity to express feelings. In our society, men often seem to seal off their tender or soft needs and feelings. Conversely, women often block off parts of the self that have to do with natural, human expressions of assertion and anger. As we mature, however, there is a tendency for these gender-related personal styles to change.

Mike is a good example. A burly, "macho" kind of guy, he works as an auto mechanic, and is known to his friends as a somewhat gruff but nice guy, a hard worker, a good athlete and a "rock." People turn to him in times of crisis and he fixes things. He's solid, strong and capable. I met Mike when he came to see me for help regarding some "weird experiences" he'd had lately. He was rather embarrassed to talk about them, but gradually his story unfolded. Mike told me that he had watched a couple of movies at home and found himself feeling very sad and tearful. (Crying was not common for Mike. Until recently he had lived all of his adult life without shedding a tear.)

On closer inspection, we uncovered something in particular in these films which had touched him: the movies involved scenes in which a father expressed love and affection for his son. Over the course of two months of therapy, Mike started to recall that he had been extremely neglected by his father. When he talked about this new awareness, he felt a wave of strong emotions: sadness, fear, anger, love. His expression of these feelings was at first very cautious and tentative, but little by little he let himself connect with the inner emotions.

One part of this process was Mike's willingness and ability to remember past experiences with his father more clearly. At the same time another change was taking place. He had rarely if ever actually experienced the emotions of sadness or tenderness; he had never really known of his inner need for love and connection with his father. This part of himself (this closed off room) was now starting to open up. At first he didn't understand what was happening. He saw the eruption of sad feelings and tears as a problem — "something wrong with me" — a common initial response when one first sees aspects of the true, inner self that have been locked away for many years.

After six months of therapy, Mike came to know the emotional part of himself better. The feelings, although often painful, became less and less foreign to him. He was less afraid of the emotions, and they started to make sense to him. And something interesting and wonderful began to happen. Mike started to notice that he was able to feel closer to the people in his life. He had discovered not only a room in his house that held some old pain, but also a room that contained the capacity for experiencing tender feelings. Mike now has more room in his "internal house." He's still a tough, macho guy, but he now can feel a greater sense of aliveness and closeness with his girlfriend and with his buddies.

### Sharon

Sharon became aware of disturbing feelings. At times she felt an impulse to smash a dish or to yell at her husband. Oddly enough, these feelings most often started to surface when Tim came home at 10:30 pm after a long day at work or when he somehow found time to play racquetball with his friends and managed to avoid Sharon — sometimes for weeks on end. Early in therapy as Sharon described her inner experiences, what she noticed most was that the feelings of anger scared her. She was afraid she'd lose control, that she'd explode, and that Tim would leave her. She also felt extremely guilty: "I shouldn't feel this way... in lots of ways he's a good husband. He makes a good living, he's faithful, he's not an alcoholic..." Gradually Sharon came to understand, however, that her angry impulses weren't crazy, weren't just "P.M.S." It started to make sense to her that years and years of Tim's empty promises and the reality of little closeness, little affection, was taking a toll on her. She came to understand and accept that her anger made sense.

At some point, Sharon decided to start voicing her needs and feelings in a more direct way. Tim didn't like this "new behavior." He was used to and more comfortable with the quiet, passive "girl he married." Sharon continued to feel afraid that Tim might get very angry or that he'd leave her. But she decided to "own" her feelings and to express them more openly.

As new ways of feeling, thinking and acting start to emerge, other people in your life may not like or accept the changes. Some women like the strength of a solid, unemotional man. Expressions of tenderness may shake things up and threaten the relationship. Some men need women to take care of them. They become accustomed to having someone wait on them hand and foot and keep their lives organized. A woman's newfound decisiveness — "Hey, I don't like having to do all the chores or all the child raising!" — can send shock waves through the relationship. Sharon's decision (see sidebar) to voice her true inner needs and feelings threw Tim for a loop. Her behavior was very unfamiliar to him.

Major changes in your personal style — such as those we've seen with Mike and with Sharon — almost invariably will confuse others in your life at first, but that doesn't mean the changes are bad. Your spouse (or children, co-workers, parents, etc.) may go through an understandable period of readjustment to the newly emerging behaviors and feelings, but then go on to truly accept the changes. Others who care about you may be able to see the changes for what they are: growth. However, such changes can have devastating consequences in relationships where the other cannot or will not tolerate change. This lack of acceptance can lead to serious conflicts, strife, and sometimes the dissolution of a marriage or the end of a friendship. For intimate couples, the challenge is two-fold: How can we live together as a couple *and* at the same time tolerate, appreciate, encourage and accept individual change in one another? It's a very difficult challenge for many couples.*

If a relationship ends in the wake of individual changes and growth, there's going to be a great deal of emotional pain. However, the final outcome of such growth (opening the doors to the true self) is usually an increased sense of aliveness and a more solid inner sense of self. The choice — to maintain the status quo and accept its pain and limits on growth, or to risk change and the possibility of relationship upheaval — can be an extremely difficult and emotionally stressful experience. We'll look at some ways you can work through it in Part III of this book.

### Being "Off-Time"

Psychologists Simon Budman and Alan Gurman have identified an important, but often unrecognized source of emotional distress which they refer to as "developmental dysynchrony." They state that "people are 'on-time' or 'off-time' developmentally to the extent that they *feel* that they are subjectively doing what they and others expect for a given stage of their lives" (1988).

---

*For thorough discussions of these issues in intimate relationships see: Dance of Intimacy by Harriet G. Lerner, and Accepting Each Other by Michael L. Emmons and Robert E. Alberti.

Throughout life people are more or less aware of major life events. These events can serve as markers of progress through life. Some of these events are either expected (e.g., getting married or having children), or at least not a total surprise when they occur (e.g., the death of a very elderly relative). These events occur in their own season of life; they are "on time" events. Yet other life events may not seem expected, anticipated or timely. The middle-aged single woman who had hoped to marry young, the businessman who experiences a heart attack at the age of forty, the twenty-five-year-old woman who is suddenly widowed are common examples. These events are not typical experiences during these times of life. Few people of the same age groups are going through similar experiences. In a major way, these individuals are "off time." (Figure 4-A notes other examples of off-time — dysynchronous — life events.)

---

### Figure 4-A

#### Common Dysynchronous Points in Life*

1. Late teen or young adult has been unable to separate from parents.
2. Young or middle-aged adult has been unable to develop an intimate relationship.
3. A woman or couple nearing the end of childbearing years has been unable to have children.
4. A young or middle-aged adult becomes a widow(er).
5. Middle-aged adult becomes increasingly aware of a long-standing lack of satisfaction in marriage or career.
6. Adult, looking forward to a free life after the children leave home, is either still supporting an adult child (a person who is immature, mentally retarded or handicapped) or elderly, ailing parents.

---

Finding yourself "off time," say Budman and Gurman, can lead not only to painful feelings of loss and grief, but also can result in feelings of inadequacy (e.g., "What's wrong with me?), confusion, uncertainty and demoralization.

We look to our social environments, our inner "social clocks," our interpersonal context in order to orient ourselves. Just as a sailor

---

*Adapted with permission from Budman, S., & Gurman, A. (1988) Theory and Practices of Brief Therapy. *New York: Guilford Publications, Inc.*

may use astronomical signs to note his position while at sea, as we go through life, we look to others to define "Where am I?" and "What is expected of me at this point in my life?" To an extent, even very individualistic non-conformists do this, at least unconsciously, to gain a sense of grounding or stability in an uncertain life.

Individuals going through a time of feeling "out of step" with their cohorts can begin to feel fragmented, disoriented and confused — an ill-defined inner sense that "something is wrong." They know they're not in synch with others, but may not know why. It's common for people to enter psychotherapy feeling distressed or depressed without a clue about what is causing the discomfort. Sometimes, after making time to really talk about their lives, it starts to become clear — the source of the distress is developmental dysynchrony. They may consciously acknowledge their distress but may, at the same time, be perplexed by underlying feelings of confusion. Recognizing and clarifying the "off time" nature of a life crisis can be an important step toward reducing those feelings of confusion and uncertainty.

---

### Sharon

"I guess I've been fooling myself. I think that down deep inside, I've been sad and hurt and angry with Tim for years. But I just kept hoping something would change. It was kind of like when I was a kid and I kept waiting for my mom and dad to spend time with me. The few times they did, it seemed like a chore for them. That's how it is with Tim. Sometimes he'll sigh with disgust and say, "OK, let's go out to eat tonight...," but he's not really there. How can I have been so blind? And I guess what I notice most here lately is that I'm getting older. My best friends have kids and I don't. Tim's saying, "Maybe some day we'll have kids" is a bunch of B.S. He doesn't want kids! And in a few years I'll be too old to have children. I just don't know what's wrong with me. I feel so mixed up."

### Emotional Pain and Beyond

During my career as a human being and as a psychotherapist, I've discovered that we all encounter difficult life situations that can cause significant emotional suffering. Yet as people come into my consultation room, they frequently make three primary errors. The first — a misconception about human suffering and emotional healing — is to believe that stressful life events are "no big deal," and if hard times do occur, the pain should go away quickly. The fact is that for most human beings, many of these emotionally painful experiences *are* "a big deal," and simply are not subject to rapid healing.

The second error is to engage in a form of self-condemnation. Rather than treating themselves from the perspective of care and compassion, they engage in a ruthless attack on their worth as human beings: "I shouldn't feel this way," "I must be crazy," "There's something wrong with me." It's rare that self-attack will *ever* promote healing, and for many people, self-attack is the major element that prevents the wound from healing.

The third error is to compare their pain with that of other people. People frequently say, "Well, it could be worse," or "Well, others suffer more, I shouldn't complain." Psychotherapy patients remark, "I shouldn't waste your time with my problems. They aren't that bad. I'm sure you have other people who need your time more than I do." These comments are an attempt to minimize the loss or emotional pain. This very common action is sometimes a way to deny the person's own worry or despair. But, to judge "whose pain is worse?" doesn't help; it goes no where. We all suffer and our pain is our own. Something either hurts or it doesn't. And whether it seems like a big deal to others or feels "legitimate," really doesn't change the fact that *it is painful*.

One of my friends once told me that he had made a valuable discovery. He had recently gone through a difficult time, and he had resisted the urge to say, "Oh, it's no big deal." Instead, he simply and honestly said to himself, "I hurt." It helped him to heal. His simple statement acknowledges an inner truth; it's a very important way of showing respect for your inner self.

I hope the discussion in chapters 2, 3, and 4 has helped you to identify with the emotional pain of various life experiences, and to become aware that such sources of distress are common to us all, occuring alongside the positive experiences in life.

With this exploration of the common sources of emotional pain as a "launching pad" for our journey, let's move on to examine the wonder of our human emotions, how they develop, and how emotional pain can be healed.

# PART II: UNDERSTANDING HUMAN EMOTIONS

## Five

## Why Does Emotional Pain Last So Long?

> *Significant experiences of early life may never recur again, but their effects remain and leave their mark... they are registered as memories... Once registered, the effects of the past are indelible, incessant and inescapable...*
>
> *The residuals of the past do more than passively contribute their share to the present... they guide, shape, or distort the character of current events... they operate insidiously to transform new stimulus experience in line with the past.*
>
> — Theodore Millon

*I*s it possible to be hurt when you are a child of five and to still feel the pain thirty years later? Doesn't time heal all wounds?

The answers to these two questions are "yes" and "not always." It is tempting to use analogies to compare physical injuries with wounds to the psyche. Sometimes these analogies work, sometimes they don't. Thankfully, most physical injuries heal, and heal to a degree that years later — or even days later — actual physical pain is completely gone. It is only a dim memory and it doesn't hurt now. This physical healing takes place because of wondrously complex biologic mechanisms that restore normal function. And healing is facilitated by proper care and medical treatment following an injury.

But the effects of a physical injury can be long-lasting. Inadequate recovery may be due to impaired immune functioning; improper treatment can lead to complications (deterioration, secondary infections, bones that do not grow back in proper alignment); and repeated re-injuries may retard recovery. In such cases, the initial problem produces long-term consequences. In the realm of emotional injuries, I think it's helpful to see these consequences as falling into two categories: persistence of actual pain and changes in perception and behavior.

## Persistence of Pain

If you burn your hand, it starts to heal. Yet if you repeatedly knock the scab off, the wound can stay active indefinitely. Active wounds remain open often on an emotional level, too, as people are re-exposed to psychologically destructive relationships and situations.

If you react to the burned hand by wrapping the wound excessively with bandages, you'll protect the wound — for a while. However, over-bandaging for a long period of time is not helpful. A massively-bandaged wound that is unwrapped a month later is not healed. Physical wounds eventually must be exposed to the air; otherwise they are prone to infection. People often bury painful emotions under layers and layers of repression — an understandable act of self-protection that can backfire. Authors Ellen Bass and Laura Davis have this to say about burying emotional pain: "Buried grief poisons... when you do not allow yourself to honor grief, it festers. It can limit your vitality, make you sick, decrease your capacity for love" (1988). Although their remarks focus on grief, the same is also true for other painful emotions.

Some injuries are so devastating that even in spite of proper care and some healing, the pain persists. It may only hurt when you bump into something that touches that spot. Or it may be one of those wounds that cause persistent, constant aching, which is true for some kinds of emotional injuries, too. Recalling emotionally difficult events touches on and reactivates the old pain. Memories and haunting images of the past have the power to reignite the pain of old wounds.

### Changes in Perception and Behavior that Keep Pain Alive

Joaquin suffered a rather serious knee injury while playing tennis. It was quite painful and a frightening experience. After medical treatment and a successful period of recuperation, he made what his doctor called "an excellent and complete recovery." He experienced no lasting pain. But Joaquin was changed.

Prior to the accident, he had loved tennis. It was the first sport he had ever tried, first learning to play at the age of thirty-five. It was fun and a source of exhilaration for a man who used to see himself as "athletically retarded." After the accident and recovery, Joaquin attempted to play tennis again. But each time he went on the court, he felt afraid of re-injury. This wasn't a conscious choice; rather, he found himself "automatically" holding back. He was afraid to move around quickly, felt inhibited and cautious. When this fear persisted for several months, his game deteriorated, and he became increasingly frustrated. What once was a passion, a source of great joy, was becoming an exercise in personal failure. Eventually Joaquin quit playing altogether. His knee no longer hurt, but his *view* of tennis — and of himself — was changed. Though the injury happened five years ago, and the original pain was gone, the lasting effect was his change in perception and ultimately the loss of this favorite sport. His loss of self-confidence and concern for his safety on the tennis court changed his life. *This* is the legacy of that injury.

Many emotionally traumatic experiences, long after the initial pain subsides, continue to dramatically affect the victims' view of the world, their choices in life and the resulting changes in their lifestyles.

Psychiatrist Aaron Beck has proposed an important theory which can help us understand how past experiences can dramatically influence our living in the present. Almost all of us have been profoundly affected by the day-in, day-out emotional atmosphere that existed in our early families. Recall your own childhood. The family is a child's entire world. At times, sudden, brief, highly distressing events do affect the developing personality of the child. However, by-and-large, it is the repeated contacts with his parents which begin to give shape to his view of the world.

Keith is an infant. Like all young children, his first experiences with people are severely limited in scope. Aside from occasional brief visits by neighbors and grandparents, his world of human interactions is exclusively that of his family. These early encounters with his parents will influence the boy tremendously as he starts to form his first impressions of the world. If most of the time Keith notices periods of hunger or other discomfort quickly followed by relief — holding, soothing, feeding by his mother, very likely he will begin to lay down some extremely powerful beliefs and expectations about the world. Maybe the beliefs will be, "There is comfort in this world," "There is reason to be hopeful that others can help me," "I can trust that any pain I feel won't last forever," or "My needs matter." At this early stage of development, such beliefs are not really thoughts or words in Keith's mind, but are more an inner sense about the world. It's a bit like when you're thirsty and take a drink, you don't really think about it, but you know and absolutely believe that the water will quench your thirst. This belief has always been your experience throughout life. This belief also leads to an expectation: "If I'm thirsty, I know what to do. I fully *expect* water to quench my thirst." Emotional expectations also operate on a similar automatic and unconscious level.

The earliest human beliefs and expectations center around what famed psychoanalyst and author Eric Erickson calls "basic trust" — trusting that others can be counted on to provide nurturing, soothing and protection. It is this trust which leads to the capacity to form attachments. Very severe adverse conditions — betrayal of trust — during the first year of life can result in the laying down of powerful negative beliefs. If Keith were profoundly rejected, neglected or abused during infancy, he might grow into adulthood without the inner ability to form attachments. Such children believe the world is harsh, and people do not comfort. These beliefs color their perceptions of life. Everywhere they look, they see rejection, abuse and harshness. They could never count on love or nurturing as infants, and even if there is the good fortune to encounter a loving person later in life, the early , severe deprivation has left its mark. Pervasive, severe emotional trauma early in life may, in a sense, set these beliefs in psychic concrete. Such people often go into the world profoundly detached — the schizoid personality who wants absolutely nothing to do with closeness, intimacy, or the human race. Or they may become self-centered narcissists and psychopaths who can never genuinely give to others, but rather only use others to meet their own needs.

These inner beliefs usually develop into the nucleus of one's self-concept. And they define "who I am," "who others are," and "what to expect from human interactions." Deeply etched negative beliefs ("Negative Core Beliefs") can be seen to emerge in two forms. The first somewhat more malleable Negative Core Beliefs are pes- simistic views of the world that, under the right circumstances, can be altered by later positive experiences with others.

Jennifer was ignored by her workaholic father and largely rejected by her mother. She came to strongly believe that, "There is something wrong with me. I am defective and in a very basic way, unlovable." Yet during her childhood, from about ages five to ten, her next door neighbor, a kind and gentle older woman, did provide her with a considerable amount of warmth and affirmation. Jennifer periodically continues to have times of feeling unlovable, but this belief is not rigid; it is not etched in stone. She is able to remind herself of her good qualities and can recall times when she has been in positive, meaningful relationships with others. The early experience left its mark, but later relationships have modified her beliefs so that they do not dominate her life. The malleability of Jennifer's negative core beliefs probably has to do with having experienced moderately severe neglect/rejection, and yet the positive effects of the relation- ship with her neighbor provided a buffer. In the end, her early experiences were certainly painful, but not of a magnitude con- sidered to be traumatic.

A second version of Negative Core Beliefs can arise in conditions of very severe emotional harshness. This version is chacterized by rigidity and unshakable negative beliefs. Bruce grew up in a home environment of pervasive harshness, brutality and ruthless criticism. Daily his father told Bruce he was worthless, evil and a "piece of shit." Bruce's incredibly passive mother would shrink into the shadows and seem to disappear at these times, offering no protection from his tyrannical father. Bruce is now a man in his mid-forties. He is single, lonely and chronically depressed. He interprets his inner belief, "There is something wrong with me. I am defective and in a very basic way, unlovable," as an absolute fact. He has never thought for a moment that the belief was untrue. Very severe early emotional trauma often results in such rigid and unshakable negative beliefs.

It is important to note that Bruce rarely thinks about his father or his childhood. He is not feeling any kind of direct pain from childhood wounds. But the powerful beliefs, laid down years ago, wreak havoc in his daily life. Negative core beliefs influence here-and-now perceptions and expectations. Let's take a look at how this process continues to happen in Bruce's life.

Bruce's firm conviction that he is unlovable influences his perceptions of the world. He is quick to notice any events that confirm or even come close to confirming his beliefs. At a recent social event taking place at his office just after business hours, he entered the room full of fellow employees. For the first two minutes he was there, no one spontaneously came up to greet him. He looked around the room, but no one met his eyes. He very quickly concluded, "They don't give a damn whether I'm here or not." This perception, this conclusion was very likely to have been exactly what he anticipated. At that moment, he abruptly left the party, went home, and felt lousy. He has had similar experiences many times before. And many more times he has been so convinced that he would be rejected or un-wanted that he didn't even attend social functions.

Bruce's inner belief has taken its toll in three ways. Current perceptions (and conclusions) are greatly influenced by the beliefs. Possibly there are times that his perceptions are accurate, but very likely his quick conclusions may not be completely accurate or realistic. Like many whose core beliefs about life are essentailly negative, Bruce is always ready to see rejection in social contacts and, as a result, is likely to jump to unwanted or distorted conclusions. In addition, powerful expectations have often led to choices (e.g., don't go to parties) that keep him further cut off from interpersonal contact. Also, a person who rarely attends gatherings and never initiates social interaction is likely to be seen as disinterested: a loner, a snob or a grump. Often others are likely to start treating the person in the very manner anticipated: with rejection. Is time healing this wound? Of course not. The scab is being actively knocked off over and over again.

### Can Core Beliefs Ever Change?

Deeply ingrained and severe maladaptive beliefs are extremely resistant to change or alteration by later benign life circumstances. In most cases, recovery and emotional healing will require involvement in psychotherapy. People who suffer these long-lasting and profound psychic wounds almost never felt a real sense of trust or safety with other human beings. Because psychotherapy involves a deep and confiding relationship with another person, the whole idea about seeking out treatment can be understandably terrifying for these people. Choosing to enter psychotherapy represents an act of tremendous courage. Fortunately, if the person finds the right therapist, treatment can be helpful, although the road to recovery is long and rocky. Successful treatment is what psychologist Stephen Johnson has termed, "a hard-work miracle" (1985).

In healthy, growth-promoting families, children are felt to naturally develop positive and realistic inner beliefs. However, it is probably true that most of us encountered at least mildly "psychonoxious" experiences at least some of the time while growing up. The experience of the majority of people lies somewhere between the extremes of optimal positive experience and severe trauma. When this is the case, as mentioned before, negative core beliefs and self-concepts are not likely to be as pervasive or rigid. Such people may not feel inadequate continuously, but from time to time, this inner belief is triggered or reactivated by life events. It's as if the core belief lies dormant and is periodically awakened by certain stressful events. The negative beliefs for most people are also more malleable

— they can be more readily modified by positive, corrective experiences throughout daily life or in powerful ways can be changed by the experience of psychotherapy.

All sorts of negative core beliefs may result from early experiences in your family. Psychologist Jeffrey Young (1990) has given us a brilliant analysis of the areas of life in which negative beliefs develop (see Figure 5-A). Most people will probably notice one or two primary negative core beliefs that are dominant undercurrents in their emotional lives.

It's a common experience for people to encounter stressful life situations and to respond with extremely powerful emotions. At first glance, such emotions may appear to be inappropriately intense. Upon close inspection, however, we find that a particular stressor has evoked such a strong reaction because it has activated an underlying negative core belief. Although such core beliefs sometimes are noticeable day-in and day-out, for many of us these "psychological Achilles' Heels" may lie more-or-less dormant. Particular stressful events bring such issues to the surface.

In attempting to understand yourself, it will be helpful to take inventory of your inner core beliefs and ask the question, "Is there anything about the stresses in my life right now that touch this emotional chord in me?"

## Figure 5-A
## Negative Core Beliefs*

| | CORE BELIEFS | HEALTHY, GROWTH-PROMOTING ATMOSPHERE | MILD TO MODERATELY STRESSFUL | SEVERE TRAUMATIC |
|---|---|---|---|---|
| **Autonomy** | Dependence | I am able to take care of myself and stand on my own two feet. | I often feel unable to function on my own. | I am *totally* unable to function on my own. |
| | Subjugation | I may care about others' needs, but my own needs are important too. | I often feel that others' needs must come first. | Others' needs *always* must come before my own. |
| **Safety** | Vulnerability to Harm | By-and-large my world is generally a safe place. | I need to be cautious because often the world is unsafe. | The world is an *extremely* dangerous place. |
| | Mistrust | Most people I am close to can be trusted in and counted on. | I must be on guard with others. | Others will *always* hurt, abuse, use, or take advantage of me. |
| **Love/Connectedness** | Abandonment/ Loss | My relationships are stable and enduring. Can allow intimacy. | I often worry about losing people who are close to me. | Ultimately I will lose those whom I love. I *will* be rejected. |
| | Emotional Deprivation | There is hope that I will be able to find love in the world. | I often feel a lack of love and support. | My needs for love and support will *never* be met. |
| **Self-esteem** | Defectiveness/ Unlovability | I am basically an OK person. I have worth. I am lovable. | I often worry that if others really know me, they wouldn't like me. | I am *profoundly* defective and unlovable. |
| | Incompetency | I have confidence in my ability to deal with the demands of life. | I often doubt that I am capable and competent. | I am *completely* incompetent and destined to fail. |
| | Shame/Guilt | I may make mistakes, but I am basically a good, decent person. | I often feel ashamed or bad about myself. | I am morally bad, shameful, and deserving of criticism and punishment. |

*Adapted with permission from Young, J. (1990) Cognitive Therapy for Personality Disorders. Sarasota, FL: Professional Resources Exchange, Inc.

## Six

## *"You Always Get What You Need "— Or Do You?*

$O$n a very basic level, all stressful events hurt because they interfere with the meeting of fundamental human needs. As you encounter difficult times, you will find the following questions helpful: "Why does this event hurt?" and "In what way is this event striking an emotional cord within me?" Often you'll discover the answers when you become more clearly aware of your inner needs and how life events affect the meeting of these needs, the focus of this chapter.

Though people are vastly different, philosophers and psychologists have observed that we are similar in some basic ways. I remember learning this lesson from my grandfather who taught me, "Always remember son, that no matter how important someone is, everybody has to take down his pants to go to the toilet." This somewhat crude, but very true lesson helped me appreciate one area of common human experience: we all share identical biological needs and limitations. Everyone must eat, drink and sleep. No one is immune to all illnesses or to the inevitability of death.

Beyond this purely physiological commonality is a powerful force that very likely springs initially from biologic sources and that influences much of human development: the drive to survive. This innate need to survive is built into every human being. Survival encompasses both physical survival and emotional survival, both types intimately connected, especially early in life. A number of studies have documented the finding that infants who are given all their necessary physical needs (food, warmth, etc.) but are deprived of contact, love, and soothing, will often lapse into a profound state of biological shut-down — a state called "failure to thrive." Such children stop eating, waste away, and — if the circumstances are prolonged — eventually die.

As we get older, emotional survival usually is not as closely tied to biological survival; other more purely psychological needs come to the forefront.

### Important Human Needs

Emotional survival depends on meeting several basic human needs. A great deal of work has been done to determine just what those needs are. The most widely accepted view is the model developed by psychologist Abraham Maslow. Before we consider this broad view of human needs, however, let's focus on the needs I consider to be most important: the need to be loved by others, the need to love yourself, the need for safety, and the need to hold stress and stimulation at an optimal level.

### The Need To Be Loved

Every human being begins life in the presence of another; the biological union between mother and the child in the womb is followed by a highly dependent relationship after birth. The child is completely helpless and needs the care and love of parents. This extremely close, dependent connection gradually yields to increasing autonomy and independence as the child grows up — assuming healthy emotional development toward adulthood. The mature adult continues to want and need love from others, yet can simultaneously stand alone and act in an autonomous way.

Though people express their inner need for love in a variety of ways, most people experience this need as a feeling within. However, many do not notice, feel, or express it at all. Some life experiences can dramatically affect one's awareness of the need for love. People who have lived through traumatic and harsh experiences as young children may come to see the world as a dangerous place, void of true love. These experiences can, if severe enough, profoundly influence expectations and perceptions of the world. For these people, closeness may automatically mean vulnerability and hurt. So they have learned to survive by blocking or numbing the inner need for love. As we shall see, all basic human needs can be blocked, denied, or buried; people generally still survive, but at great emotional cost.

Feeling loved represents a collection of experiences: the expectation that love exists in the world, feelings of worthiness, connectedness, and unconditional love. People need these experiences to survive and to grow emotionally.

The first aspect of the need to feel loved has to do with expectations. Only if a child has experienced love early in life will she have an inner expectation or hope that there is love to be found in the world. A child who has never felt love or only experienced emotional pain may abandon all hope that others might be loving. One result is that, as an adult, she never seeks out closeness or contact with others. The child who genuinely felt loved while growing up may be afraid to approach others and may find out that not everyone is loving, but she likely knows in her heart that there is hope.

Psychologist Jeffrey Young writes that an important part of feeling love also has to do with an inner experience of worthiness: "Worthiness is the sense that one... is worthy of attention, love and respect..." This inner feeling is a natural outgrowth of living in a home where one is truly loved and shown respect. Dr. Young also describes another aspect of feeling loved, what he refers to as *connectedness:* "The sense that one is connected to other people in a stable, enduring, and trusting manner." This feeling develops naturally when a child sees that on a day-in, day-out basis, others continue to be there for him, that others will continue to care and love him even when times are hard.

A final aspect of feeling loved is the sense that you are loved unconditionally for who you are. The late British pediatrician and psychoanalyst D.W. Winnicott talks about the importance of maternal love early in the life of the infant. He refers to a special kind of relating in which the mother "holds" the child. Holding, for Winnicott, goes far beyond physical holding, to include the mother's provision of a safe environment where the child is not overwhelmed. She prevents intense physical distress by feeding, comforting, protecting and soothing. And finally, mother provides a "non-demanding presence." Winnicott's concept can be illustrated by a mother who, at times, makes no demands on the baby, but simply watches her child and holds him in her heart. Presumably, the child experiences the feeling that "I am loved just because I am me. No matter what I do, there is love." Parents, of course, will make demands on their children (e.g., expecting them to learn certain rules for living in the family and in society). Yet, in healthy families, children experience times of a non-demanding presence or what the late reknowned psychologist Carl Rogers called "unconditional positive regard."

<u>Sharon</u>

"You know... Tim says the words "I love you." But day-in and day-out, I don't feel it. I don't see it in his eyes, I don't feel it in his touch... in my heart I know his words are hollow. This experience reminds me so much of my Dad. He was *so* busy. He never had time for me. I just wanted and needed him to really love me... no wonder I felt so alone... no wonder I feel so alone now."

## The Need To Love Yourself

Human beings also have a need to love themselves. Healthy self-love has many elements: recognizing that I have the right to feel good about myself; valuing myself; feeling proud if I accomplish something; acknowledging my needs; at times, putting my needs first (while also being sensitive to the rights and needs of others); making sure that demands put upon me are realistic and reasonable; and having compassion for myself. This last point — compassion — deserves some elaboration. Everyone will make mistakes; everyone will fail. Many people greet such mistakes or personal shortcomings with intense self-criticism. There is nothing wrong with experiencing disappointment; it is a normal human experience. A sense of failure or falling short of the mark spurs people to learn more, to try again to master difficult tasks. Unlike the overly self-critical person who damns himself for failures, a person who has learned self-love and compassion can live through times of disappointment or failure with much less distress. (Basically, you have a choice to treat yourself in a critical, harsh, judging way or in an understanding way, as the Introduction made clear.) Psychologist Pam Butler says that an alternative to the harsh, inner critic, is an inner "guide": a voice of understanding and reason within you who might say, "Yes, I did make a mistake. It hurts. And it's a disappointment. These are normal human feelings. I have a right to want to do better. I may need to work harder, yet I will *not* be harsh with myself."

Self-love also involves acceptance of your limitations. You may think to yourself, "I don't completely like the fact that I have a particular short-coming. But, at the same time, I care about myself and have worth despite the limitation."

One form of "self-love" is extremely egocentric behavior, in which a person is so self-centered that he always puts his needs above those of others. Pathological self-love has been referred to as *narcissism*. The narcissist believes that he is the center of the human universe, that he is special and that he is entitled to all sorts of special favors, such as success, good health, wealth, and love. Such people have not developed the capacity to love others. All of their love is self-directed.

The narcissist often skates through life feeling special, only to wake up one day in middle or old age and discover that no one has ever truly loved him. When all of life is led in an egocentric way, sooner or later other people decide that they want no part of this one-sided relationship, and they leave. Many narcissistic people find themselves tremendously empty and alone later in life. By contrast, extremely self-critical people experience an excessive amount of inner pain and turmoil because they feel the sting of inevitable life disappointments and then launch into a tirade of self-condemnation. Children who grew up in homes where they were seriously neglected, unloved or even blatantly hated, have a common experience. When they talk about themselves they say, "I'm no good. There is something wrong with *me*." Although there are exceptions, these kids do *not* say, "My parents were inadequate" or "My parents weren't able to love me." Rather, the focus of the person's perceptions is on the self: "I didn't get love; therefore, there must be something bad about *me*." Most often if you have been loved, the repeated experience of being valued instills a powerful belief within the your heart: "I have been loved. I am worthy of love. And, therefore, I must be OK." This belief is lacking in those who, as young children, lived in an unloving environment. Self-love develops in family atmosphere where a child feels loved by others.

Other early-life experiences also seem crucial for developing the capacity to love yourself. One experience is suggested by child development specialist Margaret Mahler: parents' expressions of joy when their young children do something on their own. When a child takes some independent action, for example, spontaneously stacking a few blocks, and a parent expresses joy — "Good for you!" — Mahler believes that three things happen. For the moment, the child also has the experience of accomplishment and joy. The child also receives support from the parent, which gives her courage to further express herself. And on a deeper level, the message that "It's OK for me to feel happy and proud when I am being myself," starts to sink in. Mahler states that this early experience forms the foundation for the later ability to value yourself. The child internalizes this belief that it is o.k. to direct positive feelings toward herself.

If children are subject to ridicule, humiliation, or neglect, the results can be damaging to the developing sense of self-worth. Bill, as a boy, once built an airplane out of wood scraps. Because his father was a carpenter, Bill wanted to be like "Dad." When he showed the airplane to his father, the man laughed, made jokes about the simple little plane and held it up, showing it to a couple of his buddies who were visiting. Bill was profoundly humiliated. From then on, Bill felt very inadequate about his artistic skills and never attempted to do woodworking again.

---

Dale

"One thing about Joyce that I will always love and always miss was her total belief in me. Oh, she certainly knew when I screwed up and certainly disagreed with me at times. But down deep inside, she so honestly and completely accepted me and believed in me... and after years of being with her, I felt that acceptance. Somehow her acceptance of me made a very profound difference... for the first time in my life I really started to feel OK about myself."

---

### The Need for Safety

People have a basic need to feel reasonably safe. Three factors play an important role in maintaining safety. The first is predictability. Many life events are very predictable. Some of these are rooted in our environment: you can predict with great accuracy that the sun will rise and set, that almost always there is air to breathe, that water will quench your thirst. This kind of stability or sameness in the world gives us certainty. To use a popular term, predictability helps us feel "grounded."

In the early months of life, a child's repeated predictable experiences of interaction with mother and father can serve this same purpose. The child comes to know in a deep way that even though pains of hunger periodically arise, she can count on relief and comfort from loving parents. As a child grows older, she learns that certain behaviors are acceptable and other behaviors are not. Many children can predict with unfailing accuracy that if they track mud on the new carpet, they will be scolded. Kids don't like to be scolded, but there is comfort in being able to predict. Even if something bad is going to happen, it's always easier and feels safer to anticipate the consequences based on past experience.

People have a remarkable tendency to recreate environments that resemble the familiar and known. Sometimes children from abusive families grow up and intuitively seek out abusive marital partners. A dependent man who feels inadequate and wants to stand on his own two feet somehow manages to marry a controlling, dominating woman. He again feels stifled. But on closer inspection, his powerful, underlying (and unrecognized) need is to keep the environment familiar. Even in the face of emotional or physical pain, this need for sameness and predictability can be the driving force behind repetitive life scenarios. People who repeat maladaptive or hurtful patterns of interaction, for the most part, are not dumb. Rather, they are people who are inwardly in great need of feeling safe.

A feeling of being in control also plays a role in maintaining a sense of safety. If people feel they have at least some control over events, they will feel less anxious. Exercising control (e.g., taking action) can often reduce or eliminate problems. However, even when efforts to change events fail, a person often feels better if he knows that he at least was able to have some influence on the outcome. Ann is a middle-aged woman whose mother recently died from breast cancer. Ann told me, "In the end, we couldn't do anything to stop the cancer. But, we did a lot to help. I found her what was probably the best care she could have. I persuaded the doctors to do everything they could to reduce her pain. And most importantly, my mother and I really opened up to each other and told each other 'I love you'." Having even a small degree of control matters to people; they feel less helpless, powerless, and hopeless. In fact, even recognizing the events over which we have no control gives us some sense of safety. The world seems somewhat safer when we can take action and have some impact on the outcome of events. (Plans for just such action follow in Part III of this book.)

### The Need To Hold Stress and Stimulation at an Optimal Level

All we humans need a certain amount of stimulation. There have been isolated, bizarre cases of children who were raised in conditions of extreme stimulus deprivation. If this deprivation continues long enough, and the child survives, the lack of stimulation profoundly interferes with normal brain maturation. The rich connecting pathways between nerve cells (dendrites) fail to develop adequately, resulting in severe mental retardation. (Such findings are also borne out in numerous animal studies on stimulus deprivation and brain development.) Kids come into the world literally hungry for stimulation; experiencing excessively low levels of stimulation can retard development and cause discomfort.

Each of us begins life with a certain, optimum level of activation, and when the environment provides stimulation at this particular level, it feels right for us. If the level drops below optimum, we feel bored. If this state of boredom continues for a while, we either fall asleep or try to do something to reduce the boredom (e.g., go out to do something fun). A little boredom may be restful. A lot can be very uncomfortable. More severe levels of boredom may become intolerable, and people are highly motivated to jazz up their lives.

A higher level of stimulation (above the individual's optimum) may feel like excitement. If you like the particular kind of stimulation, and it lasts for fairly short periods of time, the experience can be challenging or fun. However, if too much is going on, the experience can be overwhelming and can lead to feelings of anxiety, and in the extreme, can cause you to feel quite disorganized. The optimal level of stimulation is different for everyone.

Some people require a very low level of activation to feel comfortable. Such people may feel perfectly content to lead quiet, sedentary lives or may desire little in terms of novelty and excitement. In addition, these people may feel overwhelmed by what others consider to be relatively mild levels of stimulation.

Figure 6-A illustrates the concept of levels of stimulation:

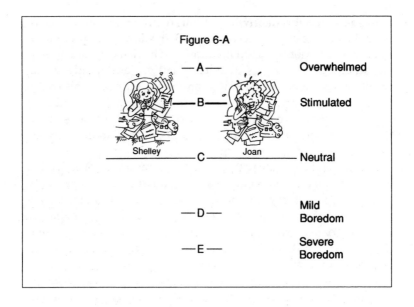

In this hypothetical case, Joan has a lower innate level of activation. The amount of stimulation that feels comfortable and right for her would bore Shelley to tears. Shelley's daily life at her optimum-level (B) would be too much for Joan. It would probably be hard for Shelley and Joan to appreciate each other's differences. It's not that one is right and one is wrong. They simply are different, unique individuals.

Even when we are infants, these principles are in operation. According to many child development specialists, good parents can sense their children's unique needs. Some kids are simply more sensitive and more overwhelmed by stresses and stimulation, while other children need and demand more activation from their environments. Throughout life, many of us struggle to find some middle ground between boredom and over-stimulation. Finding some balance is important.

### The Needs of Human Beings

When biological needs are met and basic emotional needs are at least partially met, you can pay more attention to higher emotional needs, which include a sense of aliveness, a search for meaningfulness, a desire to give something back to the world (e.g., to make a contribution, to raise a child, to take a stand for a just cause), spiritual development, and discovering your "true self."

In a model similar to one proposed by psychologist Abraham Maslow, I would like to suggest a hierarchy of human needs. Lower level, basic needs usually must be met, at least to some degree, before people are able to pursue higher needs (See Figure 6-B). As in building a house, if the foundation is inadequate, all other structures built on top remain unstable. Likewise, when biological needs are not met, striving for higher needs is unlikely or at best, difficult. For instance, a young person growing up in a third world country may wage a constant battle against starvation. This potentially life-threatening state of need will dominate his life. Developing meaningful, loving connections to others or deepening his spiritual self may simply not be possible for him.

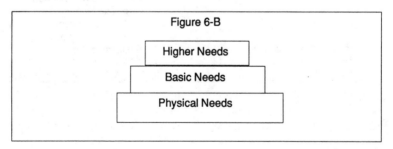

Figure 6-B

Higher Needs

Basic Needs

Physical Needs

For many people, when basic emotional needs are not met, a state of deprivation exists. For example, a young woman victim of severe child abuse each day struggles with painful memories and perceives the world of human interaction as a very frightening place to be. When her basic needs for love and safety are missing, the emotional pain demands her attention. The pain can be all-consuming, and the pursuit of higher emotional needs may be an impossibility.

Most painful emotional experiences in life, in one way or another, create distress by affecting these fundamental human needs (see Figure 6-C). The emotional pain or symptoms (e.g., distress, depression, irritability) can be seen as a voice from within, speaking out and saying, "I need something." Emotional symptoms are unpleasant; understandably, people are motivated to get rid of them. At the same time, such signals alert us that something is wrong, just as physical pain alerts us, tells us we are cut, we are ill, or we need medical help. Pain is an expression of need. Likewise, states of emotional pain and need are the mind's way of saying, "Hey, pay attention! Like it or not, you are human and your needs are not being met."

---

### Figure 6-C

| Human Needs | States of Need Deprivation |
|---|---|
| 1. Love | 1. Loss, grief |
| 2. Self-love | 2. Low self-esteem |
| 3. Safety | 3. Fear, insecurity, anxiety |
| 4. Optimal Stimulation | 4. a. Too much: Overwhelmed |
| | b. Too little: Boredom or emptiness |
| 5. Biological | 5. Illness or death |

---

## Seven

## One Size Fits All:
### *How Parents and Society Shaped You*

*A*s mentioned in Chapter 6, the drive to survive is a fundamental
aspect of the human condition. Obviously, children have no control
over the kind of environment into which they are born. Whether the
early family environment is growth-promoting or severely
emotionally damaging, the drive to survive is wired into all
children's biology and psyches. Adaptation — the mechanism or
tool of survival — is a blend of two powerful forces: *self-expression*
and *accommodation*.

### Self-expression

Self-expression means being who you are: expressing your feelings, needs, thoughts, opinions and actions. Self-expression arises
spontaneously out of the "true self" — the authentic, natural expression of who you are. Self-expression can aid adaptation
tremendously. For example, the infant who feels hungry cries.
Crying is a natural response to an inner state of need. Many times
crying works; it is an action the baby makes that gets a response. His

parent responds by feeding him, which serves the goal of survival. In adulthood, self-expression also aids adaptation. If you are being mistreated, hurt or used, to take a stand and say, "Stop treating me this way" or "I want you to take my feelings into consideration," can be an important survival tactic, and may dramatically improve the quality of an on-going relationship.

In addition to serving adaptational needs, self-expression is a primary source of feelings of aliveness. Throughout life, most of us will experience times during which we feel a zest for life, a desire to be in the world, and a sense of hope for the future. Many times these kinds of feelings naturally arise when life is going our way. Such feelings are also promoted by actions that express our true, inner selves (our unique inner feelings, ideas and beliefs).

### Accommodation

The second force of adaptation is accommodation: to change something about yourself so that you'll get your needs met (be loved, feel safe, etc.).

Let's consider this process of accommodation by looking at Figure 7-A. Diagram A represents an infant's natural, spontaneous, random behavior (crying, laughing, sleeping, spitting up, smiling, knocking over mom's house plants, etc.).

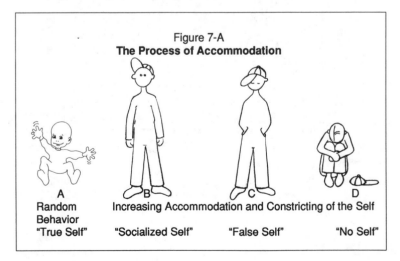

Figure 7-A
**The Process of Accommodation**

A
Random
Behavior
"True Self"

Increasing Accommodation and Constricting of the Self

"Socialized Self"     "False Self"     "No Self"

These random behaviors are expressions of the true self, of who you naturally are. With time, certain behaviors or ways of being develop that parents do not like or do not tolerate. Let's say, for instance, in Diagram B, that the child has learned to inhibit his expressions of temper and his desire to cling to Mom. In this particular example, this child's parents, in a very significant way, disapprove of these behaviors. Parents communicate disapproval in many ways. Sometimes it's very explicit: scolding a child, spanking him, sending him to his room. Often, disapproval is a more subtle, but quite powerful non-verbal message to the child: a "You should be ashamed of yourself" facial expression when the child exhibits a forbidden behavior.

---

### Shame: The Great Inhibiting Emotion

In all cultures people teach children the ways of society by example, by encouragement and by the use of punishment. Without this experience youngsters do not internalize society's values. With time, these messages become the inner voices of conscience that guide a child's behavior. One version of punishment seen across cultures is shaming (humiliation, ridicule, embarrassment). Shaming goes beyond normal "shoulds" and "shouldn'ts" — in its extreme forms, it gives the child a severe message: "In a basic way there is something wrong with you... you disgust me." At the emotional core of this message are two critical elements: 1) an attack on the basic worth of the child and 2) an implilcit communication, "Shape up or get out of my sight." The implied threat is abandonment.

Shaming is a powerful emotional experience that shapes and molds the child's emerging personality, inhibiting honest self-expression. It can be an ongoing source of despair.

_Parents' obvious or subtle messages of disapproval touch upon the child's strong inner need to be loved and to feel safe. So the child accommodates by altering her behavior. As many parents can attest, the effects of this accommodation can be temporary, or they may be profoundly long lasting. When this is the case, the child may completely block out an entire aspect of his being. (In Figure 7-A, behaviors #1 and #2 are eventually suppressed and inhibited). This type of accommodation indeed often lasts a lifetime.

> Sharon
> "I'd sometimes go and sit by my Dad's feet and look up at him. He'd be reading the paper, and then he'd just look down at me with this look on his face that said, "Well, what do you want?" He seemed annoyed... impatient. I'd just walk away... at some point I guess I just stopped going in to be with him."

Carl is an example of lifelong accommodation. He is a young man who grew up in a home where his father reacted to Carl's expressions of anger, or even the strong voicing of opinions, with explosive abuse. As a young child and now as a young adult, Carl has taken this entire part of himself (i.e., the natural human impulse to feel and express anger and to express opinions) and locked it away. Not only does he not express anger; he doesn't even feel it. He has cut off a part of his true self and locked it away.

This type of accommodation usually begins very early in life. It is generally not a conscious choice. Almost always a person blocks the true self to avoid emotional or physical pain. In a very real sense, this avoidance is a desperate attempt to feel love and safety in the early home environment. Carl has paid a price for this accommodation, however; he is very passive and non-assertive. People take advantage of him. He doesn't know how to take a stand for himself. To call serious passivity "neurotic" might be accurate, but when you know the context, such passivity can also be appreciated as an act of survival. Within Carl as little boy was an inner guide or compassionate protector — a part of his mind with one goal: "I am here to protect this boy, no matter what." That inner guide continues to be present, maintaining safety and protecting Carl. Rather than labeling this process as maladaptive or neurotic, it's more helpful to see it as a self-protective, adaptive solution while being aware of the possible emotional effects. For example, in the last chapter we talked about Jill, whose adaptive solution was to maintain interpersonal distance. The cost for her was loneliness.

The process of accommodation is an absolutely necessary part of growing up. It's the way all people learn to be socialized, civilized human beings. Just how much you accommodate, however, does make a difference. The process itself is not inherently maladaptive. But the price of socialization is always an inhibition of the true self: "...we always abandon some of our nature for the sake of our surrounding social order," says psychotherapist Jim Doak.

Accommodation and socialization are all a matter of levels or degrees, as may be seen on the continuum in Figure 7-B.

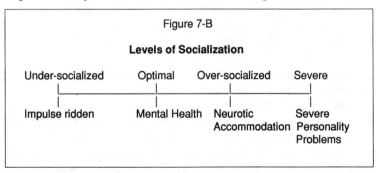

Figure 7-B

**Levels of Socialization**

| Under-socialized | Optimal | Over-socialized | Severe |
|---|---|---|---|
| Impulse ridden | Mental Health | Neurotic Accommodation | Severe Personality Problems |

People who have rarely been required to alter their behavior are at great risk for entering life situations without internal controls over their actions. They freely act out all of their feelings and desires. (To use psychological lingo, they are "under-socialilzed," or "impulse ridden.") These people exhibit blatant disregard for others and constantly violate social values. Those who have experienced extreme under-socialization are referred to as "psychopaths," and they often end up living their lives in prisons or mental hospitals.

At the other extreme, many people are subjected to experiences of over-socialization. As constriction of the personality becomes more pervasive and severe (in Figure 7-A, moving from A toward D), people start losing track of their true selves. The self that is out in the open for the world to see and for the individual to experience has been reshaped by compliance with the demands of others. The child has gone to such extremes to comply and accommodate that the majority of what she experiences as "self" may be quite different from her true inner self. This compliant self may properly be called a "false self."

Many human experiences can be blocked out of awareness. All the basic needs can be denied. The dare-devil thinks, "I don't need to feel safe; I can laugh in the face of danger." The aloof, detached person believes, "I don't need love...I don't need others." The anorexic thinks, "I don't need to eat." People can lose touch with their anger, their sexuality, their creativity, their needs to be dependent and seek nurturance, their desire to be the center of attention, their need to grieve or to seek out intimacy.

Most of us inhibit true expression of ourselves somewhat. Sean may be passive and compliant at work, but he expresses power and aggression on the racquetball court. Fiona is distant and close-mouthed, except with a special, trusted friend. While many people feel only a whisper from within, a faint inner awareness of some feeling or need (such as sadness or love), in the extreme, some have had to massively cut off and inhibit their true selves. Their true selves actually feel phony and superficial to these people. This feeling is often seen in individuals who have lived through very traumatic experiences early in life.

Inhibition or constriction of the true self can result in an impaired ability to heal from painful life events. An analogy with the human body may help to explain this idea. A number of important bodily systems operate to promote survival and to aid in the process of healing following disease or trauma. The nervous system has the capacity to rapidly perceive danger in the environment and imme-diately to elicit the so-called "fight or flight" response, a complex hormonal and neurochemical reaction that mobilizes the body to take action. This action is designed either to remove you from danger (flight) or to directly alter the situation (e.g., put out a fire, kill an attacking bear, or tell your spouse to stop criticizing you).

On a different level, the immune system has especially developed, complex mechanisms for detecting the presence of foreign organisms (e.g., bacteria) or mutant cells (as in cancer). After recognizing invading organisms, the cells of the immune system orchestrate a multi-level attack to destroy the infectious agents. Other bodily processes simultaneously aid healing by the development of blood clots, scar tissue, etc. Thus, a number of different biological systems cooperate to fight disease and to promote healing. When the immune system is suppressed or shut down (as is the case in AIDS or other immune disorders), the natural capacity to heal becomes seriously impaired.

Likewise, certain natural emotional healing processes and mechanisms exist within the human psyche. These healing systems naturally emerge during the course of emotional development. They are aspects of the human personality, characteristics of the true self. In positive, supportive, growth-promoting environments, such characteristics emerge spontaneously. However, adverse life experiences can interfere with the development of these emotional processes. Most people will, in the course of growing up, cut off or inhibit parts of the self, a process which often leads to problems. Some aspects of the true self are especially designed to promote emotional healing. If these parts of the self are unavailable, the person will experience significant difficulties when encountering painful life experiences. Inhibition of healing may be the result.

For example, following such major losses as the death of a loved one or a divorce, the normal human response is to experience grief. (Grieving is a complex process that will be discussed in more detail later in the book.) Central aspects of grieving include the ability to talk about the one you have lost, to feel the emotion of sadness and to cry. This type of human emotional expression is common in most cultures throughout the world. Something about crying promotes healing. Yet, many people have learned early in life that they should not cry. For them, crying is a sign of weakness or inadequacy.

Allowing the tears to come may be accompanied by feelings of shame or embarrassment. For other people, crying represents vulnerability (a threat to personal safety), and sadness evokes feelings of anxiety and fear. In such cases, people may grit their teeth and fight back the emotions. In more pronounced cases, the parts of the self that naturally would respond with sadness have become so stifled, so cut off, that the person is totally unaware of any sad feelings at all. This individual feels nothing but a sense of numbness. In such cases, an emotional loss is not resolved and like any unhealed wound, may continue to be a source of tremendous (psychological) pain for many years to come.

---

### Dale

"I know these days it's "in" for men to be emotional. . . you know, the "men's movement." But the truth is that the men I know aren't emotional! They seem to handle things pretty well. I never saw my father cry, except once at my mother's funeral. . . . I've been crying all the time lately. I even broke down at work once. God, that was embarrassing. I just wonder what's wrong with me.

Sometimes when I cry, I think I'm holding my wife. I sort of hug my pillow and imagine it's her. It hurts, but sometimes it's OK. I miss her, and I know I love her, and after I stop crying I feel very tired and kind of relieved.

I just wish I didn't hurt so much."

---

The second example of the inhibition of healing was seen earlier in Carl, the passive and non-assertive man. He endures on-going problems in relationships when some people continue to hurt and take advantage of him. The part of his self that is cut off naturally wants to express anger or to voice protest when he is being hurt. Carl may continue to be the victim of others for a lifetime because of his difficulties in asserting himself.

Everyone wants to be accepted and valued. To meet those needs, most of us accommodate and inhibit parts of our true selves. If this constriction of the self is severe, we lose touch with our sources of aliveness and our natural capacities for emotional healing and growth. But there are actions we can take to encourage the development of an emotionally healthy self. In the following chapter we'll take a look at the kinds of environments that can help.

## Eight

## "Hide Your Feelings" & Other Ways
## To Keep on Hurting

*T*hough people talk about feelings and emotions in many different ways, for the purpose of this book, I would like to define and discuss feelings and emotions in a particular way.

In many respects, says psychiatrist David Viscott, feelings are like a sixth sense and share characteristics in common with the other five senses. Let's look at taste as an example. When you put food into your mouth, you experience the sense of taste as the food comes in contact with your taste buds. This experience may have its origin in the mouth, but the actual sensation is registered in the brain. In a certain area of the brain, the nerve impulses arriving from the taste buds evoke a chemical reaction, referred to as a "sensation," which you notice. This sensation may be combined with other sensations simultaneously being received in other parts of the brain (e.g., smell and vision). Taken together these sensory experiences are recognized as a particular taste.

One way of understanding these sensory experiences is to view them as ways of *gathering information* about our environment. Taste tells you a lot about what you have just put into your mouth. Beyond this very basic sensory experience, you may experience other sensations that immediately come into your awareness, such as recognizing the taste as being familiar, or sensing the taste either as pleasant or as unpleasant. You may also have thoughts about the sensation, e.g., "This is delicious!" And finally, the sensation and/or resulting thoughts may lead to certain behaviors. For example, if you bite into a very sour apple, you might think, "Yuck, this is sour," and respond with a specific behavior, spitting out the food.

Thus, in a basic way, taste leads to a sensation which can be seen as "information." This "information" may or may not lead to thoughts about the taste or to resulting behaviors. Likewise, pain functions to alert you to the presence of danger. If you touch a hot stove, the stimulus is the heat; the inner sensation, the pain; and the response, taking your hand off the stove. Without sensory experiences, people don't survive well. Sensory organs have evolved and serve an adaptational purpose: to give us information about the world and to guide our behavior so we can survive.

Likewise, emotions can provide complex information about the world which we can use to guide our actions. If a child is scolded, his inner emotional experience (perhaps shame) can be seen as information that can help direct future behavior.

Emotions also can serve three additional purposes. Some emotions result in physical reactions that alter bodily functions. These reactions may be accompanied by the release of certain neurochemicals or hormones that produce relaxation or analgesia (pain control). Some researchers suggest that crying, for example, may be accompanied by the release of endorphins in the brain. These naturally occurring morphine-like neuropeptides lead to feelings of relief and exhaustion following a good, hard cry. Another example is seen in war-time situations where intense fear or anger can produce chemical changes that numb physical pain (as in case of men who are seriously wounded but temporarily feel little pain and are able to keep fighting or run to safety). Emotions also evoke behavior that elicits help from others. A baby animal, for instance, when separated from its mother, may call out a distress signal which immediately alerts the mother and brings her to help. Of course, this behavior also occurs in humans, as many new parents can attest.

The expression of emotions almost always is a way of conveying personal values. The reasons for feeling strongly about something relate directly the way I perceive events and what matters to me on a very personal level. People are not just stimulus-response organisms or computers. We attach important, personal meanings to all perceptions. Our reactions are not only directly connected to the stressful event, but also to who we are: what we value, hold dear, and believe.

Anthropologists have studied emotional responses in numerous cultures around the globe. Although many societies have unique emotional expressions or culturally determined emotional "dialects," it is clear at least seven basic, universal human emotions exist: happiness, fear, anger, surprise, disgust, sadness, and shame.

These emotions are a part of our human fiber. They are naturally occurring responses to certain kinds of situations. For example, it is natural to feel sadness if you experience a loss, to feel anger if someone attacks or belittles you, or to feel fear if your security is threatened. And yet, in many cultures, people have decided that certain emotions or the outward expression of certain feelings are not appropriate. Children are taught early to inhibit certain emotions (not to express the feelings or, in the extreme, not even to feel them inside). At times, the rules for "appropriate" emoting are based on one's sex, e.g., it's ok for women to cry, but not for men; it's ok for men to get angry, but not for women.

Why societies have chosen to inhibit the expression of particular feelings is not entirely clear. One answer may be that emotions have been misunderstood. According to psychologist Kenneth Isaacs, "A funny thing happened to the human race on its path of development. The whole race got entangled in a misunderstanding of emotions... 'Affect phobia' (mental health professionals use the term "affect" — it basically means "emotion") became a way of life, universally. Consistently, emotion was considered to be an enduring, disruptive, wasteful, interfering burden... a trouble." He says "the blessing of emotion" has been thought of as an evil opponent, and emotion, as a result, "became something to be cured." Contrary to this negative perception, Isaacs believes that in their basic form, emotions are potentially useful, benign and constructive. They provide people with information about their world. He compares emotions to color perception. People simply perceive color and integrate it into their more global views of on-going events. People do not fear color nor do they criticize other people for seeing color. It is a sensory event that conveys information. However, we know that most societies have, in fact, developed powerful rules and expectations governing the expression of certain feelings. In many respects, as we shall see, these rules do not seem to help people and instead, impede emotional healing.

### Affect Phobia

How does "affect phobia" develop? Why does an emotion, something quite natural, with time, become something that people fear? Often parents do not accept or tolerate the expression of certain emotions. Let's say that a young child runs down his driveway, slips and skins his knee and begins to cry. His father is nearby and comes to his aid. Upon inspection, Dad finds a very minor scrape on the boy's knee and says, "There, there, it'll be ok." But the child continues to cry. Next let's assume that his father is having a frustrating, stressful day and besides this, Dad himself was brought up being told, "Don't be a cry-baby. Boys need to be tough." After a moment or two of the child's continued crying, Dad says, "For heaven's sake, stop crying. It's just a little scratch!" He looks and sounds rather angry and disgusted. The boy very well may be getting the message, "Dad's angry at me," and the boy begins to feel afraid of his father's anger. Or, possibly the child thinks, "Dad is ashamed of me and won't like me if I keep crying" and begins to fear disapproval or rejection. The boy feels ashamed. If this is a repeated experience, in all likelihood in the future, the cycle will repeat itself: child's physical hurt → child's crying (a natural response to pain) → child's worries and fears about Dad's reaction → child grits his teeth and doesn't cry.

Is this experience so bad? It all depends on the intensity of the situation. Let's consider the same basic scenario, but instead look at two different extremes. In example A, the boy falls and scrapes his knee. Dad comes to him and comforts him but says, "I know it hurts. But it's a scrape. I think it'll be better in a minute or two. I think you can handle it," and gives his son a hug. In example B (from my psychotherapy practice), the boy falls on a nail which punctures his knee deeply. His father says, "What are you crying about?! It's nothing." The boy says, sobbing, "But Daddy, it hurts." His father replies, "No it doesn't; you're just a sissy." Father then carries his son to the garage and pulls the nail out with a pair of pliers.

In the first example, the father not only provided comfort and validated the pain, but also conveyed the belief that his son could cope with the pain and that the pain would pass. This boy gradually comes to know that minor pains do go away and that he has the capacity not only to feel the pain but also to tolerate it (i.e., not to see it as a catastrophe). This boy does not develop "affect phobia."

In the second case, the boy's pain was grossly invalidated. He grew up learning to numb himself to pain or at least to keep it to himself. He has never felt OK about saying "I hurt." Years later this boy, as an adult, told me, "I thought I was insane. How could I hurt so much, but Dad said it didn't hurt? It didn't make sense to me. I just felt crazy!"

The long-range outcome for each of these boys is vastly different. To a degree, the first child does learn to inhibit emotional expression, but he still can feel the hurt and know it is a natural feeling. When he experiences hurt as an adult, he will be much more likely to acknowledge and express his feelings. In the second example, the boy was forced to massively inhibit his true feelings. The basic emotion (hurt and sadness) has now become associated with other feelings (e.g., shame, fear of Dad's anger, or fear of abandonment), and thoughts such as, "I must be crazy to have this feeling. There is something wrong with me." Later in life, should he be hurt physically or emotionally, he won't show his feelings, not because of fear of the basic emotion (hurt), but rather, because of a fear of the associated feelings (shame). In a true sense, he has become "affect phobic." He is afraid of his own natural feelings and is strongly motivated to avoid expressing or even feeling emotions such as sadness or hurt.

### *Overwhelming Emotions*

Any sensory event, if too intense, can lead to pain. If a light is too bright, if a stove is too hot, if an odor is too strong, the sensory experience exceeds a certain threshold of tolerance, and we experience it as unpleasant or painful. Certain amounts of pain can be tolerated, but beyond a certain point, pain can be overwhelming for everyone. Emotions, likewise, if their intensity is fairly low, can be felt and understood as "information." But, at high levels of intensity, emotions can also be overwhelming. Pop psychology has suggested that it's good to "get in touch with your feelings" and to an extent, this process can often be beneficial. However, it is important to realize that certain emotions, especially if they are very intense, can result in significant pain. And, all people have an understandable right to avoid pain. Thus, caution is important.

Psychiatrist Mardi Horowitz and his colleagues have suggested a useful model for understanding our experience of emotions and the resulting impact on our ability to function (Marmar, 1991). We can respond to an emotionally powerful event in one of three ways: by *over-control* of our emotions; by losing control (*dys-control*) of our emotions; or by *emotional tolerance*. Figure 8-A offers a graphic representation of this notion. The following pages discuss it in some detail. (See Figure 8-A).

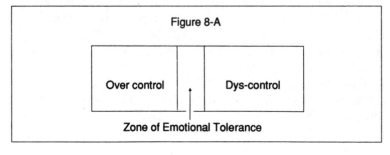

Figure 8-A

Over control | Dys-control

Zone of Emotional Tolerance

## Over-control

Let's say that the painful event is learning that a close relative has contracted a very serious disease. Many times people deal with such news by entering a state of over-control. Although this state may be a conscious choice, most often it is an automatic process that results in the person's experiencing little true emotion. A person in a state of over-control certainly may know that the news is terrible and have a vague awareness of inner emotional pain. But in a number of ways, she has sealed herself off from her feelings. Over-control is maintained by avoiding situations which potentially could trigger emotions, (e.g., avoid calling the relative); by distractions, (e.g., involving yourself in work to direct your thoughts and attention away from painful inner feelings, or watching T.V. in order not to think about the relative); by rationalizing, (e.g., "Well, he's an old man... he's lead a full life. These things are bound to happen." Such comments and thoughts partially acknowledge the painful event, but operate to minimize the emotional impact.); and by emotional numbing, which can be brought on by the use of alcohol, tranquilizers or other drugs, or can occur on a very automatic inner level. Many people are surprised at how in the face of quite painful news, they feel nothing because inner emotional defenses have come on the scene, automatically blocking out underlying pain (More will be said about this process in Chapter 11).

Over-control is a very natural, normal way of responding to painful life events. It often can help us to function and to cope. Yet, if carried to an extreme, it can become a major problem, interfering with the process of emotional healing, as we shall explore in later chapters.

## Dys-control

Emotional dys-control, conversely, is a state of mind in which inner emotional defenses seriously fail, and a person is flooded by extremely intense emotions. It is important to emphasize that dys-control is much more than just feeling strong emotions. The flooding of emotions is almost intolerable and can potentially result in severe fragmentation or disorganization of the personality (e.g., developing psychotic symptoms such as hallucinations, experiencing severe states of confusion, suicidal behavior, etc.). *Many* people encounter significant, intense periods of sadness, fear, anger and so forth, but may never truly enter a state of complete emotional dys-control. Actual personality fragmentation is generally seen only in individuals with serious mental illnesses or in mentally healthy people who encounter catastrophic emotional stress (e.g., witnessing the death of several family members or being confined as a prisoner of war or held in a concentration camp).

## Zone of Emotional Tolerance

The zone of emotional tolerance is a state of mind in which an individual does, in fact, experience very strong emotions and yet can tolerate the experience. In such instances, a person may become flooded by sadness, fear, etc., which may "feel" overwhelming, yet the experience does *not* lead to disorganization. The person lives through the wave of intense emotion, it passes, and she re-enters a less intense, less painful state of mind. As a person starts to move from a state of over-control to one of feeling (zone of emotional tolerance), she may begin to fear the emerging feelings, anticipating that she is about to be overwhelmed by sadness (or other emotions). This anticipatory fear often motivates people to engage in activities that move them back into a state of over-control. Examples of such actions might include changing the topic of discussion, fighting back tears, telling yourself, "Stop thinking about it... you're just upsetting yourself," or having a couple of beers to numb the feeling. In addition, many people notice that friends and relatives often try to prevent them from becoming emotional by saying, "Now, now, don't take it so hard," "You've got to to pull yourself together... don't let it get to you," or "Look on the bright side." All of these messages have a central theme: "Don't express strong feelings. Get back in control." The friends' intentions may be positive, but the result can be that the distressed person stifles natural feelings.

> Dale
>
> "I had literally gone through my whole adult life and never cried. Since my wife died, everything has changed. I cry a lot now. At first, a giant tidal wave of sadness would sweep over me. A couple of times I'd start almost uncontrollably sobbing. I felt really out of control. But in the past few weeks I guess I've gotten kind of used to it... I still cry, sometimes even sob, but what's different is that crying doesn't scare me as much. I guess I've figured out that tears don't kill people. Even in the middle of it, I know that it will pass, and I know that I don't literally lose control."

One basic key to successful emotional healing is the importance of letting yourself *experience* your inner emotions. Yet, I want to be clear about two points. First, inner emotions are often scary. Everyone has a right to determine when, where or even *if* he wants to feel inner emotions. Some approaches to self-help and psychotherapy advocate techniques that quickly break through defenses and unearth strong emotions. *These techniques can be counterproductive for many people and actually traumatic for some.* In fact, there are documented instances in which some individuals have become psychotic while participating in emotion-evoking encounter groups. Thus, the unearthing of strong feelings must be done at the proper time and in a proper context. People generally must open up to strong inner feelings only in an atmosphere of safety and trust. They must go at their own pace and be able to appreciate that there may be times when it's OK to experience feelings, but also times to back away from feelings.

Second, although we all share similar emotional hardware (e.g., the same basic human needs and emotions), our life experiences and our responses to them vary tremendously. Exactly the same event may have drastically different impacts on different individuals. Though people vary in many respects, three important dimensions of emotional functioning appear to be central to understanding differences in people's emotional make-ups: emotional sensitivity, emotional responsivity and emotional history.

*Emotional Sensitivity.* People are born into the world with varying degrees of sensitivity which can be seen in many different biologic systems. Sensitivity to sunburn varies. All of us know people who can spend all day in the summer sun and not burn, while others severely burn after a half hour. Comedian Woody Allen says, "When I go to the beach I don't sunburn... I stroke." The sensitivity of the skin to the rays of the sun is a part of your genetic endowment. Likewise, some people are exquisitely sensitive to loud noises and feel keyed up in situations where loud noises predominate. They may prefer to live in a small town or in the country away from the constant noise of the big city.

In a similar fashion, people are born into the world with varying degrees of sensitivity to emotionally arousing events. Although this characteristic is undoubtedly influenced by their upbringing and other psychological factors, probably a certain amount of this sensitivity is biologically rooted. Child development specialists assert that many infants exhibit temperamental characteristics: emotional withdrawal, risk avoidance, emotional sensitivity. From early in life these children seem to have lower thresholds for emotional and environmental stimulation. They shy away from novel or stressful situations and quickly seem to be overwhelmed by exposure to even mildly distressing stimuli. Early evidence of these traits has been shown to have incredible stability over time and is evident in predominant personality characteristics years and years later. Other kids reveal responses at the other extreme. These children not only tolerate stress and novelty, but often seek it out. From early in life, they appear to be biologically equipped to manage emotional stimulation in a robust and resilient manner.

*Emotional Responsivity.* Here we are talking about the outward expression of emotions. Sometimes some people show little overt emotional expression because they are feeling nothing internally. But many times people are quite emotionally sensitive inwardly, but they prefer to keep a lid on outward expression. Many people are private, and they prefer to deal with emotional concerns by themselves or to share feelings only with a few trusted friends or relatives. Other people are very emotionally responsive. They show their feelings and have no qualms about sharing their emotions with the world. As a therapist helping people to work through painful life experiences, I must always remind myself that everyone has his or her own style of dealing with feelings. Though my client and I share similar human characteristics (the basic "emotional hardware"), the client's style with respect to both emotional sensitivity and responsivity may be quite different from mine.

*Emotional History.* Emotional history plays an important role in understanding your emotional functioning/style. Going back to the example of the two boys falling and hurting their knees, we saw that in Example A, the boy was fortunate to have a father who understood and allowed the expression of emotions, while in example B, the father not only disallowed emotional expression, but also profoundly invalidated the child's inner feelings.

People encounter thousands of situations during childhood in which their natural human emotions erupt and from which they receive some sort of response or feedback from others. These responses may show understanding and comfort or they may powerfully forbid the *expression* of feelings or in the extreme, forbid feelings altogether. Single events (like falling and scraping your knee) generally do not leave lasting impressions on your personality, but repeated experiences do. To the extent that feelings are allowed, the experiencing and expression of emotions will remain a part of a child's emerging self. If the injunction, "Don't express emotions" predominates, a child will learn to stifle the emotional expression. And in the extreme, when parents massively invalidate emotional experiences, the child will, in order to adapt and survive, squelch even the inner sense of feeling.

People exposed to non-acceptance of feelings develop a secondary fear, the fear of feeling (affect phobia). Let's consider an example: Marilyn has been rejected in an important love relationship. The natural human response to such an event would be sadness, hurt and possibly anger. If Marilyn has been raised in a home environment where feelings were *not* accepted or were discounted, very likely as she begins to feel sad, hurt and angry, she will

### The Brain and Behavior

Nature, nurture and fate. Although I have focused almost exclusively on the latter two, clearly, biological factors do play a major role in influencing emotional development.

During the past fifteen years we have witnessed an explosion of new technologies in the neurosciences. New theories regarding the brain and behavior have emerged, finding support from exciting new laboratory techniques such as PET and SPECT scans (sophisticated brain imaging techniques), computer assisted EEG brain-mapping devices and neuropsychological tests.

Even a basic overview of new insights regarding the influence of biological inheritance on the emotions is well beyond the scope of this book. However, I would like to highlight a sampling of recent findings. (Readers interested in more detail are referred to books by Ornstein and Thompson and Andreason, listed in the References.)

• Several mental disorders that were long-held to be caused by severe stress and adverse conditions in childhood, are now understood to be primarily physical illnesses (neurological and neurochemical disorders). The list includes: autism, schizophrenia, manic-depressive illness and hyperactivity (attention-deficit disorder).

• Alcoholism and related substance abuse disorders have been shown to run in families and very likely are influenced by genetic factors.

- Many personality characteristics are evident early in infancy, and remain as core traits well into adulthood. Such characteristics may have little to do with learning or environmental experiences, but rather are manifestations of biological temperament. All the data is not in yet, but here are a few of the features that have been studied: timidness, risk-avoidance, adaptability, emotional sensitivity, decisiveness, vigor, flexibility, sociability, activity level and impulsivity.

- Structural differences in brain anatomy have been found in studies comparing the brains of homosexual and heterosexual men. This may suggest that biological factors play an important role in sexual preference.

- Biological factors can modify emotional and personality functioning. Under some conditions, for example, treatment with certain antidepressants can not only decrease symptoms of depression, but also reduce worry, excessive self-doubting and the internal pressure to do things in perfectionistic ways.

- Psychological factors can modify biology as well. A recent study demonstrates that abnormal brain metabolism, seen in severe obsessive-compulsive disorder, can be reversed (normalized) by patients' involvement in a treatment program using behavior modification techniques.

It is entirely possible that many of your basic characteristics, your personal "style," even your "quirks" may be rooted in variations of biology. Emotional sensitivity, stinginess, intuition, the need for order, gregariousness, risk-taking and a host of other human traits *may* say more about the wiring of your nervous system than the experiences you encountered in childhood.

also feel fear. She is afraid that others will criticize her for feeling sad, that they will belittle her, reject her, or say she is "too sensitive." Thus, Marilyn has two powerful sources of emotional pain. The first is the primary, natural emotions associated with a significant loss; the second is the fear of how others will respond to her if she shows her emotions.

It is common for people in Marilyn's situation to respond in one of two ways: to feel the primary emotions, but then feel ashamed, inadequate or crazy, or to make drastic attempts to block inner feeling and stay in a state of emotional over-control. The unfortunate consequence of the latter option is that over-control can result in an inability to heal emotionally.

### *People with Special Vulnerabilities*

Some people have certain conditions/disorders that increase the likelihood of emotional pain. Especially during the past ten years, it has been very clearly determined that a number of people suffer from emotional and mental disorders partly or entirely caused by biological malfunctions. A number of these disorders are transmitted genetically and include major depressive disorders, bi-polar illness (manic-depressive illness), schizophrenia, a host of neurologic disorders, certain types of panic disorder, alcoholism and hyperactivity (also called attention deficit disorder). All people affected by these disorders share common characteristics: they are more emotionally sensitive, i.e., painful life events hit them harder, and the process of emotional recovery can become much more difficult for them. For many people suffering from these disorders, psychotherapy and, at times, psychiatric medication treatment may be necessary. In Appendix A, the various signs and symptoms of these psychiatric disorders are discussed.

Our human emotions are a sort of "sixth sense" — giving us information about the world, helping us determine whether the people and events in our lives are pleasant or unpleasant. Emotions help us make connection with others and express our values and personal beliefs. They are our main source of aliveness and — at times of severe stress — of tremendous human suffering. For some, fear of emotions has led to over-control; others seem unable to handle their strong feelings at all. Neither of these extreme responses will promote your emotional well-being. It's healthiest to allow yourself to experience your feelings within your own "zone of emotional tolerance."

## Nine

# What Does It Mean
# To Be Emotionally Healthy?

**W**hat experiences help children grow up in an emotionally healthy way? What kind of family environment can we describe as "optimal"? Three main factors are responsible for emotional growth and development: nurture, nature and fate. Let's talk about each of these in turn.

### Nurture, Nature and Fate

Famed British pediatrician D.W. Winnicott said that you don't need to be a "super parent" to raise children. In fact (and I personally take comfort in this), he believed that most children simply need *nurture* from a "good-enough mother" (and father). This belief rests on a tremendously important assumption: that all human beings come into life with in-born potentials: a sort of basic "hardware" of the personality — muscles, sensory organs and a highly developed nervous system — which will grow and develop into an array of skills, talents and abilities, and a natural tendency or movement toward emotional health and growth. A part of this movement toward emotional health and growth includes a desire to be and express who you truly are (either to allow the blossoming of the true self or to re-own dimensions of the true self which have been previously locked away).

Allowing a child's true self to develop fully is a crucial component of parenting. Thus, Winnicott's notion of a "good-enough mother" perhaps deserves some elaboration. All parents make mistakes. We all lose our tempers, feel overwhelmed and preoccupied from time to time. Often we just simply don't know the right way to deal with a child regarding certain issues at various points in their development. But parents don't have to be perfect all of the time. Children are tremendously resilient and can certainly live with occasional parental blunders. The key to allowing the child to develop her full potential is providing a predominantly positive, loving atmosphere of respect for and sensitivity to her basic needs. The "good-enough" parent must also try to prevent overwhelmingly traumatic experiences. The final ingredient of nurture is providing age-appropriate frustrations and challenges. The infant, for example, needs close contact and monitoring. The kindergartner, however, must be encouraged to gradually do some separating from Mom and Dad and venture out into the world of others.

*Nature* — the influence of hereditary and environmental factors — may interfere even when good-enough parenting is abundant. Children with severe handicaps, perceptual disorders, brain damage or certain biologically-based mental illnesses may encounter tremendous problems despite adequate emotional care from parents.

Finally, *fate* plays a role. One of the examples of fate's role can be seen in the death of a parent. The ravages of war, poverty, famine and extreme social conditions (e.g., racial harassment) can derail what otherwise is movement toward emotional health.

In optimal circumstances, people will quite naturally unfold in the direction of mental health, aliveness, and the expression of the "true self." As this process of growth occurs, certain characteristics of mental health emerge.

### Characteristics of Mental Helath
Psychiatrist James Masterson has described in some detail the characteristics of the "real self" which I have summarized. In many respects these are aspects of healthy personality development and

embody the major elements of inner emotional healing mechanisms. Let's examine his list of seven:

1. *Spontaneity and aliveness of affect.* Affect is a term used by psychologists and psychiatrists to refer to the expression of emotion. This characteristic reflects the ability to experience the full range of human emotions and to feel these emotions deeply. It is natural to feel pain and to withdraw if you burn yourself; it is normal to feel a pleasurable sensation and to savor it when you taste delicious food. Likewise, it is a natural human experience to be aware of inner emotions.

2. *The ability to identify inner feelings, wishes, needs and thoughts.* This ability is more than just noticing inner experiences; it involves the capacity to have some understanding of one's feelings, needs, etc., i.e., to attach some meaning to these inner experiences. For example, John, who has been recently divorced, notices his inner sense of loneliness and says to himself, "I feel sad and alone. It's not pleasant. I long to have companionship." His inner experiences are not those of vague discomfort, but rather emotions and thoughts which can be understood in the context of his life.

3. *Self-entitlement.* A person has an internalized sense that "it is ok for me to feel good about myself when I accomplish things... I am entitled to have feelings of pride and to value what I do." As mentioned earlier, this inner permission to feel good about yourself is probably an outgrowth of having had early experiences with parents who provided support and praise, not only for accomplishments, but simply for being alive and a part of the family. A related characteristic is *the ability to internally generate feelings of worth and self-esteem.* Everyone likes to receive praise from others. It feels good to be acknowledged or to get a pat on the back. However, the psychologically mature person is not constantly in desperate need of affirmation from the outside. She can often draw upon her own inner source of self-worth. For example, Janice selflessly gives an anonymous gift to a charity or feels proud of earning a promotion even if no one else notices.

4. *Self-assertion.* This is a two-fold process. It begins with the inner belief that it is ok for you to express your opinions, feelings,

needs, etc. and to defend yourself if you are being hurt by others. In addition, you have the ability and willingness to put these inner beliefs into action, i.e., to take a stand, to voice an opinion or express yourself. Mature people have the capacity to act in an assertive way but are not necessarily assertive all of the time or in every situation. You assert yourself while taking the rights, needs and feelings of others into consideration.

5. *The ability to provide self-soothing.* This very important point deserves a lengthier discussion. All people will ultimately experience losses, set-backs, and personal failures — absolutely unavoidable events in life. The person who denies such experiences is incredibly lucky or extremely self-deceiving. The personal pain that results from losses and failures can be tremendous. Self-soothing, a sort of nurturing that takes place within oneself, encompasses a wide array of attitudes and behaviors.

The first is a deep, inner belief, an attitude of compassion toward oneself: "I am hurting and I have a *right* to do something to ease my pain." Remarkably, many people do not feel ok about this basic human right. They may think that they deserve to feel awful or think "I'm just feeling sorry for myself." This attitude often reflects their early experiences of unsuccessfully seeking comfort from others. Many children are told directly to stop being cry-babies... to stop feeling sorry for themselves. The parental message is that it's not ok to hurt and (especially) not ok to ask for comfort. The child internalizes this message which can become a lifelong inner belief. The emotionally mature person usually has been fortunate enough to be genuinely cared for early in life and has developed an internalized capacity for self-compassion.

Self-soothing also takes the form of remembering and calling forth positive images of past successes or love. Susan just experienced a very painful rejection. Paul, whom she had been dating, told her that he was fed up with her and had, in fact, been seeing another woman for the past month. He said to Susan, "You are a loser. I should have left you a long time ago." In the midst of her sadness and hurt, Susan would often tell herself that she wasn't a loser. When she reminded herself of the many good friendships in which she had been valued and loved, she remembered a number of occasions when she had made a difference in the lives of friends and family members. These thoughts and memories were not mere rationalizations designed to deny her hurt. Rather, they were real facts about her and her life experiences that helped her to preserve a sense of self-worth in the wake of Paul's rejection.

One of my former professors was dying of cancer. He told me that he would frequently recall his years of teaching and the numerous students whom he had taught. He recalled the many occasions in which he knew he had made a real difference in his students' lives. These memories gave him comfort and a sense of meaning as he was living through times of intense physical pain and facing the reality of death.

Another type of self-soothing can be seen in the willingness to do things for yourself. Shortly after experiencing several agonizing months of being with my father as he was dying from lung cancer, I gave myself permission to get some massages simply to release physical tension. In a sense, I was saying to myself, "You have been through a lot... it's ok to do something for yourself to provide some pleasure." In addition, I turned to my wife periodically to say, "I need to talk." Although I noticed an inner voice sometimes saying, "You shouldn't burden her," with her encouragement, I was able to talk about my father, to cry and to release some of my grief. My wife encouraged me and comforted me, but the decision to feel ok about turning to her came from within me. This decision is often hard for people to make. For so many of us, strongly held attitudes, such as, "I need to handle this on my own," block the seeking out of support from others. And yet, how crucial to discover the truth that shared pain is easier to bear.

A final aspect of self-soothing is the decision to be kind to yourself and to avoid harsh self-criticism. A lawyer friend of mine, Bernard, failed his bar exam, probably because of experiencing a good deal of anxiety during the tests. He initially berated himself. But he soon became aware that his own harsh attitude was hurting him all the more. Then he began consciously to remind himself, "I'm a bright guy. I've done well throughout my school years. It's not that

I am stupid or a failure. I was simply scared during the exams. It's unfortunate that I didn't pass. But it's not a sin." He decided to see a therapist for help to deal with test-anxiety and resolved to again do his best the next time took the exams. Bernard's decision to be kind to himself is yet another example of self-soothing.

6. *Intimacy.* The capacity for intimacy involves the ability to express yourself in an open and honest way with someone you love. Openness often carries with it an element of risk, however. When you let yourself feel very attracted to another, you may feel a haunting fear: "What if I lose him?" Sally avoided having children for many years. She told me that she was afraid to have a child because she knew that she'd get *very* attached to the child and then be afraid that the child would die. This fear of possible loss paralyzed Sally, until finally, after the course of psychotherapy, she decided that despite the risk, her desire to have a child was stronger. Though she now has a young daughter, she still sometimes thinks "What if?", but the love and the fulfillment she enjoys are more important. The capacity for true intimacy also involves the willingness to make sacrifices for others. In the words of M. Scott Peck, love is "the will to extend oneself for the purpose of nurturing one's own or another's spiritual growth."

The risks of intimacy are potential loss and vulnerability. However, the rewards are many, including one very important resource during times of emotional pain: the relationship with another human being to whom you may turn for comfort and support. As we shall see, as people live through difficult life experiences, their emotional healing processes occur at internal/personal levels. But recovering from emotional trauma is greatly facilitated by turning to others, by counting on a social support system, by sharing deep feelings with those you love, and/or by successful psychotherapy.

7. *Commitment.* This is the ability and willingness to "stick with it" during difficult times. Commitment is evident, for example, in a relationship in which the couple is going through a period of distress and frustration, yet the partners manage to stay connected and "hang in there" until the stress subsides. I am not talking about the decision to stay in a *very* pathological relationship for a long time. In some

instances, staying in very destructive relationships can be extremely emotionally damaging. Rather, I am referring to involvement in an important relationship in which the couple is willing to endure some degree of distress for a period of time because they have committed themselves based on true love. Again, this capacity to rise above emotional pain and maintain a loving connection probably reflects the influence of early life experiences. Fortunate children growing up in emotionally healthy homes have experienced at a deep level the knowledge that they will continue to receive love and not be abandoned even during difficult times.

To Masterson's list of seven crucial characteristics of the "real self," I would like to add another.

8. *Being able to have an attitude of profound understanding for your humanness.* This concept is captured well by the writings of psychiatrist Cliff Straehley: "By humanness, I really mean fallibility or imperfections. This is part of the fabric of life and inescapable... [I can] have understanting for myself that this is so, and not condemn or judge myself because of it... if we can indeed wholeheartedly admit this to ourselves, then a tremendous burden may be lifted from our shoulders. The price for the removal of this burden is humility. Paradoxically, when we are able to admit to ourselves that we can't control everything and only can offer life our best at the moment, it gives us a profound permission to be ordinary."

The eight characteristics I've described in this chapter can be seen as the critical components of a sort of emotional immune system, the parts of the true self that are designed to help us live through painful times, to heal, to recover and to grow (see Figure 9-A).

These characteristics emerge naturally, given positive experiences early in life (in terms of nature, nurture and fate). However, I would caution you that attaining this favorable state of emotional development in no way provides you with *protection* from emotional pain. It does, however, equip you with the basic personality characteristics that help assure that as you encounter inevitable emotional pain, you can work toward healing and recovery.

---

Figure 9-A

**Characteristics of the Emotional Immune System**

1. The ability to feel emotions deeply
2. The ability to identify and understand inner feelings and needs
3. Self-entitlement: entitled to feel good about yourself
4. Self-assertion
5. Self-soothing
   - An attitude of self-compassion
   - Calling forth past soothing images
   - Doing things for yourself (self-comforting, seeking support from others)
   - Adopting a non-critical/non-harsh attitude toward yourself
6. The capacity for intimate relationships
7. The development of commitment
8. Permission to be human, to be ordinary, and to love myself for the simple reason that I exist

---

It is hard to know how many people are fortunate enough to be blessed with extremely positive early experiences. I would hazard to say that they are the exception rather than the rule. However, it is entirely possible for those who have gone through difficult, painful, or even traumatic childhoods to still move toward emotional growth. The road is harder, but not impassable. Many people have the inherent capacity to develop the aforementioned characteristics; the potential is there, but may as yet be undeveloped or under-developed. Often, good, healthy relationships with others during adolescence or adulthood can help many people unlock hidden potentials. For others, psychotherapy may be an important catalyst for emotional healing and growth. In addition, there is much that you can do for yourself to reduce emotional pain and to nurture your emerging true self. This process will be the primary focus of Part III of this book.

# PART III: ACTION PLANS FOR HEALING

## Ten

*Action Plan #1:*
*Do No Harm*

$N$ow that we've examined common sources of psychological pain and explored the ways our human emotions work, it's time to move on to *what you can do about it*. This chapter begins the "action plans" part of our journey beyond emotional pain. In this and the following chapters you have work to do. If you really want to change your life, now is the time to begin!

The first action plan toward dealing with your emotional pain is to *stop making it worse!* Before we discuss emotional healing per se, it is very important to understand that some events and processes can interfere with recovery and growth.

Hippocrates stated that the first rule of medical healing is to "Do no harm," a wise statement. A break-through in surgical procedures was the use of sterile techniques. The mortality rate dropped dramatically when physicians learned how not to infect the patient with dirty instruments. This was not a new curative technique per

se; rather, it was an approach that prevented additional complications. And clearly, although major advances have been made in
medicine, many of our modern treatments are interventions
designed to boost and facilitate natural healing mechanisms.

Similarly, people also possess natural *emotional* healing
capabilities. The first rule of emotional healing should also be, "Do
no harm." Yet as we shall see, people very often do things which
completely derail emotional healing. Most of these behaviors may
seem to be merely misguided, if desperate, attempts to reduce suffering. However, they are solutions that can backfire and account for
a tremendous amount of unnecessary emotional pain.

There is nothing inherently noble about suffering great pain.
Some people say that it builds character or is some kind of test of
strength or spiritual fiber. But pain hurts, and it seems awfully
normal to want to reduce suffering. At the same time, some emotional pain is absolutely unavoidable. Pain will be encountered as one
begins to work through the effects of difficult emotionally-charged
life events. In fact, it seems that you *must* experience some pain if you
are going to heal from emotional wounds. However, it is important
to distinguish between *necessary* and *unnecessary* pain. According to
psychologist Steven Johnson, "Necessary emotional pain is that
which is a natural organismic outgrowth of a life circumstance... this
may mean mourning the death of the spouse or child, feeling the
betrayal of a friend or feeling anger when seriously frustrated"
(1987).

One way to distinguish between necessary (normal, constructive) pain and unnecessary (neurotic, destructive) pain is to ask some
basic questions: Is it helpful? Does the pain ensure survival? Does it
lead to corrective action? Does its expression result in a sense of
relief/release? Does it bring you in closer contact with loved ones?
Of course, these are often very difficult questions to answer with
certainty since a good deal of necessary pain initially hurts so much
that it's hard to imagine that it can serve any helpful purpose.
Unnecessary pain is suffering that goes beyond the core emotional
response. It is exaggerated, intensified, and prolonged suffering
which is an outgrowth of two common processes I will call

*pathological blocking* and *pouring salt in the wound.* These two processes are the topics of the rest of this chapter.

## Pathological Blocking

People reduce pain in a number of ways. Some of these are deliberate, conscious attempts to avoid awareness of distressing realities. Glen is a forty-two-year-old dermatologist who lost his young wife to breast cancer six months ago. He now works twelve-to-fourteen-hour days, seven days a week. He doesn't want to reduce his workload because he knows if he works less, he will begin to feel his grief. Barbara is a thirty-one-year-old housewife and mother of three, who has been emotionally dying inside since learning that her husband is having an affair. She extinguishes the emotional aching by drinking heavily every day. Barbara does not want to feel because it hurts too much. In both of these cases, conscious awareness could open the gate to Glen and Barbara's emotions.

*Consciousness is both the cause of our pain and also the root of our salvation. It is the cause of our pain because of course were we not conscious we would not have any pain. And in fact one of the things that one will do for people who have unconstructed, unnecessary suffering is that we give anesthesia to help them to lose consciousness.*
— M. Scott Peck

In contrast there is Megan, a twenty-eight-year-old woman who has for the first time started to vividly recall extreme physical and sexual abuse by her uncle. She is willing to face the pain; however, she just feels incredibly numb. She tries to talk, she tries to remember, but she feels dazed, as if swallowed up in an emotional fog. The numbness is not intentional but rather, entirely automatic, as if a part of her mind has decided to put her to sleep. Her emotional awareness is blocked.

In many respects the blocking of pain makes sense. Whether it is conscious or not, it is certainly understandable that people do not want to hurt. Sometimes the intensity of emotional pain is God-awful. I have heard people quite honestly say they would rather be dead than to sink into an engulfing sense of inner darkness and despair, or to have to face tragic realities. It is no sin to want to avoid pain. In fact, it's a blessing that most people are able to block out at least some of the pain, some of the time. However, excessive numbing, blocking and distracting for a prolonged period of time can create even greater emotional problems. Many people who consciously or unconsciously refuse to mourn, carry around deep, unhealed wounds for many, many years. In the long run, profoundly sealed-off emotions and walled-off psychic wounds fester. In many cases of excessive numbing/blocking, people are at a high risk for developing severe bouts of depression or psycho-somatic illness. Some move through life with a sense of inner emptiness. The blocking has snuffed out their aliveness and passion, along with the pain. And if they self-medicate with alcohol or tranquilizers, they may eventually become addicted.

Often the decision to "grit my teeth" and refuse to feel inner emotions is prompted by unrealistic, maladaptive beliefs (injunctions, see page 165). Many of us have been taught to be tough, don't cry, get on with life, and so forth. These inner voices urge us to move away from the experience and the expression of normal human emotions, warning that to be emotional is to be weak, inadequate and shameful. Such beliefs protect us from ridicule, embarrassment, shame or rejection, and in that respect these are voices of compassion. But, the injunctions are often misguided. In the wake of emotionally painful events, completely blocking out feelings for a prolonged period of time is almost never helpful. Normal, brief periods of numbness and blocking certainly occur and are entirely appropriate, but such periods alternate with times of awareness and feeling. In order to heal, you've got to feel.

However, excessive emotional blocking is not just a matter of listening to your own internal voices. For many people, the voices heard are those of friends, relatives, clergy and sometimes even from therapists: "You've got to stop being so emotional," "Don't take it personally," "Aren't you over it yet?!" "Honey, maybe you need to see a shrink." The messages are either "Don't feel" or "If you do feel, there is something wrong with you." Often my clients who are going through periods of normal grief have become convinced that they are crazy or neurotic or clinically depressed, largely because many of their friends and relatives are telling them so.

### Pouring Salt in the Wound

Exaggerated, intensified, and prolonged suffering is an outgrowth of a second common process, "pouring salt in the wound," which can occur in a number of different ways.

### Salt in the Wound — Version 1:

*Excessive and unrealistic self-criticism.* Three versions of self-criticism are typical: inaccurate conclusions, negative labeling, and unrealistic "shoulds."

• *Inaccurate Conclusions:* If you're feeling intense physical pain, for example, if you were to suddenly catch on fire, having a rather unclear perception of events happening would be entirely normal for you. You certainly would know you were on fire, but perceiving any other aspects of the moment accurately would be difficult. Likewise, as people experience waves of emotional pain or face very difficult realities, they commonly misperceive situations and jump to unrealistic conclusions. These misperceptions can often undercut self-worth and result in excessively low self-esteem. Cognitive therapists have described two types of unrealistic conclusions: All-or-none thinking (Beck, 1967) and mind-reading (Burns, 1980).

Henry is a good illustration. A recently divorced man who is living through a period of considerable sadness and loneliness, he recently asked Sarah to go out for lunch. She declined, and he quickly concluded that no one likes him; no one wants to be with him. Maybe that statement is 100% true, but it is more likely to be an example of all-or-none thinking. The reality probably is that Henry *does* have friends who want to be around him, but *this particular woman*, Sarah, turned him down for lunch — once. However, this unrealistic conclusion — no one likes me — results in the intensification of his pain (unnecessary pain added to the natural distress he was already feeling). To explore this process a bit more, let's say Henry further concludes, "Sarah probably thinks I'm a jerk." Again, maybe she does, but how can he know this for sure? He is engaging in "mind reading," — acting as if he knows what's in her mind. There may be many reasons Sarah turned him down: maybe she was busy; maybe she recently broke-up with a man and is feeling that it's too early to get involved with someone else; maybe she likes a lot of things about him, but simply doesn't want to date him; maybe she does think he's a jerk. The point is that Henry doesn't somehow magically *know* Sarah's true thoughts and feelings. To conclude, "She probably thinks I'm a jerk," generates feelings of worthlessness (more unnecessary pain).

• *Negative Labeling:* When people make mistakes or experience losses, rejections, or disappointments, they often tend to engage automatically in negative self-labeling. This is attaching pejorative labels to oneself: "I'm a loser... I'm a failure... I'm a jerk... I'm so stupid." These labels have an all-or-none quality to them and are a powerful source of feelings of inadequacy and worthlessness. This kind of labeling never helps and only further intensifies emotional despair.

• *Unrealistic Shoulds:* "I *shouldn't* take it so hard... I *should* take it like a man... I *shouldn't* be so sensitive," "I *shouldn't* cry... I *should* be over this by now..." And the implication of these unrealistic shoulds is that if you do take it hard, if you do cry, if you are sensitive, somehow you are inadequate. Most of the time these harsh inner judgements are based on an inadequate understanding of human nature, human emotions, emotional pain and the possibility for healing. Besides, these "shoulds/shouldn'ts" — a major source of unnecessary pain — rarely help people cope well or recover.

Figure 10-A illustrates some more helpful and compassionate alternatives to the statements we've been talking about. In each case, the more compassionate statement is characterized by three crucial qualities: First, the statement is *realistic*. It is not an attempt to deny reality or to fool yourself into believing that everything is ok. Sometimes life is absolutely not ok, and self-deception rarely helps. The compassionate statement sticks close to the known facts and attempts to portray an accurate perception or conclusion. The statement also *acknowledges that it's natural* to feel bad if you have been hurt. In a sense, you give yourself permission to have and to experience normal human emotions. Finally, the goal of each compassionate statement is to help *promote emotional healing*. Excessive and unrealistic self-criticism is a potent way to keep knocking off the emotional scab. Self-criticism *always* intensifies and prolongs emotional pain.

---

Figure 10-A

| Critical Statement | Compassionate Statement |
|---|---|
| 1. "No one wants to be with me." | *"This* woman did not want to go with me to lunch. That's disappointing. Maybe other friends *will* want to be with me." |
| 2. "Sarah probably thinks I'm a jerk." | "I don't know exactly why Sarah turned me down. It's hard to know without asking her." |
| 3. "I'm so stupid." | "I made a mistake and I feel bad about it." |
| 4. "I shouldn't be so sensitive." | "I do have strong feelings about this situation. It hurts. I don't like to hurt this much, but it's human." |
| 5. "I should be over this by now." | "I would like to be over this by now, but the truth is that I'm not, and it feels bad." |

---

Here's a simple exercise which will help you to see if your thoughts are self-critical and damaging or compassionate toward yourself: When you're aware of what you are thinking or telling yourself, write the thought down on a piece of paper. Then ask yourself three simple questions:

Is the thought (or perception or conclusion) *accurate?*

Is this thought *the whole truth* and nothing but the truth?

Is this thought *helpful* to me, or *hurtful?*

At times, intense self-criticism may be a deeply ingrained habit, not simply or easily eradicated. However, for many people, the brief exercise just noted can increase awareness and disrupt what may have become habit. The result can be a reduction in unnecessary pain.

### Salt in the Wound — Version 2:

*Negative Predictions & Tunnel Vision.* A magnifying glass when held in sunlight will intensify the rays of light and burn a hole in paper. In a similar fashion, two very common mental events have a powerful effect on emotions; they can magnify and intensify core emotional pains.

• *Negative predictions:* These are frequent when people move through difficult times. Predicting the future accurately is really impossible, but people often act as if they can see into the future: "Things will never get better," "No one will ever love me," "I will be alone the rest of my life," "I know the cancer will come back," "I'll never be able to stop drinking," "I'll never get over the grief." These statements are entirely natural and arise very easily at times of emotional suffering. In many respects, thinking about the future in pessimistic ways is normal. But it never helps. First, most people's predictions are notoriously inaccurate. But even more importantly, to say "I'll never feel better," makes the future look extremely bleak, which almost *always* turns up the volume on feelings of hopelessness and powerlessness. Any core emotional pain is always intensified if accompanied by perceptions of hopelessness and powerlessness.

A more helpful (and accurate) view to take is to acknowledge honestly and clearly your present realities and emotional pain, but to curb the attempt to predict the future. The divorced man can choose to stop thinking, "I will be alone the rest of my life," and instead decide to say to himself, "I'm alone a lot now. I don't like it. I feel sad and I miss my wife. But I *cannot* predict the future. I will cross those bridges when I get to them." The cancer patient can refuse to slip into helplessness by saying, "This cancer *could* come back, but it may not, and I can't tell the future. I hate having cancer, but now my job is to do whatever I can to heal myself and to live." These are not statements of self-delusion. These people know that continued loneliness or recurring illness are *possibilities*. But both people are deciding not to predict negative outcomes and instead are actively deciding to reduce their hopelessness, stubbornly refusing to believe that they can somehow magically read the future. Your present emotional pain is probably enough without inadvertently magnifying it!

• *Tunnel Vision:* This is a second powerful pain magnifier: looking almost exclusively at a source of pain, disappointment, or loss and perceiving it as the whole picture. Kevin, recently laid off from his job, says, "I've got nothing going for me in my life." At that moment, he is failing to consider that he has a loving family and a successful record of finding employment. Cynthia, an author who has just had her manuscript rejected by a fifth publishing company concludes, "No one wants to publish my book." She fails to remind herself that there are hundreds — thousands — of publishing houses she hasn't contacted, and initial rejections are the rule rather than the exception for authors. Kevin and Cynthia are noticing the source of disappointment or pain, but tuning out other realities, a very natural thing to do. If you seriously cut your finger, you immediately notice the pain — all of your attention is focused on the pain. In such a situation, you're not likely to say, "Yes, my finger hurts, but my back, face and heart feel great!" Your attention is automatically drawn to pain like iron filings to a magnet. But if you can notice the pain *and* try to look at the "whole picture," you can intervene in the process of magnification. When Kevin stops to remind himself of his supportive family and his track record, he is *not* denying the fact that the lay-off is depressing and a pain in the neck. Self-deception rarely helps (at least not for long). But the awareness of his family's support and love, and the acknowledgement of his own strengths and talents (e.g., being a hard worker and having had the skills to find work in the past) do help ease the blow of the lay-off. By reminding herself about the publishing companies she hasn't yet approached, Cynthia *does* feel disappointed, but also gathers the energy to send her book to another publisher. She has avoided tunnel vision and reduced her feelings of hopelessness.

<u>Gary</u>

Gary found himself increasingly preoccupied with worries about his cancer returning. One day he hit upon a helpful idea. He knew that he had a number of positive, meaningful activities in his life, but he would more or less automatically tune them out and focus on his inner worries. So he made a list of positive things in his life. He taped one copy on his bathroom mirror and kept another copy in his desk at work. He made a point to review this list often.

Gary's List

1. My hobby: carving and painting wooden decoys
2. My involvement in the local Lion's Club and fund-raising for a children's hospital
3. Gardening
4. Spending time talking with my wife and children
5. Working as a C.P.A.
6. Driving in the near-by country with my wife
7. Going to church
8. Reading science fiction novels
9. Listening to music
10. Taking walks on cool evenings

His goal was not to fool himself into believing "everything is wonderful. Everything is ok." That sort of self-deception is not helpful. Everything is not ok, and he knows it! He has recently had a very serious illness with an unclear prognosis; however, at the same time, he has many important life activities which do give him a sense of happiness, meaning and stability. In the midst of his despair and fear, staying focused on positive aspects of his life has been damned hard. His list wasn't a magic solution, but it did help. These reminders serve as anchors that he can hang on to, especially during times of concern and anxiety.

### Salt in the Wound — Version 3:

*Repeating Destructive Relationships:* If you touch a very hot stove and are badly burned, you're not likely to do it again. We learn some lessons in pain quickly. However, a very common source of continuing emotional despair is to stay in a highly destructive relationship, or to leave one bad relationship only to jump into another. Why do abused kids marry abusive spouses? Why do battered wives divorce one abusive man and soon become involved with another? Why do people who grow up feeling terribly criticized or dominated by a parent enter relationships that look remarkably similar to those in their family of origin? Are people just stupid? I don't think so. But many friends and counselors seem to act as if these behaviors are a matter of mental retardation. They tell the abused person, "You need to realize that this relationship is hurting you. You need to get out" as if the abused person never felt the hurt; as if this enlightening knowledge will lead to rapid insight and emotional growth. Friends and counselors make another mistake when concluding that people must "like" abuse or they wouldn't stay in the relationship. "They must be masochistic."

The fact is, nobody *likes* to be abused, belittled, abandoned or beaten up. Then why is this compulsion to stay in toxic relationships so common and so difficult to change? As you might guess, there are a number of reasons.

First, despite painful realities, many people manage desperately to feel *hopeful.* It is not the verbal or physical slap that keeps them in the relationship, but rather the thought or belief that "maybe it'll get better... maybe if we just try harder... maybe if I can just love him enough... maybe if the financial stress eases some." These hopes give people something to live for. The pain really doesn't keep them there; the dream born of the desire to feel loved and to feel valued does.

People often enter relationships with unrealistic/inaccurate perceptions of the other person. They think they have found "Mr. or Ms. Right." Often people stranded in the desert see mirages. The images are based on intense needs, not on realities. We often project hopes onto others and then see in people what we most want and need to see. Perceptions and hopes get mixed up. Sometimes initial perceptions are accurate. However, often in relationships, one person gradually and more clearly perceives who the other person really is. This more accurate view of reality may lead to greater closeness and truer love in some cases, or to an increasing sense of disillusionment and disappointment in others. Hope-driven perception may account for both the decision to stick it out in a bad relationship or the tendency to jump from one painful relationship to another.

---

### Sharon

"When I met Tim I was absolutely convinced that he was the man for me. He was kind, he was strong and he was ambitious. I *never* would have thought for a moment that our life would turn out the way it has. I don't know if he's really changed or not, or if maybe it's just taken me nine years to see him for who he really is."

---

The second reason people put up with abuse is that it's *familiar*... it's known. People have very powerful needs to feel safe and one way to ensure safety (at least partially) is to seek out what is known — *even if it hurts*. To allow abuse to become familiar is not inherently masochistic — at its core it is motivated by the very human need to feel safe. It is very hard for most of us to truly understand how terribly abusive relationships can feel safe. Friends and counselors who sense the abuse victim's tremendous fears of the unknown and need for safety have taken an important step toward providing true support.

Third, at times people stick with bad relationships because they feel either that they *deserve to be hurt* and/or they don't deserve better. Inner feelings of worthlessness coupled with pessimism can lead to choices to remain in damaging relationships for years.

Fourth, for better or worse, some people decide to stay in a bad relationship *"for the sake of the children."* They may be clear about the negative aspects of the marriage but willfully and consciously decide to put their own needs second. It is not clear, however, that an abusive parental relationship *is* actually better for children than a single-parent family environment.

Reason number five is *financial*. More commonly for women than for men, owing to the nature of social roles in our society, the consequences for leaving a bad relationship may be a hit in the pocketbook. Many women have spent years as homemakers and do not have the kind of job skills or experience required to earn a decent living. To leave a bad marriage often means serious financial strife for a woman and her children. In a poor economy, it is often necessary to have the wages of both spouses, just to pay the bills. Moreover, women are often paid less well than men and therefore cannot afford to launch into the world alone.

Finally, some people endure destructive relationships because *the idea of being alone in the world is frightening*. Even in very bad marriages, a sense of companionship can still exist; it's easy to get hooked on having *someone* around. Divorce holds the prospect of experiencing and enduring a period of aloneness. Ultimately, divorce may be worth the price, but it isn't fun.

The compulsion to repeat destructive patterns in relationships can be very hard to change. Many people enter psychotherapy in order to deal with this common human problem. Whether in the context of therapy or in the course of daily living, however, healing must deal with several key issues: first, becoming aware of underlying, healthy motives — the desire to search for love, to hope for nurturing companionship, and to seek out safety — is important. Your inner needs must be appreciated and honored. Second, you must make a realistic and honest assessment of the likelihood of true change in the relationship or the other person. Third, you'll need to acknowledge the reality of the pain and grief of lost hopes and dreams. Finally and most important, you can take actions to strengthen your sense of self. Whether ultimately deciding to leave a bad relationship or deciding to weather it, the more solid you feel about yourself, the better you will fare. (Ways to strengthen your sense of self will be discussed in Chapter 12.)

As you begin to take action for your own emotional healing, you'll find it helps to stop making things worse than they need to be. In this chapter we have examined pathological blocking of painful feelings, "rubbing salt in the wound," and other actions people often take which create unnecessary suffering, and we've looked at some ways to start changing those counterproductive patterns. "Doing no harm" is a good place to start your journey toward emotional health.

Now let's move on toward the heart of the emotional healing process and how to enhance your own healing.

---

## Eleven

## Action Plan #2:
## *Understand How People Heal*

*"Those creatures who find everyday experience a muddled jumble of events with no predictability, no regularity, are in grave peril. The universe belongs to those who, at least to some degree, have figured it out..."*

— Carl Sagan
*Broca's Brain*

*I*n the last chapter, we saw some of the common ways people often inadvertently interfere with emotional healing. In this chapter, let's begin to take a look at the natural healing process. What happens to people when they encounter painful life events? How does healing take place? What promotes or enhances healing? Although obviously there are tremendous differences among people's styles of dealing with emotional distress, there are also some remarkable commonalities.

During the early part of this century, Sigmund Freud was beginning to develop the basic foundations of psychoanalysis. He had already forged many of the early theoretical ideas of this emerging school of thought when World War I began. As a medical officer in the Austrian military, Freud was responsible for treating a number of soldiers suffering from what then was called "shell shock." (More recently this has been referred to as "war neurosis" or "Post-

Traumatic Stress Disorder.") In his private practice prior to the war, Freud had been fascinated by the variety and uniqueness of his patients' problems — their symptoms, their histories and their unconscious conflicts. But his war-time experience made him aware of a multitude of emotional problems that appeared not unique, but quite stereotyped and predictable. Almost regardless of the soldiers' personality styles or backgrounds, countless hundreds of them returned from the front suffering from remarkably similar psychological symptoms. They had a tendency to move back and forth between two seemingly opposite states of mind: from a state of tremendous emotional upheaval (e.g., anxiety, trembling, fearfulness, crying)to a state of withdrawal (numbness, distance and lack of emotion).

These WWI combat veterans also showed two additional symptoms. The first was *a tendency to repetitively recall horrific, traumatic events* as if they couldn't help it; their conscious minds were flooded by these memories. They frequently relived the traumatic experiences, in waking hours and in recurring nightmares. They were troubled by intense emotions when recalling the traumatic events, and they actively attempted to repress the memories. The second symptom was *a variety of physical complaints* for which no organic (medical) cause could be determined. Headaches, insomnia, abdominal pain, and poor appetite — now understood to be stress-related psychosomatic symptoms — were mysterious to Freud and his fellow military doctors seventy-five years ago.

Freud's patients returning from the front by-and-large were not people with mental illnesses; they were relatively normal people who had been exposed to extremely severe stress. This same rather stereotyped reaction pattern has been seen in subsequent wars, and was brought into public awareness most notably following the Vietnam War.

Twenty-five years later, Eric Lindeman, a psychiatric researcher and clinician, had the opportunity again to observe and study closely the effects of severe stress on normal people. In 1942, during a post-football celebration at the Coconut Grove nightclub in Boston, a disastrous fire claimed the lives of 499 people and stunned the community. Lindeman and his colleagues quickly rushed in and provided free counseling services for a large group of people, including survivors of the fire and relatives of the victims. The researchers established what amounts to the first community-based mental health intervention in the country. At the same time the mental health team was able to study carefully this group of people. Like the soldiers in Freud's studies, these were normal people caught up in the wake of disaster. Lindeman, too, discovered tremendous regularity in the symptoms that people reported: again, the vacillation between overwhelming painful emotions and periods of numbness; again, a strong need or impulse to repeat the tragic events in their minds over and over again; again, a host of psychosomatic symptoms.

Prior to the 1950's, many theories regarding emotional stress and psychiatric symptoms had been developed primarily from experience in treating severely mentally ill people. Little was really understood about emotional distress among relatively normal people. However, the observations of Freud, Lindeman and subsequent researchers were beginning to shed light on what might be a rather general pattern of response to significant emotional stress.

### The Stress Response Syndrome

In 1976, Psychiatrist Mardi Horowitz published a book entitled *Stress Response Syndromes*. In this landmark publication, Dr. Horowitz carved out a very useful model for understanding what appears to be a common pattern of human emotional response to significant stress. Horowitz developed this model based on his review of numerous field studies (like that of Lindeman), a good deal of clinical work treating mentally healthy people who had experienced major stresses, and even some experimental studies. The experimental studies included, among others, research with college students in which the volunteer subjects were exposed to fairly intense, stressful movies (e.g., films of Nazi concentration camps). Horowitz concluded that across a broad spectrum of stressful events (deaths of loved ones, physical assaults, natural disasters and even viewing upsetting movies), most people exhibit a typical pattern of response: the "stress response syndrome." This model can be very helpful in understanding common human reactions to stressful events. And, as I will explore with you later, embedded in this model are some important keys to understanding the emotional healing process.

Let's take a look at the stress response syndrome. The full stress response syndrome is seen most clearly in situations where the stressful event is sudden and intense. Although a host of events may trigger this reaction, we'll use the example of a sudden loss (e.g., the death of a loved one). Less intense or less sudden stressors also elicit similar responses, but we'll first consider what happens in the wake of more serious events.

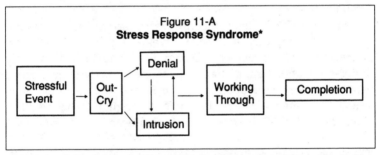

Figure 11-A
**Stress Response Syndrome\***

Each of the boxes in Figure 11-A represents a state of mind or emotion. The stress response reaction begins with your awareness of some painful event.

The first phase is *Outcry*. In a sense, a state of outcry is simultaneously an eruption of intense, unpleasant emotion (sadness, fear, etc.) *and* denial, ("I can't believe it... it can't be true.") The person is in a state of shock and may be engulfed by very strong emotions. This phase of the reaction can last for just a few minutes, a few hours or a few days. Rather quickly, the person moves into phase two, which may be either a state of *intrusion* or a state of *denial*.

*Intrusion* occurs when a person experiences waves of intense emotion and a strong impulse to think about, imagine, remember or mentally relive the stressful event. These experiences are deemed as "intrusive" because generally the strong feelings and repetitive

---

*\*Reprinted with permission from Horowitz, M. (1976). Stress Response Syndromes. New York: Jason Aronson, Inc.*

thoughts are not brought on willfully. The person does not choose to feel or remember; it just happens.

---

Dale

Following the accident, Dale had to identify his wife's body. In the two weeks following her death and during periods of "intrusion," he would continue to imagine seeing her at the morgue. He would have extremely vivid memories of looking down at her body and then being overwhelmed by horror and grief. Dale said, "I know it sounds morbid, but I keep thinking about it over and over again. Sometimes I can't help it, the memories just come into my mind... sometimes I kind of want to think about it or need to think about it." Dale thought this impulse or need to remember sounded "sick" and "morbid." But this is a very common and natural experience for many people who have witnessed something horrifying or who have experienced a tragic loss.

---

During a state of intrusion, emotions feel very raw, people feel extremely vulnerable, easily overwhelmed and close to tears; they startle easily, don't sleep well, and often have nightmares. In these times, a familiar song or a fragrance can trigger a surge of sadness or anxiety. It is as if the mind is in direct contact with the full force of the painful feelings and realities. People don't choose to be in this place; they find themselves there automatically.

Most people living through a period of intrusion will experience very strong emotions. Such emotional intensity may be unfamiliar and very frightening, but generally these intense emotions do not lead to dyscontrol. They exist but can be tolerated (recall Figure 8-A, page 110).

Phase two also includes a stage of *Denial*. Denial may occur directly following outcry or may come on the heels of a period of intrusion. As noted earlier, denial is a state of emotional numbness. People often feel nothing. Feeling nothing may seem odd or crazy in the wake of a disaster, and such a state is sometimes misunderstood by others as a lack of caring or shallowness. But the person is not uncaring or shallow. In a sense, she has been hit by extremely painful stressors and her mind is now numbing itself. This numbing takes many forms: actual denial (e.g., denying the significance of an event: "Well, it's not that bad... I'll get over it"); emotional blunting or numbing (a conscious awareness of the stressful events, but an inner sense of deadness, emptiness, absence of emotion); withdrawal (withdrawing from work, from friends, from life in general); and sometimes a peculiar sense of confusion, disorientation, fuzzy thinking and feelings of unreality.

> ### Dale
> Dale also reported these experiences when Joyce died. "For two weeks I was an emotional basket case. Then suddenly I felt nothing. Like somebody pulled the plug. I kind of felt like I was on drugs. I was sleepy and lethargic... I started feeling guilty. I loved my wife so much, how come I can't even feel anything for her now? I can't even cry." This period of numbness lasted about six weeks and was followed by yet another wave of intrusive pain.

People typically go back and forth between periods of denial and periods of intrusion. Each state of mind may last for a few days or even for a few months, and then the shift occurs. Many people think that they are "over it," having lived in a state of denial and numbness for a number of weeks, only to be surprised when suddenly they are hit by a new wave of grief or distressing memories. Friends and relatives may begin to believe that a widow is coping well with her loss, and yet a month later wonder why she is upset and easily brought to tears. This alternation may be hard to understand at first glance. But it is not entirely random. There appears to be a pattern to these ebbs and flows of emotion. Let's consider the possibility that the human mind somehow inherently knows that painful realities must be faced and that difficult emotions must be experienced, but people cannot cope with these demands all at once. It is a gradual process, a pacing, a rhythmic shifting back and forth between pain and psychic anesthesia.

Perhaps an analogy, a situation familiar to most parents, will more clearly explain this process of shifting emotions.

I'm surprised my kids haven't turned me in for child abuse when it comes time to remove splinters. Most kids hate this because it hurts and it's scary. So parents learn to remove splinters a bit at a time. You go in with the needle and remove a bit; it hurts, the child cries and then you back off, hug him and say reassuring things. After a few moments, it's back to the splinter. And this rhythmic "dosing" of pain and soothing continues until enough of the splinter is removed so the skin doesn't become infected. The pace of this dosing mostly depends on the depth of the splinter and the child's tolerance for pain. To go after the splinter all at once would be too overwhelming, too traumatic. Likewise, facing the full intensity of painful realities can be traumatic. So it appears that automatic checks and balances exist in the human mind that push toward awareness and feeling, and retreat to numbness, a sort of "psychological R & R." The process is not conscious; it's more-or-less automatic.

If this vacillating rhythm of pain and anesthesia continues long enough, the intensity of emotional intrusion starts to lessen. Usually the pain does not completely stop, but the volume is turned down, bit by bit. Repeatedly experiencing the thoughts, memories, images and feelings surrounding painful events over time drains away some of the more intensely distressing emotions.

It is important to understand and respect this natural process. Knowledge about the seasons of the year allows us to be prepared for changes. Similarly, knowing the terrain and direction of emotional reactions helps us cope.

Often problems occur when people misunderstand the phases of the stress response reaction. Following a painful loss, a physical or sexual assault, or other very stressful event, when the individual enters a time of denial and numbness, others may assume "she's over it." At that point, supportive and caring friends gradually become less available; they assume that the worst is over. But a month or two later, as the person then shifts into a period of intrusion, a couple of things commonly happen. With new waves of feeling and emotional rawness, she finds herself alone. Many widows and widowers will attest that there was a lot of support just following the loss of their spouses, but in the wake of this new upheaval of pain, people aren't there. Often, concerned friends and relatives react to this new surge of emotion in unhelpful ways. Their intentions may be good, but the messages have a critical edge to them: "I thought you were getting over it"; "What's wrong now?!", and so forth. They don't fully understand the workings of the human mind. The re-emergence of feelings, in most cases, is not a sign that the person is worse but rather, simply another in a series of *phases* in the healing process. The

---

Dale

Dale endured a good deal of grief during the first six months after his wife died. Then things started to simmer down. But two months later around the time of their wedding anniversary, he encountered a new welling up of emotion. One day he was with his friend Bob who had had close contact with Dale over the past year and probably was relieved to see Dale feeling less pain. But on this particular day, Dale got tears in his eyes as he told Bob, "God, I just miss her so much." Bob said, "Dale, you just need to get on with your life and not dwell on it. Gosh, you've been doing so much better lately. Don't let it get to you." Bob may be sincere, but he just doesn't understand. Dale walked away thinking, "He's right; what's wrong with me?" He started to think that he just wasn't coping well. The result was that Dale now experienced two sources of pain: his loss *and* feeling as if there was something wrong or defective about him. This just added to his pain. In addition, after the incident, Dale felt very inhibited about expressing his feelings around Bob and others. He put a lid on his feelings and rather than sharing them, had to endure them alone. The process of mourning and healing had now become complicated for Dale. Bob's reaction was not a crime nor was it unkind. It simply was an act of compassion, but it had come from a friend who did not fully understand the healing process.

hurt is normal and healthy. People don't choose to hurt; it just happens. In the long run, the periodic reawakenings of strong emotion are absolutely necessary for emotional recovery and healing to take place. And yet, when the person hears, "I thought you were over it," she often begins to think, "There must be something wrong with me."

This very same cycle of vacillation between intrusion and denial can occur when people begin to recall very painful events from childhood. As mentioned before, many if not most times, when children are exposed to very abusive situations, the memory of and emotion associated with such events are blocked out of awareness, to remain entombed in the unconscious mind for a lifetime, or to resurface during adulthood. Beginning to recall and relive these old memories sets in motion a stress response syndrome in adult survivors of child abuse.

Reliving terrifying memories of child abuse can be one of the most unpleasant types of human suffering, but it's not insanity. And again, the vacillation between emotion and numbness is the mind's way of facing reality, periodically providing doses of numbing escape from the overwhelming emotions and, fortunately, gradually overcoming the pain (like removing a psychic splinter).

This process may feel or look crazy, but it is not. It is predictable, understandable, and probably necessary to the operation of the mind. Just as bleeding and clot formation are aspects of physical healing, the oscillation between intrusion (awareness and feeling) and numbing are the phases of emotional healing. I try to help my clients understand this and, at the same time, I want to respect the process, i.e., to know where someone is in the healing process, appreciate that and accept it. If you or someone you know is going through difficult times, I believe it is also important for you to understand and respect this process. When people are in a state of denial, forcing them to face reality is *generally* not helpful. When people are feeling strong emotions, giving them the message — "Don't be so emotional" — is *generally* not helpful. The work of healing is difficult and painful, but most times, necessary. People will

Katherine

At age thirty-six, Katherine started to remember episodes of severe abuse and sexual molestation that had occurred when she was a young child. Until recently she had completely banished these memories and feelings from her conscious awareness. She had no idea that she had been victimized.

Recently, she has come face to face with very intense feelings from the past. At first, there were simply times of panicky feelings and tearfulness that seemed to come out of the blue. She thought she was going crazy; the waves of strong emotion made no sense. But little by little she started to recall, first in the form of nightmares and in bits and fragments of images and memory. During the past six months, these hazy and disconnected recollections have started to make sense. Yet Katherine found herself frequently shifting back and forth between times of intense emotion and poignant awareness of her prior abuse and times of profound numbness and denial. During such times, she would question the reality of her memories: "I'm just making this up. It couldn't have happened!" She would also feel distant, detached and emotionally stupefied. This radical shift from emotional anguish to anesthesia was perplexing to her. She felt as if she must be insane.

have their own time and place for experiencing emotions, and they have a right to back away from the pain when it hurts too much. There is no absolute or right time frame or schedule for living through this process. The stages may be similar for many human beings, but the pace is always unique.

Finally, the stress response syndrome is also seen in situations where the event is much less intense or sudden than that described in the sidebar, "Katherine" above.

<u>Sharon</u>

Sharon has recently become more and more aware of her sense of aloneness and of the emptiness in her marriage. The problems in her marriage did not develop overnight, so in a sense, the stressful "event" in her life is not sudden. But it is intense. These issues mean a lot to her, and her feelings have become stronger in recent times because her awareness of her problem has increased. Sharon also moves back and forth between times of tearfulness and despair and times when she feels better, less hopeless and kind of numb. From time to time when she is feeling especially bad, she will mention her concern to her husband, Tim. On several occasions, he's said to her, "I thought you were over that. We've talked about this a hundred times before. I thought you were better now. Why the hell are you letting this get to you again?!" Her "problem," her dissatisfaction and loneliness, did not really go away or get better, but she did enter a state of partial denial in which the intensity of her emotions lessened. During these times, she would think "Oh, I'm ok. I'm just making a big deal out of nothing." But she was not ok. The real concerns, the real pain was simply in temporary hibernation.

Intrusion and denial do not necessarily alternate in a predictable cycle. Sometimes the predominant state of mind is one of intrusion. There may be a relative absence of denial. In this situation, a person seems chronically plagued with repetitive thoughts (e.g., repeated images about something bad that has happened) or worries about the future. Earlier in this book, I told you of my feelings when I had to fire someone once. In the days before I took action on this, all I could think about was the coming event. Believe me, I did not want to or choose to be preoccupied with these thoughts and feelings; they came to me automatically. Throughout the book, we've followed the experience of Gary, the man plagued by frequent worries that his cancer will come back. Often such worries involve images not only of possible, realistic outcomes, but also of extremely scary, negative events. Worry has some times been referred to as "What-ifing," repetitively wondering, "What if this?" "What if that?" The repetitive, intrusive nature of such thoughts and feelings seems remarkably similar to the that which people encounter during the intrusion stage of the stress response syndrome.

Indeed, what-ifs can drive people up the wall (and in that sense be a non-productive, non-necessary source of pain). At the same time, some degree of repetitively going over events in your mind can be helpful, a way to anticipate events and consequences (so you can be prepared). It can be a way to rehearse plans of action in your mind ahead of time to evaluate and refine your strategies. And it can be a way to desensitize yourself so if bad things do happen, you aren't completely caught off guard or overwhelmed. My thoughts while I was on the airplane enroute to visit my ailing father included awful and scary images of him. Thinking those thoughts wasn't pleasant, but in a sense, prepared me to face some extremely painful realities.

### When the Healing Process Gets Bogged Down

Following painful life events, many people will go through the aforementioned stages of intrusion and denial over and over again, (a process known as working through), and sooner or later, the intensity of grief, fear, etc. begins to wane. It is not time that heals, but the effects of repeated exposure to reality and strong inner feelings that make a difference. (We'll discuss more about this idea shortly.) Many people navigate these waters fairly well; they suffer, they struggle, and they heal. However, a number of people also can get bogged down or stuck. Dr. Horowitz describes three such complications (see Figure 11-B).

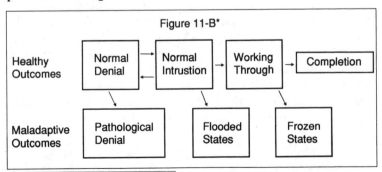

Figure 11-B*

| | | | |
|---|---|---|---|
| Healthy Outcomes | Normal Denial | Normal Intrusion | Working Through → Completion |
| Maladaptive Outcomes | Pathological Denial | Flooded States | Frozen States |

*Adapted with permission from Horowitz, M. (1976). Stress Response Syndromes. *New York: Jason Aronson, Inc.*

*Pathological Denial* goes beyond normal withdrawal and emotional numbing. Presumably the pain of feeling the emotions is so scary and so intense that a person becomes very strongly motivated to avoid feeling at all costs. We discussed this concept — Pathological Blocking — in Chapter 9. It can take the form of certain actions that distract you from inner feelings (working all the time, sexual promiscuity, shop-till-you-drop); consciously and willfully avoiding talking or thinking about the painful event (e.g., in the case of the death of a loved one, you may never mention the dead person's name, may avoid going to familiar places that are a reminder of that person, take down photos of the deceased loved one, change the subject if conversation drifts toward mention of the deceased person); taking drugs and alcohol to chemically numb the pain; and in general to massively shut down and withdraw from life. If these actions are carried to an extreme, real healing comes to a halt. The pain remains as an open psychic wound, but the emotion is at least partially avoided. The results can be disastrous: serious depression, drug and alcohol addiction and psychosomatic illness. Denial in small doses is not only ok, but probably necessary. Pathological denial derails healing and creates a new set of problems.

*"... there is merit in forgetfulness. It is one of the gentlest forms of healing and one of the most dangerous..."*

— Pat Conroy
*The Lords of Discipline*

People can also get stuck in a state of intrusion, which Horowitz calls *Flooded States.* The intense emotional experiences are too intense and do not relent. A person can become engulfed in incredible, on-going emotional anguish that can lead to dyscontrol. The result may be the serious fragmentation and disorganization of the personality, very severe bouts of panic or depression, and sometimes suicidal impulses.

A final negative outcome can be what Horowitz terms *Frozen States,* when the person does not successfully work through the emotional pain. Rather, the more acute distress becomes at least partially sealed off from conscious awareness *and* the person adopts a new lifestyle that is in some way markedly constricted. For example, a person who has lost a loved one decides (unconsciously) never to get close to others again. To love again is to be vulnerable to the risk of yet another loss. The victim of a severe car accident never again drives on the freeway. The survivor of child sexual molestation never allows herself to experience sexual feelings or sexual closeness; the whole sexual area of her life has been quarantined. Such people pay a heavy price for such unconscious decisions. There is safety in avoidance, but there is a loss of freedom, vitality and aliveness.

Psychologists estimate that somewhere between 80 and 85% of people without a history of emotional disorder manage to move through the phases of emotional healing to a successful completion, without making detours into these maladaptive states of excessive denial, flooding or frozen lifestyles. For those who do get bogged down, suffering is prolonged and increased considerably. Professional psychological counseling is indicated and often extremely helpful.

What do we mean by the term *completion*? This term does not have exactly the same meaning implied by the phrase, "Getting over it." Major life events that cause emotional pain, in some respects, stay with us for a lifetime. Ask any person who has been raped, or who has lost a child or gone through a divorce: "Are you completely over it?" Even years and years after the experience, the the typical answer is, "No. Not completely." These tragic, painful events matter to us; they are a part of the fiber of our souls. It makes sense that very major events have lasting effects. However, thankfully, with time and emotional healing, changes do occur. The anguish decreases in frequency and intensity, new realities come to the forefront of life and the memory of the painful event slips into the background. Finally, at some point, people start to feel "normal" again. Some painful memories are still there, but life gets back on track.

The time frame from event to completion varies considerably. However, it has been found that major stressful events (deaths, physical and sexual assaults, divorces, etc.) typically send a series of intense emotional shock waves through a person's life that last from one to four years. Some events (e.g., the loss of a child, child abuse, multiple deaths/losses) take much longer to resolve.

So when we discuss arriving at a place of resolution or completion, let's consider that this emotional state can be characterized by less intense and less frequent pain; life is, more or less, back on track; and life is truly beginning to feel "normal" again.

The stress respone syndrome and other natural responses to emotional trauma are powerful automatic healing processes within the human mind. One of the most valuable things you can do to promote your own health is to aid and abet these automatic processes. At the same time, however, you don't have to rely solely on the work of the natural systems. There is much you can do actively to move through the journey of healing, and that brings us to the next chapter.

## Twelve

## Action Plan #3:
## *Promote Your Own Emotional Healing*

*T*he movement through the various stages of emotional healing, toward completion and resolution, is probably set in motion in a more-or-less "automatic" fashion by the human mind. You could, of course, simply sit back and let time take its course. But what if you'd like to take a more active role in your own healing? Are there things that can be done to facilitate this process?

You may not actually be able to speed up healing tremendously, but you can remove road blocks and keep from getting bogged down. We've already talked about the first two steps to take: *Do no harm* and *understand how people heal*. Rather than seeing the various emotional reactions as random, chaotic and crazy, it is helpful to view them as rather predictable, often necessary and very human experiences. Now it's time to talk very specifically about what actions seem to *promote* effective emotional healing.

*Time heals all wounds, and it's true to a certain extent... time
will dull some of the pain, but deep healing doesn't happen unless
you consciously choose it.*

— Ellen Bass and Laura Davis
*The Courage to Heal*

Psychotherapists like to use a term that I mentioned briefly in
Chapter 11: "Working Through." This important, but rather vague,
concept has also found its way into everyday language; in that
context it seems to mean getting through hard times or getting over
an emotional crisis. But what does "working through" really mean,
when it comes to healing long-term emotional pain?

It's important to note that working *through* is not the same as
"getting over it" or "going around it." The emphasis is on the word
*through;* it inevitably involves a passage through the reality of personal meanings and painful feelings.

Psychologist Stephen Johnson has a shorthand prescription for
the process of working through: "Claim it, name it, aim it and tame
it" (1987). "Claiming it" means to notice, acknowledge, feel, express
and own a feeling. "Naming it" means to put words to it, to understand it, to find meaning in the feeling. "Aiming it" is to make
connections; to understand where the feeling comes from. And
"taming it" means to eventually get to the point where the intensity
starts to diminish. Not that you are blocking out the pain or gritting
your teeth, but that you can openly and honestly talk about painful
events, and the emotions are bearable: when you have talked about
and "hung out" with the emotions long enough that the memories
no longer devastate or overwhelm. The mind will naturally enter the
various phases of the stress response syndrome, but working
through is a process you can *choose* to actively promote healing. The
decision and courage to willfully go through this process (whether
with a friend, relative or a therapist) can make a significant difference!

And if you do want to work through a problem, what specifically
can you do? There appear to be at least four separate-but-related
elements of this working through process: emotional expression,
talking, sharing the pain and taking action. Let's take a closer look.

## *Working Through 1: Emotional Expression*

> *When such as I cast out remorse*
> *So great a sweetness flows into the breast.*
> — W.B. Yeats

In the 1880's Sigmund Freud and his colleague Joseph Breuer developed a revolutionary new treatment for emotional disorders which would eventually evolve into what is now called psychoanalysis. At that time in history, there were virtually no effective treatments available for those suffering from emotional illness. One of Freud and Breuer's early discoveries was that encouraging their patients to recall vividly and talk about painful events would often lead to the expression of very strong emotions. Following sessions in which strong emotions were released, patients often noticed the lessening of or disappearance of psychological symptoms such as phobias, tension, depression and so forth.

One of Freud's well known patients, Anna O., described the approach as "the talking cure" and likened it to chimney sweeping, because after a session she felt somehow cleansed. This particular approach has also been called *abreaction* or *catharsis*. Catharsis is not just a technique of psychotherapy, however. In many cultures across the globe, rituals are designed to help bring people in close contact with their inner feelings, particularly common in many forms of bereavement ritual. The evoking of strong emotions is seen to occur in healing practices of shamans, faith healers and witch doctors. In western societies, people give permission and support to others to openly grieve after the loss of a loved one. Etched into global human wisdom is some awareness of the value of outwardly expressing painful feelings. Release of strong feelings, especially by crying, helps to discharge tension and may also be accompanied by the release of pain-reducing brain chemicals. Expressing feelings involves not only a physical expression of emotion, but also a change in your perception of these emotions: noticing, acknowledging and admitting these inner experiences.

### Encountering Strong Emotions

California psychologist India Fleming has proposed the following metaphor — the experience of deep emotions as analogous to her sensations as a white water kayaker — to describe the difficult, but important movement through periods of strong emotion.

*As one paddles through fairly calm and placid pools, one notices the river narrowing, the current moving faster, the rocks on the riverbed become closer to the surface. Then the waves begin. Suddenly one is surrounded by exploding waves as the river moves with tremendous energy and force. One's attention becomes very focused on the rapids and on navigating a course through it. One strives to keep one's balance and to work with the force of the river because it is much too powerful to fight against. In the midst of the chaos, one also may notice the beauty of water and sunlight reflecting off waves. Then the waves get smaller, the river slower and deeper, and one ends in a quiet pool closer to river's end. As a therapist, this image has given me a sense of calm and confidence in my ability to stay centered and navigate with my clients through their distress rather than fighting or fleeing from their pain.\**

Giving yourself permission to have and to express feelings appears to be an important part of emotional healing, but spilling your guts or crying alone is rarely enough, and at times it is not helpful. For catharsis to be healing, two important conditions need to be met. First: most strong feelings *can be endured*, if you experience them within the zone of emotional tolerance (see Figure 8-A, page 110). These intense emotions can seem awful, scary and almost overwhelming, but they don't kill people, and they don't lead to fragmentation or emotional disorganization. However, some emotional pain is simply too intense, or the person truly may not be able to tolerate the feelings, and may suffer a loss of control. Catharsis can bring forth overwhelming emotions which may be traumatic and can under such circumstances actually *retard* the

---

*\*Reprinted by permission from the author.*

healing process. Second: *it is important to make sense out of and find meaning in the experience,* not just to feel it. The best way to accomplish this is to talk about what's going through your mind while you're experiencing strong emotions. Talk about the memories, the thoughts, the images and the feelings. In the words of Kansas psychologist Mary Jo Peebles, "Words carve out coherence from a blur of feelings."

### Working Through 2: Talking

When Anna O. called it the "talking cure," not the catharsis cure, she was onto something. How many times I've heard people say, "Oh, talking about it won't help," or "How can *just* talking help?", or "I've talked about it a lot; it hasn't helped!" Well, *can* talking help?

How? Clearly some types of talking don't help at all. We'll look at this type first. (You may wish to review the discussion of "Pouring Salt in the Wound" in Chapter 10). Certain kinds of talk intensify misery in a powerful way. You'll often hear inaccurate conclusions, critical or negative self-labeling, and unrealistic "shoulds" if you listen to someone talk in the aftermath of a stressful event. This type of talking does not lead to healing.

Many kinds of talk also take people far away from their honest inner emotions. Language can help us avoid or distort truth. Let's look at several examples.

Quick Closure
"Yes, I know it's bad, but I'll get over it." (then changing the subject)
Minimizing
"Oh, it's not that bad."
"Well, other people have gone through worse things. I shouldn't complain."
"I feel sad, but I'm OK. I can handle it."
Injunctions
"I need to be strong."
"I shouldn't cry."
"I can't get emotional... I've got to get myself under control."

Outright Denial
"I'm not upset. I'm OK." (choking back the tears)

In each of these cases, the words (or thoughts, if not spoken aloud) direct your focus away from inner emotions or the awareness of painful realities. Sometimes this process is temporarily helpful, especially when you're feeling very overwhelmed. These natural human maneuvers are designed to protect us from too much pain. But all forms of defense can, at times, backfire and result in excessive blocking of honest emotions.

In a very different way, some forms of talk can open doors to inner feelings and promote healing. Many times, in the course of psychotherapy, I encourage clients to recall troublesome events in great detail, and while recalling, to talk to me about what happened. For this talking to be helpful, it cannot be rushed or forced. The person needs permission to imagine and recall vividly, and then to put any thoughts, feelings, and memories, into words at his own pace.

Why does this *apparently* simple type of talking help? For a number of reasons. Often during times of emotional crisis, people are beset by a wash of vague, ill-defined, but disturbing emotions and sensations. Many people feel confused and unclear about their inner experiences during these times. They may notice only an intense uneasiness or tension in their bodies, a lump in their throats or tightness in their stomachs. They may feel a confusing array of mixed emotions, and this state of inner emotional confusion and ambiguity intensifies their sense of anxiety, uncertainty and help-lessness.

When a person is able to gradually talk about inner thoughts, feelings and experiences — a process of progressive articulation — bit-by-bit the inner experiences start making sense. Vague feelings become increasingly clear. The person makes connections between the events and her feelings, as if she's shining a light into a dark cellar and gradually seeing more clearly what is inside. Because we humans don't like feeling uncertain and confused, the increased clarity and understanding leaves her feeling a greater sense of mastery and control. To "come to terms with" a situation literally means to put words to the experience. To understand is to begin to "get a handle" on a situation. In other words, talking gives coherence to vague feelings and helps us better understand inner emotions.

A small sample of dialog from one of Sharon's therapy sessions illustrates this process (see sidebar).

| | |
|---|---|
| *Sharon:* | Today at work for no reason, I started crying. It was crazy. Nothing bad happened. What's wrong with me? |
| *Therapist:* | Well, let's look at what was happening today. What went on in the office? |
| *Sharon:* | Nothing really. |
| *Therapist:* | Well, maybe not, but just start talking. Tell me about today. |
| *Sharon:* | I was at work. My girlfriend Diane was talking about her love relationship and how it wasn't working out. She's talked about it before, but all of a sudden, I just started feeling terrible. I felt like I was going to cry... I don't really care that much about her love life... |
| *Therapist:* | You said her love relationship wasn't working out. |
| *Sharon:* | Yeah. (She looks sad.) |
| *Therapist:* | I wonder if there was something about your conversation with her that struck a chord with you... tell me what comes to your mind. |
| *Sharon:* | I guess I thought, "Yeah, I know how you feel... things never work out for me either. I'm married and I'm unhappy." (She starts to cry.) |
| *Therapist:* | That hurts... do your tears make sense to you? |
| *Sharon:* | Yes. |

In a brief interchange about the events of the day, the meaning and source of Sharon's pain became clear to her. This is not a fancy psychotherapeutic technique nor is it magical. People help other people do this sort of thing all the time: one person is simply listening to and encouraging another person to talk. Whether I'm listening to a client or to my child relate upsetting events, in the back of my mind, I'm thinking, "Let's see what's happened... I bet we can make sense of this." The keys are to *really listen* carefully; to avoid jumping to conclusions or trying to dazzle the other person with brilliant interpretations; to avoid pretending to understand when you don't; and to encourage openness. If the therapist had made statements such as, "Well, I'm sure it was nothing," or "Well, you're over it now," or "Well, it was probably just PMS," the process would have been quickly ended. Sharon would be just as much in the dark as before the session.

Sharon had initially tried to close the door herself:

*Therapist:*  Can you tell me what went on in the office?
*Sharon:*      Nothing really.

The therapist nudged it open again, and she started to talk. This is not just talking or "chit-chat" but talking about events with the goal of *understanding,* by looking inward to discover true feelings (and thereby to discover what is really important to her). This talking brought Sharon more in touch with her true self. Her sadness and confusion were replaced with greater understanding. As she became more aware of her own emotional turmoil, her feelings of sadness became an important issue to explore. It is one thing to feel sad and confused; it is quite another to feel sadness and to understand its source. Thus, talking aloud about feelings and events helps open up emotional doors, helps us get in closer touch with true inner feelings, helps us understand ourselves better, and helps us view past and current realities more clearly.

All people develop a view of the world made up of many elements that give structure and familiarity to everyday life. This view is made up of familiar places (home, work, school); it is populated with familiar people; and it is supported by a number of basic assumptions about the world (e.g., I know where my next meal is coming from. I can go to doctors if I get sick. I feel competent to take care of myself. My world is relatively safe. Honesty is the best policy, and so forth). These familiar images, people and beliefs provide sameness, stability and support for everyday living. They help us feel more solid and grounded as we move through each day. Major life events, however, alter these familiar sources of support. The loss of a job, the death of a loved one, the break up of a marriage, or a physical assault can dramatically erode these fundamental aspects of our everyday reality. Life isn't the same after we experience major stresses. The ordinary, familiar realities that provided support are now shaken up or taken away. In addition to feelings of loss, fear, and/or vulnerability, major stressors also tend to destabilize people. In most cases, the result is a sense of fragmentation, anxiety and uneasiness. Among the many professionals who have contributed to our understanding of these issues, the work of Dr. Mardi Horowitz (1976) and Dr. Ronnie Janoff-Bulman (1992) has been particularly important.

By repeatedly talking about the stressful events (e.g., a divorce) in a context of understanding, one may gradually piece together two views of reality: "How it was" and "How it is now." It is tempting to try to do this quickly. Some people may think, "I know we've gotten a divorce. I see that clearly. I don't need to talk about it." Yet getting a divorce, or being raped, or losing a child are not simple events. These are extremely powerful experiences that send ripples of change into many, many parts of a person's life. Coming to a deep awareness of "how it is now" often times takes a long time and a *lot* of thinking, reflecting and talking. Many, if not most, people feel an impulse or need to repetitively talk about the painful event and their current lives, a part of the natural, repetitive urge seen in the intrusive phase of the stress response syndrome discussed earlier. Yet, many people also think, "I shouldn't belabor this... I shouldn't beat a dead horse," and quite often they think, "I shouldn't burden others with this. They'll get tired of hearing me complain." Some folks do get into a pattern of non-productive complaining, but in the aftermath of painful events, the impulse to talk about things over and over again is entirely healthy and normal.

If you are in a stage of emotional recovery, it is very important to give yourself permission talk it out. At some point, this process finally will lead to a clearer view of the realities of stressful events and of your current life. At some point, the vague sense of uneasiness, anxiety and fragmentation will begin to subside. You may continue to grieve the losses, but you'll start to feel more grounded and more stable. The world will start to seem somewhat more normal and familiar again.

> Dale
>
> "I will never forget my wife or our lifetime together. At the same time, my life is different now. It's a life without Joyce. For a number of months, I couldn't or wouldn't accept it. But over and over, as if my mind kept forcing me to see reality, the idea of life without her started to sink in.
>
> I would never choose to remember the awful details of her death, but my mind kept inflicting the memories and the images on me. And for some reason, I felt compelled to talk about the awful events in my bereavement group. I guess since everybody else in the group talked about similar experiences, I felt it was ok to do it myself. But now I know — I *had* to face this new reality. My life has changed and that's just the truth."

### Version One and Version Two of Reality

*Truth is what stands the test of experience.*
— Albert Einstein

*Your vision will become clear only when you can look into your own heart. Who looks outside, dreams; who looks inside, awakes.*
— Carl Jung

Conscious views of reality are often influenced by what other people tell us. These views may take the form of pronouncements from important others: "Your father is a good man," "You had a perfectly normal childhood," "You know, your mother really does love you," "I really want to spend more time with you honey, but I have a lot of work to do," "I'm doing this for your own good," "Of course I love you. We're married aren't we?! I don't have to *tell* you I love you... you should know it!" Views of reality are also shaped by injunctions: "You shouldn't rock the boat," "Don't be so sensitive," "I should like my job, it does pay well," "I shouldn't complain; others have it a lot worse than I do."

These thoughts and views of reality have a tendency to dominate our conscious awareness and constitute what I call "Version One" of reality. Sometimes Version One may be accurate; sometimes not.

On another level is "Version Two," which is based more on your direct experience, sensations and feelings — a type of inner truth. Recall from Chapter 2 a woman, who, during her first menstrual period complained to her mother of painful cramping. When her mother responded, "You are too young to have a period!", the young girl was now confronted by two views of reality: Mom's view (You are not having a period.) and her own view (I hurt.). A child sometimes might say, "Mom, you are wrong!" But a child will more likely focus on the mother's version and somehow manage to ignore the reality of her own inner experience. The inner reality (physical pain, emotions, needs) can be ignored by using various conscious strategies, such as *rationalizing:* "Well, I'm making a big deal out of nothing... it's not that bad," or "I'm just too sensitive... I know I shouldn't complain," or "I guess it's just all in my head," or by using unconscious means such as *repression*, in which the feeling is partially or totally blocked out of awareness. The person may be completely unaware of her inner reality.

Recall Sharon's case. She initially did not even notice her anger toward Tim. She just felt upset, afraid and tearful. For her, Version One meant "Tim is a good man. He says he loves me. It could be worse. I shouldn't complain." During therapy she started to listen more carefully to her inner experiences; she gradually became aware of her Version Two: "He is rarely at home. There is little intimacy. I feel empty, unhappy and angry. His words say 'I love you,' but his behavior tells a different story." The old saying "Actions speak louder than words," became true for Sharon.

Sharon's dawning awareness of the truth of her inner experience brought her in closer contact with her real self. Version One was fashioned on empty promises, words, and Sharon's own strong hopes. She wanted desperately to believe Version One. But it wasn't true. As she talked and explored her feelings during psychotherapy sessions, Version One began to fade and gave way to Version Two. Tim may have had good intentions and sincerely believed that his statement of love and promises were genuine. However, the "bottom-line" reality or experience for Sharon was Version Two. She didn't like it, and it hurt, but it was real.

A major part of growth and emotional healing has to do with *questioning* one's own personal "Version Ones" regarding *important others* (e.g., parents, spouses, friends, etc.); *world views* (e.g., "the world is fair," "bad things don't happen to good people," etc.); and *guidelines for living* ("Don't be emotional," "Don't be so sensitive," "Don't get angry."), and *paying attention to direct experience* — inner reactions, sensations, longings and emotions.

A passage in the Bible says, "The truth shall make you free." This phrase can have multiple meanings, and one of them applies to the process of emotional growth and healing. It's hard to define ultimate truths, but the truth being discussed here is the truth of your inner self. This truth cannot be defined or dictated from without, but must be discovered from within.

> *The individual in search of self-identity becomes a consumer of reality.*
>
> — Walter Truett Anderson

When people make time to really talk about their thoughts, feelings, and other inner experiences in the process of working through, one outcome is often an increased awareness of inner truths. Revelations such as "My childhood was not happy," "My father didn't truly express love toward me," "My job isn't gratifying," or "My mother hurt me," among many others are often the kind of discoveries that hurt and help. People then must grieve the loss of illusions (e.g., the illusion of a happy childhood or a meaningful marriage). Sometimes ultimately Version Two is ok. You may start to see your husband for who he really is. Maybe that's all right; maybe not. The more accurate awareness may ignite more open conflict or problem-solving in important relationships; it may lead to the need for marital counseling or even to divorce. But for many people, the increased awareness of inner "truth" results in a decrease of internal emotional conflict and a stronger sense of self.

It must be emphasized that within each person there are usually many "truths." Most of us have mixed feelings and varying opinions. So the search for "truth" is not aimed at finding "one truth," but has as its goal the discovery of any number of inner beliefs, needs or emotions. Only when we can clarify these truths can we then begin to sort out who we are and feel more solid about the actions we choose to take.

Talking out loud with another is also a good way to spot pain-magnifying distortions. As we saw earlier, inaccurate conclusions, negative, critical self-labeling, unrealistic shoulds, negative predictions and tunnel vision all powerfully turn up the volume on pain.

This kind of thinking can continue indefinitely and pour salt into emotional wounds, especially if the thinking primarily remains unspoken. But by talking openly with another person, you more easily catch yourself thinking in these unrealistic and pain-magnifying ways.

*So little by little, time brings out each several thing into view,*
*and reason raises it up into the shores of light.*

— Lucretius

So let's recap this aspect of working through. Talking out loud about what has happened, about your inner thoughts and feelings and current realities, can be helpful in at least four ways:

• It gives coherence to vague feelings and helps us better understand inner emotions.

• It can help us get in closer touch with true inner feelings (opening emotional doors).

• It helps us to develop an increasingly clear view of past and current realities, to become aware of inner "truths." This often reduces feelings of fragmentation, uncertainty and anxiety, and strengthens a sense of the self.

• It is a good way to spot the presence of pain-magnifying distortions (negative predictions, inaccurate conclusions, etc.).

The talk I've been describing is not social small-talk, not complaining, not "just talking." Instead, it is an incredibly important tool in the healing process. Your goal is to explore and understand yourself, compassionately. But often talking requires courage because talking can, and often does, lead you to discover more intense feelings. Also, the outcome of talking in this way depends a *lot* on the person in whom you confide. This choice takes us to the next major aspect of working through: sharing the pain.

### Working Through 3: Sharing The Pain

*...in silence we would honor our private shame and make it unspeakable."*

— Pat Conroy
*The Prince of Tides*

*"The more we are willing to share, the more we connect with a common humanity in each other."*

—John Bradshaw

It is commonly said that shared pain is easier to bear, but it depends on how your sharing is received by others. Sometimes opening up to another person makes matters worse, as in the case when the other person responds to the expression of emotion by judging. Sometimes the judging is blatant; sometimes it is subtle. Let's look at some examples:

Obvious Judgement

"You should be ashamed of yourself."

"You have no right to feel that way."

"You are being too emotional, too sensitive."

Somewhat Disguised Judgement

"Gosh, you're really taking it hard, aren't you."

"Now, now, don't cry."

"Look on the bright side."

"You need to put it behind you and get on with life."

The obvious or underlying message implied is judgement: "It's wrong to feel that way," or "There is something wrong with you." In response, the person in pain may begin to feel ashamed or inadequate, and her emotional expression may cease altogether. In addition, she is likely to become increasingly inhibited about sharing inner feelings, further cutting her off from connections with others. In such cases, sharing is hurtful rather than healing.

Another type of non-helpful sharing occurs when the listener quickly jumps in to offer brilliant insights or good advice. Sometimes this response is helpful, but often it is not. In fact, it generally closes the door on deeper emotional sharing.

A final type of non-helpful sharing occurs when the listener rather quickly or in a phony, shallow way says, "I understand." True understanding is hard to achieve. People are just so unique and so complex in their make-up that to come even close to a state of true understanding requires a *lot* of listening and a good deal of time spent coming to know the other person. The friend who says, "I understand," is probably trying to be helpful and trying to express care and concern. However, the person sharing her pain often thinks, "How can she really understand?" The result again is a closing down of emotion and a reluctance to share.

Yet, thankfully, there are good listeners in the world. Some of them have made a profession of it (healers, clergy, psychotherapists), and others are ordinary folks who are able to listen, to care and to strive for understanding, not judgement. Who is a good listener? Here are some of the characteristics.

• The ability to listen with an open mind, to accept what is said without passing judgement. A willingness to accept that what is being said is simply the truth of the other person's inner experience, and not a matter of good or bad, right or wrong.

• The ability and willingness to be patient and to understand that emotional healing takes a long time. The listener may think the other person is covering the same ground a number of times, but the *good* listener knows there is value in this repetition, and is able to transmit the message that "it's ok to ramble. It's ok to talk about things time and time again. I know this may be necessary and helpful."

• The ability to share another's painful and intense emotions, which is often *very* difficult. Not many people enjoy witnessing anguish, terror, extreme vulnerability or deep emptiness. However, some people are able to stand face to face with human suffering and not back off. When someone has been through truly horrendous emotional times, his pain is often simply too intense for another person to endure. Even genuinely loving, caring friends and relatives are often overwhelmed by the powerful emotions. In such cases, psychotherapy can be tremendously helpful. Professional therapists are trained to do this kind of work.

• The good listener strives to understand but also knows that true understanding is difficult to achieve. He is quick to say he doesn't understand or to ask the person to elaborate in an attempt to achieve increasing clarity.

• The good listener is able to admit that she does not have ready-made solutions; it is not her job or responsibility to "fix things." Rather, she wants to listen, to believe, and to care. Doing so can provide a safe, accepting and nurturing emotional atmosphere. In this setting, a person in pain can generally feel secure enough to open up and share inner feelings, memories and thoughts.

### Benefits of Positive Sharing

When sharing pain with another person, you may experience strong but manageable emotions that otherwise would seem completely overwhelming. The other person can be like an anchor, providing some degree of stability and strength, thus, lessening the intensity of your emotions.

During times of crisis, many people are flooded with a host of emotions, some of which seem either too intense or too shameful. An extremely important consequence of sharing your feelings with a good listener is feeling more "OK" about having such human emotions. You feel less guilt, less shame, and even disturbing emotions often begin to seem more normal or understandable. So many people are afraid that others will be disgusted, or shocked, or critical, but a tremendous sense of relief can result when you reveal deep inner feelings and see that the other person hears you and does not condemn you.

Sharing pain with another also gives you a chance to talk out loud. We've seen the value in talking earlier, and people can, and do, talk to themselves, but talking is more effective when another person listens.

Finally, and very importantly, sharing allows you simply to be with another human being during a time of distress. Most people feel any life crisis more acutely in isolation and aloneness. Being in contact with a close friend, a loved one or "just" a good listener is soothing and healing.

---

### Gary

While recovering from bladder cancer, Gary privately agonized about his illness for two months until he finally talked openly with his close friend Neal. Gary didn't want to burden Neal with worries Gary thought foolish. But he got up the courage to call Neal to say, "I need to talk." They talked for two hours one night. Gary openly shared his intense fears and worries. Neal didn't offer any platitudes; he gave no advice. He simply sat and listened to his friend. Afterward, Gary said, "It was wonderful. It felt *so* good to tell him. I just felt so alone and so scared. Thank God I have a good friend like Neal." Gary's worries did not completely and magically vanish, but his tense, frenzied emotional state gave way to a greater sense of calm. And he knew it was ok to talk to Neal again if he wanted to.

---

Sharing pain connects us to one another. Compassion and love can play an important role in the healing process.

### *Working Through 4: Taking Action*

Many people suffer silently, their emotional pain completely internalized. Sometimes they suffer alone because they are private people; sometimes injunctions to "be strong" or shame and embarrassment motivate them to deal with their emotional pain alone. Undoubtedly many people do heal in such situations, but many others do not heal or end up living through prolonged periods of unnecessary pain.

Taking action in working through requires three especially

important and helpful steps. The first involves a *conscious decision to do something* to help yourself. This decision must begin with honest self-assessment; that is, admitting to yourself "I hurt" or "This is painful." This acknowledgement of your pain is often easier said than done, but is essential. The second action is deciding to develop *an attitude of compassion toward yourself.* Compassion for yourself promotes emotional healing. As we've discussed before, harsh self-criticism doesn't work. Instead, you've decided, "My job now is to treat myself with understanding and kindness; whether I feel deserving or not, it is simply necessary and right." The third and crucially important action is to *find someone to talk to,* a good listener with whom you feel safe. This may be a friend, a relative, a support group or a therapist.

### How Long Does Working Through Take?

Many psychotherapy clients ask this question. The only good answer I know is Yogi Berra's, "It ain't over till it's over." Many factors come into play in determining "how long": the source of the pain, how long ago the painful event(s) occurred, how hard you want to work on the process, and more. Specialists in therapy for depression note that it can take from a few weeks to several months for recovery; divorce therapists claim two to three years. Very tragic losses or the pain from severe child abuse may require years of struggling and healing. Many times the emotions behind the question "How long does it take?" are pain, desperation and a natural desire to want the hurt to stop. So my response to this question generally is, "I don't know. But let's see if we can do everything possible to speed up the process. Let's start talking."

### Deep Wounds, Deep Healing

If you get a splinter in your foot and it goes in deep, it hurts and may become infected. So you remove it. Do you need to get every single, tiny piece of the splinter out? Often you don't, but you do need to get enough out so it does not fester, and healing can take place. Likewise, in the process of working through, a good question with unclear answers often arises: "How much working through is really necessary?" This issue is especially evident in the working through of very painful, deep emotional wounds from childhood. For these and other significant causes of emotional pain, a simple bandage or other quick fix just doesn't work. The process of working through can be long and painful. I wish I had a formula that could tell you when enough is enough. I regret that I do not. However, as in the splinter analogy, you probably don't have to get out all of the pain. Clearly a good deal of healing can take place, and yet a person (perhaps working with a therapist) may decide to back off from actively working through. This decision ultimately rests on an intuitive judgement that "we've gone far enough." The true test is then to see how you do without further therapy. Just as the body can assimilate some splinter fragments and heal, so can the human heart assimilate some splintering emotions and heal. In episodes of splinter removal with my two sons, I get to a point where I decide, "I think we got enough... I think you'll be ok," and I offer a hug and hope they'll heal.

People who have experienced truly awful life events probably never overcome them 100%. Such experiences under the best of circumstances leave tender spots in the psyche. However, the name of the game, in my view, is to actively pursue emotional healing at least long enough to reduce unnecessary suffering and to regain the capacity for living the best life possible.

The myth of Pandora's box reveals a related truth. After lifting the lid and being engulfed by all manner of misery and evil, people found the spirit of hope.

### Why Stir Up the Past?

Sometimes the legacy of childhood emotional trauma can be a daily encounter with painful memories, flashbacks or nightmares. In such cases, the trauma is hard to simply ignore; its force and reality penetrate the here and now. Facing, struggling with, and working through such memories may be the only successful path toward healing and resolution. One survivor of very severe child abuse told me that her husband asked, "Why do you go into therapy and stir up all this old childhood pain?" Her response was, "I don't choose to remember. It happens automatically. And either I do it with my therapist, or I have to face it alone, on my own."

Some people, like Katherine, are dealing with day-in and day-out emotional bombardment from the recesses of memory. However, many, if not most times, the painful experiences of childhood are not registered on a here-and-now, conscious level. Yet the influence of early traumatic experiences profoundly affects day-to-day living.

As we observed in Chapter 4, a common lasting consequence of early emotional trauma is the laying down of core beliefs. These powerful, often unconscious beliefs whisper barely audible warnings to people: "Don't get too close to others," "Don't attempt it... you know you'll just fail," "Eventually, if they really get to know me, they will abandon me," "No matter how hard I try, I still am basically defective." These powerful, inner beliefs act as stoppers — they warn someone about potential dangers and disappointments such that assertion, intimacy or self-expression inevitably feel risky. The results can be chronically low self-esteem, shame and/or loneliness.

Many psychotherapists believe that exploring childhood experiences is tremendously helpful — to talk in depth not only about the events, but especially to focus on the feelings and personal meanings of important early events. Does this process just stir up old pain? Can it help?

A man attempting to leave a boat dock untied all the ropes securing the boat to the dock and started to row, but the boat didn't move. After a careful search, he saw that one last rope remained tied to the dock, but it was out of view beneath the surface of the water. Sometimes you have to look beneath the surface of obvious day-to-day events to see why you feel stuck. Often the past is still very much alive in the present, in the form of haunting memories and negative core beliefs. Stirring up the pain and exploring your past may be like reaching in and untying that last rope.

Katherine

As Katherine retold her story of sexual abuse, her memories of the past were tremendously painful. For months she struggled with the intense emotions and often felt almost overwhelmed. But at least two things were different as she re-experienced the childhood trauma. In this encounter with the trauma she was accompanied by a companion (her therapist); this time she was not alone; this time someone supported and believed her. The trauma of her sexual abuse was greatly intensified when, as a child, she went through this so very alone, and when she experienced marked invalidation of her feelings by her mother. A second, very important difference was that Katherine experienced the original abuse as a helpless, powerless child. On retelling and refacing the memories as an adult, though the emotions have been extremely strong, Katherine has, little by little been able to face them, endure them, and survive them. She has been able to shout out, "It isn't fair!" and "God damn that man!" To face, to speak out, to acknowledge, to share and to be believed by another can change a person. The sharing with another does not change the reality of the event, but it changes personal experience from one of total helplessness and powerlessness to one of courage, survival and mastery. Katherine's response reveals this change: "I never would willingly choose to go through all these memories. But I had no choice. And by God, I faced them! My feelings are real and I know they matter to me and to my therapist." The restoration of feelings of worth and the validation of feelings and experiences contributes profoundly to the process of emotional growth and healing.

Sharon

Sharon carried around some deep-seated beliefs: "Others don't really love me... there must be something wrong with me." These beliefs and strong painful feelings of inadequacy and aloneness are often evoked by present-day events, e.g., when her husband Tim seems to avoid her for days on end. His behavior operates to verify in Sharon's mind her conviction that *she* is somehow not good enough. In therapy, Sharon initially discounted her "past," saying, "Yeah, I was alone a lot when I was a girl, but that was years ago. My problem now is in my marriage." And she's right; her childhood was years ago. Her pain now issues largely from problems in her relationships. But in the course of therapy, she did decide to explore her early life, to honestly re-encounter her memories and to see them from a different perspective.

What became clear to Sharon after only a few counseling sessions was that her parents were much more aloof and unavailable than she had really noticed before. She became increasingly aware that their top priority had been their careers, not her or her happiness. "It's not like I came to a completely new view of my parents... I kind of knew this all along. But, the more I really talked about it, the more clearly I saw that they did *very* little to really be with me. Their words were hollow, and

## Strengthening the "Self"

When living on the Gulf Coast I once experienced a hurricane. A day or two before the storm hit, we took action. The people in our community placed boards on windows, tied down trees and secured other possessions, bracing for the storm. No amount of human action could lessen the force of the hurricane's winds, but the preparation made a significant difference in how well people weathered the storm. Similarly, during times of emotional crisis people can take steps to more successfully ride out emotional storms. These actions, and over and over again I became hopeful and then was let down." As she talked, the *realities* of her past did not change (of course), but her *view* of her experience did. It shifted from "There is something wrong with me..." to "I was a lonely, needy kid... a normal kid who wanted to be included. And my parents cared more about their jobs than they cared about me."

This discovery is much more than just an indictment of her parents; it reveals a major shift in her perspective. Sharon was able to arrive at new conclusions about herself, her parents and her reality. The revised view also was different in that she came to see herself not as defective, but as a normal kid who was emotionally starving. She came to believe that her needs were and still are legitimate. She is not an unlovable person, but rather, a human being with understandable desires to want to be included, to be noticed and to matter in the hearts of her parents.

Recounting her past experiences did result in an upheaval of Sharon's emotions, but this in itself was not the goal or what turned out to be most helpful. The truly helpful results of her journey into her past were a new understanding about the context and circumstances of her childhood and most importantly, a real change in her beliefs about herself.

I believe, have one thing in common: they strengthen a person's sense of self. There are a few tremendously important steps a person can take to strengthen the self.

In Chapter 2, I discussed the emotionally destructive effect of invalidation. Judging children or adults in emotional pain with invalidating comments such as "it really doesn't hurt" or "don't be so emotional" derails healing. People often respond by feeling inadequate, ashamed or crazy. *Conversely, experiencing validation* and affirmation from others acts powerfully to relieve suffering. To feel accepted, to feel believed, to have others understand — all these provide tremendous emotional support at times of crisis or despair.

Validation, however, comes not only from others, but also from within yourself. A crucial aspect of developing an attitude of compassion for yourself is to allow yourself to believe your inner experiences. Many people may rather habitually think, "I shouldn't feel this way," or "I'm making mountains out of mole hills," when the simple truth is that they hurt. Self-validation is acknowledging inner feelings and accepting them as real and understandable. It certainly does not mean that in any way you like the experience, that you choose to wallow in the pain, or that you accept the pain as your lot in life. Rather, it is an open and honest acknowledgement of your emotional reality.

Our case examples help illustrate the point: for Gary, the truth was that he was scared out of his wits; Sharon admitted to herself that she really wasn't happy, and that she didn't believe Tim's "promises." Awareness and acknowledgement of inner truths can serve as an anchor during hard times. ("Version One and Version Two of Reality," pages 170-73, illustrates the importance of validation of one's inner experience.)

A second step to take in strengthening your sense of self is to find outlets for *honest self-expression*. Weak muscles can gradually become strengthened by exercising. Self-expression is the type of emotional exercise that gradually builds and strengthens the self. Self-expression can take the form of open verbal communication with others: expressing your opinions, beliefs, values, needs and feelings, taking a stand, saying "no," asking for change in others' behavior. Assertion groups and self-help books focusing on developing assertion skills are popular and extremely helpful ways to foster self-expression (see Chapter 14).

Sometimes direct expression of feelings or opinions may not be desirable or possible. (For example, you may have strong inner feelings directed toward someone whom you do not choose to confront or toward a person who is no longer living.) In such situations, many people have found writing — but not mailing — a very frank letter to the person helpful. The goal, of course, is not to communicate directly with that person, but to find an outlet for expressing unresolved issues. Even though the other person never sees it, this expression in writing can often lead to an important relief from inner emotional conflicts and can help you work through unfinished business from past relationships.

Many people have found tremendous value in keeping a *personal journal.* Writing down feelings, thoughts, hopes, and dreams can be a powerful way to clarify inner emotional experiences and find an outlet for self-expression.

The self always flourishes best in a healthy atmosphere, which you can create by giving yourself permission to *care for basic physical and emotional needs:* adequate rest, good nutrition, exercise, fresh air; surrounding yourself with things of beauty; making a place in your home that can be a haven of warmth, comfort and peace; making time for recreation, humor, relaxation, or meditation; establishing a reasonable balance between work and play; setting realistic expectations for yourself; and, from time to time, splurging. All of these sound incredibly simple and obvious, but these issues often go unnoticed (even by psychologists who write self-help books) and contribute to an underlying sense of dis-ease. Some people may think these ideas sound selfish. But it's a smart kind of selfishness since it helps people feel better, more alive, and in the long run, ultimately affects the lives of others in a positive way, too.

A number of therapists have found the use of *"centering exercises"* to be of help to people wanting to feel more inner solidity. One of these exercises involves making a time and place to relax quietly (even for a couple of minutes, although a ten-minute exercise seems best). Sit down in a chair, assume a relaxed posture, but make sure your back is well supported and both feet are planted firmly on the floor; close your eyes and concentrate. Notice your body, notice your breathing and in particular notice where you sense your physical or emotional "center." For some people this may be in the pelvis, for others in the spine, heart or the head. Silently talk to yourself, perhaps giving yourself what some call "affirmations" or supportive "self-talk." Examples of positive self-talk may include: "I am here at this moment. I feel and notice myself. I feel my feet on the ground and a sense of solidity and balance in my body"; "I am giving myself permission to relax and get in touch with my inner self. My inner self can be an anchor for me as I go through difficult times"; "I have concerns that matter to me. Whether others agree or disagree, I am entitled to my beliefs, my values and my feelings. No one can take these things away from me"; "As I deal with hard times, it is my choice to do my best ... to take care of myself... to honor my feelings and my values... to be gentle with myself."

Experiment with other versions of self-talk that suit you in a more personal way. Try it out. The intention is not to ignore difficult life circumstances, but to shore up your inner sense of self.

Finally, you may strengthen your sense of self by deciding to become involved in life activities that *express and affirm your own inner beliefs* and values. You sometimes accomplish this through your choice of profession. Many people realize this goal through involvement in churches, organizations and causes that have personal meaning. Dozens of volunteer agencies and support programs in every community offer many opportunities for people to give something back to the world. Not only can these activities help the community, but they also can become an important vehicle for your own self-expression. Your journey through difficult times is easier when you can feel a more solid sense of yourself.

### Whom Can I Turn To?

> *It takes two to speak the truth — one to speak and another to hear.*

> — Henry David Thoreau

Your best chance to work through important emotional issues is in the context of close, trusting relationships. Often this process occurs within your own network of social supports: friends, family and church. Excellent support groups which offer a lot of help can be found in most communities. By turning to loved ones and other sources of support, a large number of people weather major emotional crises, not only surviving but going on to live full lives.

## Thirteen

*Action Plan #4:*
*Taking Action in Your Real World*

*I*f you sustain a physical wound, such as a burn, healing generally occurs in time. However, if the burn is repeatedly re-injured, or the scab continues to be knocked off, the pain can continue for a prolonged period.

With emotional wounds, it's pretty common for the "scab" to be knocked off. Repeated emotional injuries occur as you encounter conflicts in personal relationships. Repetitive emotional abuse and on-going friction with others can keep the hurt alive indefinitely.

Unresolved, recurring problems in important relationships are major sources of ongoing emotional distress, and they appear in many forms: repeated put-downs, unrealistic demands, emotional abuse, unfair treatment, hostility, inappropriate jealousy. Unless action occurs, these common problems can continue for months or years, exacting a significant emotional toll. They occur in the context of friendships, with colleagues, at work, with relatives and in intimate relationships. Many on-going interpersonal problems are tolerated and result in chronic suffering.

You can do a lot on an internal level to come to terms with emotionally difficult times, as we have seen in the previous chapters. But your best efforts to heal from within may not be enough. It may be important to take action in the real world of your relationships; to identify ongoing problems, to reduce stressors, to ask for and negotiate for changes. Withdrawal can sometimes work (e.g., breaking off a friendship, avoiding certain social gatherings, dissolving a marriage, moving away from unhealthy family members); however, such a strategy may be difficult or impractical. Despite the decreased friction, ending a relationship may be felt as a regrettable loss.

You will find there are no magic solutions for problems with others, but some helpful tools are available. In this chapter and the next, I will be sharing with you a few conflict resolution strategies that have been shown to be extremely effective.

### *Say No and Let Go*

It is a fact that the total number of stressors you are dealing with at any given time makes a difference in how much stress you experience and how well you cope. Regardless of the *nature* of particular stressful events, simply *the more you must deal with at a time,* the more stress you feel. Stressors are always cumulative and additive.

In the days of TV's "Ed Sullivan Show," a man periodically came on the show and demonstrated his ability to spin twenty plates simultaneously atop bamboo poles. He would rush back and forth keeping the plates spinning. You can bet that this man knew his limit. I assume he discovered that by adding one or two extra plates beyond the twenty, it was too much, and all came crashing down. Like the TV juggler, everyone has a limit to the amount of stressors which can reasonably be kept in balance at any given time in life. Adding the "twenty-first plate" sets the stage for distress and ineffective coping.

During particularly difficult times there may be a single primary source of stress or emotional pain; for example, a marital separation. The separating partners feel tense and overwhelmed, and the main reason for their distress issues directly from the main stressful event.

Yet there very likely are a number of less noxious life events — everyday tasks and obligations — which are also putting demands on the person. These less traumatic sources of stress may, at first glance, seem to be "no big deal"... they are the routine chores of life. Yet even the mundane tasks sap energy and demand attention. They can be the stressors that break — or at least strain — many camels' backs.

One strategy for taking action in the real world involves identifying current life stressors, acknowledging that they may be contributing to stressful feelings, and choosing to reduce or eliminate some of them. It sounds simple, but may be easier said than done. (Remember, stressors are not necessarily painful or obnoxious events, but also include positive or neutral demands and life activities.)

A simple exercise to help you pinpoint some of the sources of stress in your life is to note how you spend your time each day for a week. You'll need to make a full-page copy of figure 13-A below and jot down very briefly almost everything you do. Obviously this would not include such very minor events as taking a drink of water or sneezing, but should include any activities that take five minutes or more of your time. In listing these, you will be prioritizing your activities along two dimensions: *necessary for life* and *quality of life*.

### Figure 13-A
#### Quality of Life

| | | High | Medium | Low |
|---|---|---|---|---|
| **Necessary for Life** | High | A | B | C |
| | Medium | D | E | F |
| | Low | G | H | I |

After you've kept track of your daily activities for a week, it's time to take a careful look at them and to evaluate how the way you're spending your time may be contributing to your stress. Here are some examples: In box C, you might write "washing dishes." This is an activity that (at least eventually) is necessary, yet it may be something that adds little to your experience of "quality of life." Box G might contain "soaking in a hot bath at the end of a busy day." This may not be at all necessary for living but may rank high as it contributes to a sense of peacefulness or relaxation. In box I it is likely you'll find tasks that are either obligations (things you think you "should do," but really dislike) or habits. The strategy then involves looking at activities in Box I, asking yourself, "Are these really meaningful or important?" and then deciding to let go of them or to say no.

For a while I had a vegetable garden that required tending. When I looked at this task critically, it became clear to me, "I hate this." I got no joy from it and mainly experienced it as an unpleasant way to sweat. Why was I doing it?! Because I think I thought it was a "good" or "right" thing to do. I had convinced myself that "lots of people like to garden, so I should too." Indeed, for many people, gardening may rank high as an important, meaningful activity. The truth is, gardening is not my cup of tea. Tending the garden wasn't killing me, but it was clearly a source of some frustration — "I guess I *ought* to go water the plants," — and it took time and some energy. That same time spent listening to music or reading would have been much more pleasant and self-nurturing for me.

What if you're going through some awful life stress? How can letting go of some tasks and obligations really help? Will it bring a marriage back together or reduce the agony of witnessing the serious illness of a loved one? Of course not. But it *can* help. It's easy to deny the significance of minor stressors. Yet in the face of serious life crises, it's important to seek relief wherever you can find it. Letting go of unnecessary tasks and obligations is an action step you can take.

### Finish Your Unfinished Business

Long-held regrets, old grudges, and unspoken words burden the inner emotional life of many, and can contribute to on-going problems in relationships. The opportunity to speak out about strong feelings may be lost by the death of a friend or relative. You can choose consciously to express yourself to important others regarding issues that you've held within yourself. This could take the form of an honest letter, a phone call, or a visit with your friend, laying your cards on the table about your feelings and beliefs.

Virginia had for many years valued and appreciated the support, concern and understanding of her college roommate, Ginny. The two had shared a lot of emotional times together back in school, yet they've had few contacts since their graduation twelve years ago. On a rainy Sunday afternoon, Virginia wrote Ginny a long-overdue letter, expressing her warm feelings and memories. She had put it off for so long, not because she didn't care, but because she simply felt inhibited and never seemed to "find the time." That afternoon she *made* the time and wrote. The next weekend, Ginny called to say how touched she was by the letter. Virginia was delighted with the outcome: "It just felt so good to write to her and to hear from her. I feel as if I did someting for both of us. It was a gift to Ginny that left me feeling more whole inside and at peace with myself."

Three months before my own father died, I wrote him a letter that included a list of very specific and important things I remembered and cherished about our relationship when I was a child. I remember feeling a bit uneasy and hesitant as I wrote; I didn't know how he'd react. But the letter meant a lot to him. I believe it opened up our relationship so that we were able to talk about other important personal matters during the last weeks of his life. Now years after his death I am so glad I found the courage to write him.

For Virginia and for me, these actions had an impact on another person and left us feeling good inside as well. In counseling hundreds of people over the last two decades, I've often heard my clients admit deep regrets about not expressing their true feelings to loved ones now gone. Choosing to express yourself about both positive and negative feelings can have an immediate impact and can be a way to avoid years of regret for missed opportunities.

### Forgive — or Not

Forgiveness is a thorny issue in human relationships. To "forgive and forget," or to "let bygones be bygones," is easy advice to give, yet incredibly hard to follow — especially if you've been seriously hurt. How can you truly forgive someone who has inflicted tremendous emotional pain and heartache?

Yet, in the absence of forgiveness we harbor intensely painful inner emotions — anger, bitterness, disappointment — which can eat away at us for a lifetime.

In their book, *Forgiveness*, Dr. Sidney and Suzanne Simon have stated well what forgiveness is not: It is not forgetting, or the erasure of painful memories; it is not condoning or excusing the hurtful behavior; it is not absolution or relief of responsibility; it is not martyrdom, denial, or giving in. Rather, say the Simons, forgiveness is an intensely personal process we do *for ourselves* as a way of letting go of the past hurt. And it is a refusal to give your life over to preoccupation with grudges or "evening the score."

Forgiveness says "what was done was wrong — absolutely not ok — whatever the cause." Forgiveness does acknowledge that people do hurt each other, that sometimes the hurt is intentional — but often it is the result of another person's own woundedness. This may be an explanation, but never an excuse. To choose forgiveness is to come to terms with and accept, on some level, that life is often not fair but despite this, we choose life. Rabbi Harold Kushner goes as far to suggest the idea that we may even choose to forgive God for creating a world that is often dangerous and unfair.

Forgiveness can be purely personal — within yourself — and not shared with the person who hurt you. Or you may choose to express your forgiveness to the other. It is my personal belief that it is never helpful to *encourage* someone to "forgive." The choice to forgive or not is highly personal and is usually the outcome of much emotional struggle and healing. Forgiveness is found only within the individual and can't be forced.

To imply that lack of forgiveness is a fault or weakness — even if innocently by declaring that "to forgive is Divine" — is an act of judgement which lacks understanding.

Finally, it is important to note that there is no psychological evidence to suggest that it is necessary to forgive in order to heal.

### Make Life-Changing Decisions

After a good deal of soul-searching and attempts at conflict resolution, sometimes it becomes apparent that a major change in lifestyle, work or relationships may be necessary. This can be an incredibly difficult decision, and the outcome ultimately may make a big difference in your life, for better or for worse.

While some folks make such decisions in an impulsive way, most of us do a lot of thinking before taking major leaps. There are some useful steps you can take to help yourself carefully think through the multitude of issues that may accompany major life changes.

For people confronted with the reality of a very painful or unchangeable situation — for example, involvement in a very destructive, unhealthy relationship — a powerful inner voice may call out, "But I *can't* leave!" The word "can't" (and the belief behind it) implies powerlessness. At such a time, it can be helpful to become clear about how you really think and feel, and to own up to the fact tha most life decisions actually are *choices*. You probably *can* leave, but to do so might be very painful.

Susan is a good example. She has been married for fifteen years to a chronically unemployed, alcoholic man, and they have two children, ages ten and twelve. There have been times of closeness and shared experiences, yet over the past five years their relationship has deteriorated. There is almost no intimacy now. On a number of occasions Wayne has become verbally and physically abusive. Susan has repeatedly asked him to seek out counseling, but to no avail. "I'm so stupid," she tells me. "Anybody in her right mind would leave him! But I just *can't*."

Let's look closely at Susan's conclusions and, in particular, at her perceptions of herself. She sees herself as somehow defective or inadequate ("Anybody in her right mind..."), and she believes that she is powerless to make a decision to leave. This conclusion about herself only intensifies her feelings of despair and helplessness.

In the course of therapy, I asked Susan to look very carefully into herself. "You say you *can't* leave him. Possibly it's not a matter of *can* or *can't*. Maybe there are important reasons that you *choose* to stay." Her first response was to focus quickly on the pain: "There's no sane reason to stay with him!" But, when encouraged not to be so harsh with herself, and to take time to sort through her feelings, she finally said, "When I was young, there was absolutely no one there. I spent night after night so scared and so terribly alone. Even though my husband is a cold S.O.B., for some reason, I feel safer knowing he is there to protect me... In lots of ways I want him out of my life... In some ways I guess I do want him to be there."

As she struggled with her own inner conflicting feelings, Susan came to view herself from a different perspective. Instead of being a helpless person who "can't leave," she began to see herself as a woman who, in fact, had chosen to stay (at least for now). And her choices were based on important and legitimate inner needs. This new view of herself, which was much less self-critical and more empowering, certainly did not solve the dilemma of her problematic relationship. But it empowered her. She now sees herself as an adult woman, making choices and struggling with extremely difficult decisions, no longer powerless and helpless.

Owning up to "choices" rather than pleading "helplessness" is hard to do, but it can be an important step toward taking action on the major issues in your life.

Another common obstacle to good decision making is jumping to very general conclusions about a difficult situation. Thomas, for example, has worked for many years in a job that is very stressful and unsatisfying to him. He began to tell me about it, then brushed it off, saying, "Oh, it's bad, but I shouldn't complain. Others have it bad too... I just need to put up with it."

Job security, benefits, the familiarity of a long-term relationship, all of these are very important issues that people take to heart. On the other hand are uncertainties: What awaits me in a new job? A new relationship? Is the grass really greener on the other side? Is there even grass at all on the other side? The lure of the familiar and fear of the unknown are not trivial issues when it comes to making major life decisions.

An important exercise that can sometimes help is to project out into the future in your imagination. Make time to really explore the question: "What would it look and feel like if I am in this same job (or relationship) five years from now?... Ten years from now?... At retirement?" The objective is not to somehow *predict* the future, but rather to allow this image of a *possible* future to help you get in closer touch with current feelings about your job or relationship. This exercise may help to clarify your current emotions, needs, and hopes, and your perception of the reality of present circumstances.

As an extension of this exercise, take a piece of paper and draw a line down the middle. On the left side write down the potential benefits of staying in your current situation; on the right, the potential risks. On a second sheet of paper do the same, but here imagine the potential risks and benefits of a major life change (e.g., leaving the situation). Many people entertain only vague notions of the risks and benefits associated with change. This exercise clarifies these issues and makes them more concrete. If you carry out this "risk-benefit" analysis honestly, you'll begin to see whether the *objective* facts favor staying or leaving. Even if you decide to go against the objective facts, at least you'll know that you took everything into account when you made your decision.

Major life changes are often incredibly difficult — and this is understandable because the consequences of such changes can be profound. While some difficult circumstances are dealt with by way of negotiation and conflict resolution, there are times when it is written clearly on the wall: "This job (or relationship) just isn't for me!" To leave, relocate, or change can be a life-enhancing choice to take a new direction in life.

As a final thought on this complex process of life decision making, remember that few such decisions are totally irreversible. Although you probably can't reclaim the job or relationship you left, you can *almost* always find another.

### Recurring Interpersonal Problems

The best antidote for recurring interpersonal problems is usually to take action toward problem-solving or conflict resolution.

Millions of people, however, have taken comfort in the sage advice of the "serenity prayer," usually credited to German theologian Reinhold Niebuhr:

> *God grant me the serenity to accept the things I cannot change, Courage to change the things I can, and Wisdom to know the difference.*

This prayer — popularized by Alcoholics Anonymous — directs us to determine what problems potentially can be changed — whether this involves true resolution or workable compromise. It is important first to identify the on-going problem, then very honestly to ask yourself three questions: 1) How important is this issue? 2) How do I really feel, and where do I stand on this issue? and 3) What specific outcomes are desirable?

Many people deny the significance of on-going problems, grit their teeth and say, "I can live with it... it's no big deal," only to enter into an ongoing, seemingly interminable "conflict dance" with the other person. Problems continue, sometimes they escalate, and emotional distress is the result. Over a period of time the relationship deteriorates, feelings of friendship, caring and love erode.

It is beyond the scope of this book to address conflict resolution in a comprehensive way. However, in the next chapter I will talk about one approach that has been found to be an especially helpful tool in problem solving and conflict resolution: learning to be assertive.

*Fourteen*

---

*Action Plan #5:*
*Assert Yourself*

*P*eople don't always get along.

Sometimes it's simply because they have different values, different styles, different needs. Problems in relationships often are not intentional or sought out, but unfold almost automatically; as a result, people get frustrated or hurt.

It's happened to you and it's happened to me. Maybe you found yourself frequently being put down (criticisms, snide remarks, sarcasm, humiliating comments). Or you were in converstaion with a group of associates, and despite your best efforts to contibute, you were being ignored. People did not really listen to you when you tried to discuss important issues.

As you read through the following list, think about times in your own life when you've felt the hurtful actions of others (or maybe you have been guilty of them yourself):

Common Examples of Interpersonal Conflict
- Broken promises (people not following through with promises). Unfair treatment or unequal responsibilities.
- Obliviousness to others emotional needs (e.g., time together, intimacy, support, etc.).
- Attempts to control or dominate the other person (e.g., keeping someone in a submissive position).
- Unwillingness to compromise.
- Blatant emotional, physical or sexual abuse.
- Racial or sexual harassment.
- Dishonesty.
- Guilt trips (others using guilt-inducing tactics to persuade or manipulate).

If you've experienced one or more of these (or similar) emotionally painful circumstances, you'll probably recognize some of the following reactions in yourself — all of them cues that it's time for you to take action to resolve the conflict:

• *Pent up feelings*, rather strong unexpressed feelings that you keep inside. Many times people notice and relate easily to pent up feelings of anger or resentment. If a person is being taken advantage of or abused or used in some way, it is very easy to quickly develop internal feelings of anger. Often people emotionally grit their teeth and keep these feelings inside. But people hold in not only feelings of irritation or frustration or anger, but also feelings of caring or love for others. For example, John may be feeling inwardly, "I'd really like to tell Joan how much I love her and care about her, but I'm afraid she may not accept those feelings." So, he chooses not to be honest, deciding instead to keep quiet. When people like John have pent up feelings, they may walk away from the situation kicking themselves: "Why didn't I tell her that I love her? I really wanted to!"

• *Avoiding people and situations* which you know inwardly are important... it is a big deal, but you're afraid to confront the issue. You may go to great lengths to avoid confronting people or even being in situations where the subject might come up.

• *Long, phony excuses, apologies* or excessive justifications. There is a time and a place to give people a short, simple explanation of why you're doing or saying certain things. However, going to great extremes to explain yourself, bending over backwards, being very apologetic, feeling that you must, in a defensive way, justify everything you say — all these are signs that it may be time for a change.

• *Chronically putting your own needs last.* Certainly I'm not suggesting that you walk through life and constantly put your own needs first. If you do that, the chances are that you'll never make it in any sort of relationship. Every kind of relationship — in marriage, in friendship, with a co-worker — involves mutual give and take. But it's not healthy if you are almost continuously putting your needs last, giving in to what other people say and what other people want, and not expressing how you really feel or what you need.

• *Putting yourself down.* Often people say, "Well, this may sound kind of silly, but..." or "This is kind of stupid, but..." When you're doing this, you are, in a sense, expressing how you feel or what you believe in, or your opinions, but in a self-downing way, degrading or minimizing your own feelings. Again, not a healthy way to act.

• *Aggressive behaviors.* Do you notice yourself very frequently exploding in a very hostile and aggressive way? This might be a sign that you need to learn to deal with the situation in an appropriately *assertive* way. I've talked to many people who are having trouble with temper outbursts or flairs of anger who say, "But gosh, look what's happening! Wouldn't you feel angry?" My response might be, "Well, yeah, probably so." And, in fact, there are many situations in which feeling angry is very human, very normal and very appropriate. To just sit on top of angry feelings would be to allow them to develop into those unhealthy pent-up feelings we talked about earlier. The key would be not to suppress the anger, but to find an acceptable adaptive outlet for expressing feelings of anger. You can be angry and express it in an assertive way.

### So What Can Be Done About These Conflicts?

Ongoing friction with others certainly accounts for a considerable amount of human misery and plays a crucial role in blocking emotional healing. Taking action in the real world of interpersonal relations can be a decisive factor in resolving emotional distress. Resolving conflicts is a major task of adult life and can often make a tremendous difference in the quality of life, in relationships with friends, at work, or in a marriage/family. Many strategies have been developed to help people resolve interpersonal conflicts more effectively: negotiation, reflection of feelings, expression of empathy, active listening, communication skills. There exists a wide variety of strategies for confronting difficult interpersonal conflicts; let's take a look at one of the most valuable resources you can add to your own strategic toolkit: *assertiveness*.

### What Is This "Assertiveness"?

When you're assertive, you are basically being honest with people about how you feel, what your opinions are, what you think about things. This may be an appropriate response in a number of situations. For example, in a common situation in which someone is trying to sell you something that you're not interested in, you're being honest by telling her, "No thanks, I'm not interested." Assertiveness could involve being honest about how you feel about the way someone is treating you. For instance, if someone is taking advantage of you or hurting you, or in some way being emotionally abusive, you're being honest by telling that person, "I don't like being treated this way; please stop." Being assertive also involves the honest expression of your positive feelings. For instance, you might wish to tell someone, "I really appreciate the work you're doing for me," or "I really like you," or "It makes a big difference to me that you're here working with me in this office," or simply that you love him or her.

When you're assertive you get to the point. It's a way of expressing feelings and thoughts directly without a lot of excuses, excessive apologies or beating around the bush.

You also temper your honesty and directness with people with a true sensitivity to other people's feelings. This addition of sensitivity would involve using good judgement and tact in choosing the right time, place and way to express your feelings to other people.

For instance, let's say that at your office a co-worker, Igor, frequently belittles you in front of the rest of the staff. You may have very strong feelings about this and want to tell Igor to stop treating you this way. However, it may not be appropriate to confront him in the middle of a big staff meeting because it would put him on the spot, and he might feel excessively uncomfortable, defensive, and perhaps hostile toward you. One way of showing sensitivity to Igor's feelings would be to wait until a more appropriate time, get him aside, and talk to him alone.

Assertiveness is a concept that has been frequently misunderstood. For example, some people mistake assertion for aggression. Others feel that a person who learns to be more assertive will begin to act in selfish or demanding ways. Although this may happen in some cases, such behavior is a misinterpretation of what it means to be truly assertive. In a nutshell, being assertive involves learning to interact with other people in an honest and adult way, learning to talk straight to others while, at the same time, showing respect for their needs and feelings.

For many reasons, becoming assertive can be very helpful for you. Being more assertive often results in more effective coping. It can increase the chances of effectively dealing with people in resolving problem situations, for example, by asking for help or by asking for changes in the way someone treats you. On an interpersonal front, learning to be more assertive can lead to the development of more honest, mutually satisfying relationships. At the same time that you're confronting and dealing with problem situations, assertion can lead to inner changes, too. Most people find that when they learn to be more assertive, their self-respect and self-esteem increase. Likewise, most people come to experience a greater sense of control over their lives. And finally, increased assertion is a potent way to combat feelings of helplessness, powerlessness and depression. There are many personal benefits in learning to be more assertive.

### But, Isn't That Something You're Born With?

Let's talk about what assertion is and what it is not. Many people think, "Well, I'm naturally a very shy person, so it's going to be hard if not impossible for me to learn to be assertive." It's easy to believe that assertiveness or non-assertiveness are *personality traits*. Not so. Assertion is a *learned* style. The fact is that many passive, shy people do learn to act more assertively without having to make major or complete "personality changes." Thus, it is best to view assertiveness as a combination of *attitudes* and *skills* that *you can learn*.

Let me emphasize that assertion is a way of behaving that you *choose* in *some* situations. Many people may read a book on assertion or attend an assertion workshop, become very enthusiastic about being assertive, and then try to be assertive all the time. If you're being assertive all the time, constantly telling people how you feel about things, or *always* voicing your opinions, your behavior can be rather obnoxious. Assertion is a skill you learn and that you can tap into or decide to use during particular times that you judge to be important and that warrant assertive action. Most people who learn to be assertive are not assertive all the time. However, when problem situations come up or conflicts arise in important relationships with other people, you can use these skills to express your feelings or opinions to deal more effectively with the situation.

### Aggressive Behavior Hurts Others

In contrast to appropriate assertiveness, being *aggressive* is a way of expressing feelings and ideas that rarely, if ever, takes other people's feelings into consideration. Sometimes aggression takes the form of out-and-out hostility or physical aggression. Many times it is "disguised" in the form of sarcasm or snide remarks. When a person is being aggressive, you can detect personal belittling or humiliation of others, if you listen carefully. There are many situations when it is absolutely appropriate or necessary to express feelings of anger or to be critical of someone's performance. There are assertive ways to do this, and there are aggressive ways to do this. You can express fairly intense anger assertively. But when people are getting angry and aggressive, you will notice that they are attacking the basic worth of the person through intimidating, belittling or humiliating comments.

For some people it feels good, at least for the moment, to get really aggressive; it's a way to feel powerful and to feel in control. However, the end result, almost always, is that people simply don't like being around someone who's aggressive. And frequently, aggressive people end up losing in the long run.

### Non-Assertiveness Is Self-Denying

The third way of acting in dealing with others is to be *non-assertive*. Some other terms that might apply are "timid" or "passive." This form of interaction with other people is just not being honest about how you feel. For example, several of your friends get together and decide to go to a movie, and someone says, "Oh, let's go to such-and-such a movie." To be honest, you really don't like that kind of movie, but you say, "Well, sure, that would be fine." We've all done this at times. What's happening is that you are feeling, for one reason or another, reluctant or hesitant to say, "I'd rather not to go to that movie. Can we go to another one instead?"

It's certainly true that everyone acts in a non-assertive way at times, and many times that's appropriate. But there are times when a situation really is important and calls for an assertive response. Let's say that the movie being suggested is very violent, and you *absolutely* don't want to go see a violent movie; you don't enjoy them, and you don't want to support them. This is an example of a time when it would be important to be assertive.

You'll end up paying a price if you are non-assertive very often. One result is that you may go along with people and end up doing things you really don't want to do and never get your own needs met. Also, when you are grossly non-assertive, your behavior opens the door to being taken advantage of and used by other people.

Finally, almost always when people are non-assertive, a lot of the time, deep down inside, they begin to develop feelings of inadequacy. They may think, "What's wrong with me? Why can't I stand up for myself?"

### Still Not Sure You're Ready To Try It?

The major problem in learning how to be assertive is learning how to feel ok about being assertive. Almost everyone can learn the right words to say, but feeling ok about being assertive is the big hurdle. (For a very comprehensive look at assertion, I refer the reader to the book, *Your Perfect Right* by Drs. Robert Alberti and Michael Emmons, which is considered to be the most helpful and authoritative book on the topic.) What I'd like to focus on somewhat briefly in the rest of this chapter is a step-by-step process for you to use that will help you prepare to be assertive. This step-by-step procedure, in all likelihood, will help you feel less anxious and more solid in your decision to act in an honest and assertive way. Effective coping and conflict resolution and changing hurtful relationships into equal relationships can play important roles in emotional healing.

### Getting Started

The most important first step is to look at the problem situation and very honestly ask yourself, "Is this important enough?" Keep in mind that learning to be assertive doesn't mean that you must be assertive all the time. There are times when the situation is simply not important enough; it's honestly not a big deal and it is not necessary to be assertive. Taking a more passive stance is fine. However, I want to caution you about something: people who are frequently very non-assertive commonly encounter situations that in fact *are* very important, but minimize that. They tell themselves, "Well, this isn't that important, it's no big deal," even when it really *does* matter. So it's essential that you look at situations very honestly and realistically!

### Consider the Potential Risks

"What are the realistic risks of being assertive?" Psychologists Richard Rakos and Harold Schroeder (1980) suggest that you consider that question very consciously. People often imagine all sorts of very dangerous or upsetting consequences of acting assertively. Whether you are aware of them or not, these assumptions about what is going to happen actually may rule and determine whether you decide to act assertively. Many times we scare ourselves by imagining that all kinds of bad things are going to happen. Sometimes unpleasant things do happen, and I think that we need to examine closely, honestly, and realistically what these risks may be. Let's take a look at a list of common risks of being assertive.

• *"The other person might become upset or angry or may feel hurt or rejected."* These are bonafide risks. However, often people tend to greatly overestimate the amount of emotional upset that actually may result when they confront another person. By-and-large, if you approach the other person honestly as an adult, treating her with respect, showing some sensitivity to her feelings, and just being honest with her — without belittling her or putting her down — the upset that does occur will be very short term. Many people put off dealing with and confronting problem situations in relationships because they are afraid the other person is going to become extremely upset. The reality is that by avoiding the situation, you may perpetuate serious interpersonal problems for months or even for years — which could take a tremendous emotional toll on both of you. Deciding to confront the issue and deal with a temporary upset may be the first step toward permanent resolution.

• *"The other person may find a way to get back at me or to get even."* I want to caution you that being assertive is no guarantee that the other person is going to respond in a positive way. It would be great if every time you were assertive, the other person said, "Oh, that's fine. I understand." Sometimes that happens. Sometimes people are somewhat irritated or upset, but these feelings pass — they're temporary. And in some situations being assertive with certain kinds of people can lead to some very serious problems. This is often the case if you are dealing with an emotionally unstable or infantile person. A very good example of this might be confronting a supervisor or boss who tends to be quite emotionally immature and who may, in fact, not like having an employee who is simply honest, direct and adult. Some rather infantile people in these kinds of positions enjoy and gain satisfaction from dominating and controlling other people; their focus is making sure that people under them are submissive and not assertive. With a person like this, you potentially risk getting seriously hurt, sometimes physically, and many times in non-physical ways that can be very damaging. You have to use your head about this possibility by asking yourself, "What do I know about this person? Based on my experience, do I feel that this person is mature enough to endure and to handle an honest confrontation?" Sometimes the answer is "No, he is not." In that case, it may pay to choose to be non-assertive.

• *"The assertion may fail."* You may stick your neck out, you may ask for something, you may confront someone, and she may say, "Forget it! No way!" Many people are very afraid to look foolish or to feel helpless or not to know what to do should the assertion fail. One response you may wish to consider in such a situation is to respond quickly, "I'm sorry you feel that way. This issue is very important to me, and I hope you'll give some thought to what I've said."

(Shortly, I will be giving you some additional helpful "backup plans" for these situations. When you have decided to approach a problem situation in which there's even a slight chance that the assertion might fail, having some pre-arranged back-up plans is important: "What am I going to do if the assertion doesn't work?")

• The other person may decide, "Well, this is my opportunity; I'm going to be assertive, too!" It's a risk we all need to consider.

### Risk vs. Reward: Short Run and Long Run

It's natural for people to tend to focus on the immediate emotional issues that might come up when they confront others and talk to them assertively. I think it's important for you to ask yourself, "Okay, I need to consider that, in fact, this other person might feel sad or might feel irritated or might get angry with me at the moment. But let me think about the long-term consequences of these responses. What do I think *really will* happen in the long run? Is she going to continue to be *very* sad or *very* upset for a prolonged time if I confront her?" Consciously appreciating this view, that negative responses may be short-term, can make the decision to be assertive easier.

Considering the longer-term positive consequences is also helpful. So many times what's really going on inside our heads (consciously or unconsciously) when we think about being assertive are the short-term negative consequences. But I think it's very important as you're preparing to assert yourself to ask yourself consciously, "Once I get through with this, even though there may be some upset, I wonder what the *positive results* could be?" These positive outcomes might be seen in terms of both the situation and yourself. You might ask yourself, "I wonder if maybe in the long run this decision to be assertive will solve the problem? Maybe this problem is something we won't have to deal with over and over and over again. Maybe I'm not going to be walking around with this pent-up anger and resentment all the time. It might make it easier for me to really get in and work on our relationship, to truly feel better about things." Another positive consequence would be that "these people are going to know where I stand. Maybe they'll think twice before they try to take advantage of me again. I'm not a person who is willing to be pushed around; I'm going to stand up for myself."

Here's another positive result: "Even though this might be tough in some ways, just maybe after I've been assertive, I can walk out of there and tell myself, 'By gosh, you know what? I did that! I'm proud of myself!'"

The goal here is not to sugar-coat the situation and convince yourself that everything is going to be ok because the fact of the matter is, sometimes when you're assertive, things don't go just the way you hoped they would. Other people don't always go along with what you're asking. But if you'll consider the long-term positive consequences, you'll be able to weigh the pluses and minuses fairly. Then when you do make the decision to be assertive, you're going to feel more ok about doing it.

### Goals of Assertive Conflict Resolution

One goal of acting assertively, of course, is to bring about a change in a situation or in another person's behavior. For example, if somebody is taking advantage of you, your goal might be, "I want her to stop doing this." However, a second very important goal is to increase your own sense of self-respect. I want to strongly emphasize that the second goal — increasing your own self-respect — really is the major goal in being assertive. Before you go to talk with somebody about an important issue, it's very helpful to remind yourself of these two goals and to tell yourself, "Obviously I want to make a change in the situation — I'm going in there to request a change. But regardless of what happens, I'm going to take this opportunity to express how *I* feel and what *my* opinions are. Even if _____ (person) doesn't give me what I want, I'm going to state my feelings and opinions firmly, and then I'm going to be able to walk out of there and feel proud of myself."

### *Planning for Action*

Systematically going over each one of the steps mentioned above, in your own mind, can be very helpful. It is a way to prepare yourself emotionally and to get to a place of feeling ok about your decision to speak out. In addition, especially if the situation is very important to you or very emotional, it also may be helpful to write out exactly what you're going to say to the person ahead of time, and then to practice out loud several times, until you are expressing your thoughts in a way that feels right. If you have a trustworthy, close friend, you may wish to sit down and practice with him or her; let your friend pretend to be the other person as you practice and practice again. Practicing an assertive response even two or three times can make a big difference in feeling ok about how you're coming across. If no one is available to help you, practicing in front of a mirror can be helpful, too, because it gives you an opportunity to watch and hear yourself and then to make some improvements. Then, when you are actually getting ready for the meeting, you already know how you're going to come across. (If you have the luxury of a video camera, that's an even better tool to help you practice and improve.)

### *Key Ingredients of Assertive Behavior*

The preceding discussion should give you a pretty good idea of what we mean when we're talking about "being assertive." Now let's consider what that "looks like," and what the different aspects of assertion actually are.

It's helpful to break assertive behavior down into three component parts:

• *Verbal content*. This is refers to the particular words that you choose to speak, what you decide to say. There are two guidelines that you can use to make sure your verbal content is assertive; one is K I S S, which stands for "Keep It Short and Simple." Many times when people are trying to be assertive, they get sidetracked, get off onto some long explanations, excuses, justifications, apologies and so forth. Getting to the point as quickly as possible will really pay off.

The second point about content is something called "I Language." When you're expressing what you feel, it's an effective strategy to say, "This is how *I* feel." Lots of times people inadvertently will say, "*You make me* feel sad," "*You make me* feel unhappy," "*You make me* feel angry" and so forth. This approach can present some problems; when you say "*You make me* feel...," in a sense, you're casting yourself in the role of a helpless person. And this role can increase feelings of anxiety and insecurity. There's simply something about saying, "*I* feel sad," or "*I* feel angry" that helps the message come across as more powerful. What's more, you're maintaining more self-control. Saying, "Look, *I* feel this way," actually increases and enhances your self-esteem and self-respect. Also, if you say to another person, "*You make* me feel" a certain way, that tends to greatly increase defensiveness. If you want to talk with others and negotiate for change or confront them about their behavior, and you make statements that increase defensiveness, you have decreased the chances of success. People simply tend to be more responsive and open to hearing someone say, "*I* feel sad," "*I* feel angry," and so forth.

• *Vocal tone*. An assertive vocal tone is firm and direct. You're not coming across in an overly loud voice, which might scare people or make them feel you're aggressive, or, by contrast, in a silent, meek, whiny kind of voice. A firm, solid, well-modulated tone of voice conveys "I mean what I'm saying."

• *Gestures, Body Language and Eye Contact.* Probably the most important non-verbal element of communication is eye contact. When people are afraid, anxious or non-assertive, it's tough to make eye contact. Just watch the next time someone's talking to you and feeling anxious. There's something powerful and convincing about looking someone right in the eye and saying, "Hey, this is how I feel; this is my opinion." It's a non-verbal message that lets people know "I mean what I'm saying."

---

Sharon

When Sharon decided to tell Tim about how she felt, she made a point to have his full attention. She started by stating, "This is very important to me, and I'd like you to listen to what I have to say." She also consciously made herself look directly into his eyes and began to talk in a firm, but non-hostile voice.

"I think I have said the same words to him a hundred times, but this time he heard me. It wasn't *what* I said as much as *how* I said it. He got the message that I meant business!"

---

### Back-up Plans

At this point I want to briefly discuss some of the backup plans that I mentioned earlier. Lots of times when you assert yourself, the other person may respond in ways designed to get you to stop being assertive and to back off. Let's say that you're confronting someone about a very emotionally charged situation in which a lot of your feelings are being revealed. Some people will respond by saying, "You're just too emotional about this" or "It's just like a woman to be so emotional." One way to respond to this is to say, "You know what? I *do* have strong feelings about this issue, and I am going to make my point again." Then jump right back in and re-assert yourself. Reasserting your point in spite of the other person's response is a very effective way of stopping the other person from using this type of manipulation. You have not agreed that you are *too* emotional. You have simply said, "Yes, I have strong feelings about this. I do have strong emotions." And then you've taken the opportunity to jump right back in and re-assert yourself.

Let's say that sometimes the other person responds to your assertion with tears and a lot of guilt messages. One way to deal with this is to say, "I know this is hard to hear, I know this is causing you pain, but I want to tell you something. This issue is important, and I want to repeat myself because we're going to work together and resolve this." Again, what you've done is to stop the other's attempt to use guilt to get you to back off from your assertive response.

In a third situation, let's say that someone begins to quibble with you about the legitimacy of what you feel. You have the right to state feelings and opinions without justifying them. A way to react to this response is to say, "Regardless of the reasons, this is my opinion" or "Well, let's face it, we may not agree on this, but all the same, this is how *I* feel." Again, you're re-asserting yourself and not bowing to the demand for justifications.

Finally, when dealing with an extremely angry and aggressive person, you might say, "I can see that you're very angry and upset, but it's important that we resolve this issue, and we are going to talk about this. If we can't talk about it now, that's okay. But I'm going to come back, and we're going to talk about it later."

### Is It Time for Action in Your Real World?

I do hope this discussion about assertion will be of help. Deciding to confront truly difficult interpersonal problems and act in an assertive way is often hard to do and may be accompanied by a good deal of uneasiness, and sometimes actual risks. Many people have found it helpful to seek out an assertiveness training group. (This is a type of group therapy that helps people learn how to act in an assertive way, provides opportunities for practice and role playing, and offers support.) Many have benefitted by reading the excellent self-help books on assertion which I have listed in the References section of this book. And for some, consulting with a psychotherapist will be valuable — particularly if you are preparing to resolve significant problems in important relationships. The therapist can provide guidance and support.

Many self-help books offer seemingly good suggestions that sound reasonable and that may be accompanied by glowing testimonials. The fact is that dealing with really significant conflicts with others is many times incredibly difficult. That's a reality which has to be acknowledged. At the same time, the approaches advocated in this chapter have been in wide use during the past twenty years and have a solid track record. Being assertive is no panacea for resolving the emotionally-charged conflicts in your life, but it certainly is an approach that has a good chance of success.

You have a right to say *no* to emotional abuse, to express your own feelings, and to ask for changes in another's behavior. I encourage you to learn to be assertive.

## Fifteen

## *Action Plan #6:*
## *Gain Control Over Your Emotions*

$A$s we've seen in previous chapters, the process of emotional healing, especially in the aftermath of major life stressors, often takes a long time. Although there are many steps one can take to facilitate healing and growth, beyond a certain point you can't rush the process. Healing must take its natural course. When it comes to deep healing and true growth, there are no quick fixes. Meanwhile, however, you may be experiencing considerable emotional distress and a host of psychological and stress-related physical symptoms. A number of strategies and techniques have been developed in recent years which can allow you to take action to reduce the intensity of some of your symptoms of distress.

These strategies are the focus of this chapter. The underlying goal of each strategy is two-fold: reducing emotional pain and regaining a sense of some control over your emotions.

### Build Your Coping Skills

In the midst of any type of difficult life experience, your sense of confidence and competence to handle the difficulty can make a big difference in how you feel. Let's examine Figure 15-A which shows a balance between the demands of life and your ability to cope with those demands.

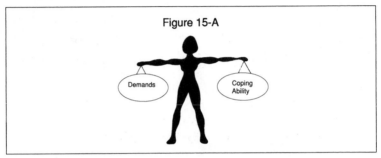

Figure 15-A

Confronted with a difficult situation, the stressed person — let's call her Steph — recognizes the demands and assesses her ability to cope with them. As long as Steph thinks she has adequate coping ability, she doesn't feel overwhelmed by the demands of the situation, though life may feel stressful to some degree. She's facing a difficult time, but feeling confident. Steph may think and believe, "This is tough, but I'm on top of it... I feel like I've got what it takes to handle this." Under these circumstances, life's stresses may certainly be unpleasant, but they are not overpowering and can sometimes even be seen as growth-enhancing challenges.

Two sets of circumstances can tip the balance, however, and result in significantly increased stress — or distress.

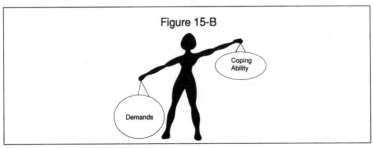

Figure 15-B

Figure 15-B illustrates a situation in which, despite adequate or even well-developed coping ability, life has dealt Steph an over-whelming amount of painful, difficult demands. When the weight of life's demands increases, she will begin to experience an extra measure of distress. She may begin to think "This is too much... This is overwhelming. I'm not sure I can manage this." The limit of distress with which she can cope and feel in control has been reached. As she feels the demands are outweighing her coping ability, Steph begins to experience the escalation of stress symptoms

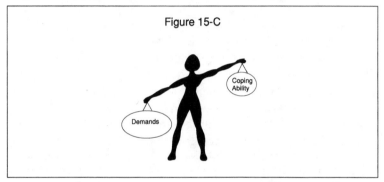

Figure 15-C

As illustrated in Figure 15-C, the demands may not be over-whelming, but the balance has shifted because of a decrease in self-confidence. Steph has, for some reason, started to think, "I can't cope. I feel helpless... powerless. I feel like I don't have what it takes to tackle and master these demands." The outcome is similar: stress symptoms begin to increase.

Why has her confidence lessened? Her *actual* coping skills may not have diminished. What has changed is Steph's *belief* in her ability to cope. Confidence in her ability to master challenges has been eroded. *Negative self-talk* is one of the primary reasons erosion of self-confidence occurs.

### Keep Your Self-Talk Positive and Realistic
All of us talk to ourselves, sometimes aloud, but often silently: "Boy this is going to be tough," "I can't wait till this is over," "What should I do next?", "I did a damned good job on that project!" These

internal thoughts involve observations, conclusions, predictions and problem-solving. Thoughts guide perceptions; they give us a chance to test out trial solutions in our minds before taking action; they provide important feedback on our performance; and they are the source of both harsh self-criticism and compassionate self-support (see Chapter 9).

As you encounter difficult times, you can count on engaging in self-talk. It happens automatically. The self-talk can clarify perceptions, encourage planning, provide positive support and encouragement, or it can be negative, self-deprecating, critical. Sometimes people are very aware of their self-talk, but many times self-talk is subtle and covert, like a barely audible whisper: "You're doing fine," "You'd better rethink this," "You screwed up again."

Cognitive psychologists have carefully studied this phenomenon and found that self-talk plays a crucial role in determining how people feel and how well they cope during difficult times. In a nut-shell, excessive negative self-talk powerfully chips away at self-confidence. (You can read more about negative self-talk in the Beck and Emery book, *Anxiety Disorders and Phobias*, listed in the References.)

Let's look at one very specific example to illustrate how self-talk works. Imagine that you're asked to give a twenty-minute presentation at work before a group of fifty people, though you have never been comfortable with public speaking. Let's look at two examples of inner self-talk that occur five minutes prior to your being introduced as the speaker.

Example A
   "Oh, my God. Look at all those people."
   "I know I'm going to blow this... I'll start trembling and forget my speech."
   "I'm going to completely humiliate myself."
   "They're going to think I'm stupid."
   "I've never done well at this kind of thing."

This self-talk mainly consists of negative predictions of failure and humiliation. Such inner thinking does not enhance performance! Instead, it increases anxiety and self-doubt. This variety of self-talk serves to scare you and increase your expectations of disaster — not a good strategy just prior to giving a speech — but an all-too-human type of self-talk.

Example B

"Oh, my God. Look at all those people."

"OK, now settle down. Sure you feel anxious. Lots of people don't like public speaking and it's normal to be a bit on edge."

"I need to encourage and support myself... I'll give it my best. I may not win an Academy Award, but I'll get through this."

"I don't like this kind of stuff... but I've done it before. I survived... I'll survive this time, too. It may be unpleasant, but it won't kill me."

In Example B, the thoughts reveal that you are certainly not blind to some feelings of anxiety, but at the same time, you provide support for yourself and avoid a flood of negative thoughts. The last thing you need to do is to scare yourself.

In Example A, self-confidence is eroded and stress increased. In Example B, stress is *not* completely avoided (of course) but the outcome is quite different — you have given yourself realistic support.

In a multitude of life circumstances, the silent, but potent inner self-talk contributes greatly to the perception of self-confidence and ultimately affects the amount of stress you experience. Let's take a closer look at how to stem the tide of negative self-talk and how to develop more positive/realistic thinking. To do so, we'll focus on the three most common kinds of thinking that increase stress: *over-estimating the danger* (risks), *undercutting your self-confidence,* and *seeing yourself as a victim.*

### Don't Jump to Conclusions

We commonly over-estimate the danger in a particular situation in two major ways. The first is to jump to conclusions about the degree of risk; that is, to assume the very worst possible outcome. Most of the time, these conclusions do not occur on a unconscious level, i.e., you may not really be aware that you are thinking these thoughts. Before giving a talk in front of people at work, you might conclude, "They're going to think I'm a terrible speaker. I'm going to make mistakes and they are going to laugh at me. They're going to think I'm a fool, that I'm a complete failure." This is an example of what New York psychologist and author Albert Ellis calls *catastrophising*, i.e., assuming or predicting that the outcome in a situation will be a complete catastrophe. You can prevent catastrophising the next time you're in a situation where you're beginning to feel anxious. When you first start to notice an uneasy or anxious feeling, ask yourself, "Ok, *what's going through my mind* right now? What am I telling myself?" By questioning yourself, you are helping yourself to focus on internal thinking, thereby bringing your thoughts into conscious awareness. As you ask the question, "What's going through my mind?", you might feel that you are arriving at some rather catastrophic conclusions.

Then, ask yourself, *"Where is the evidence?"* In asking this question, you remind yourself that "I cannot tell the future, I cannot read their minds." You don't have any evidence of a successful *or* unsuccessful talk, yet!

Your next question is, *"What do I know* about this particular situation?"* For instance, in your experience in working in this office, when people have given talks in the past and have not done especially well, do other people *actually* laugh, make humiliating comments, get up and walk right out of the meeting? By asking this question, you are using your conscious mind to critically evaluate your past experiences in particular situations.

Continue your analysis of the feared situation by asking yourself, *"Well, what if the worst does happen?"* Would it be so terrible if the feared outcome really were to occur? What would that experience truly be like? Exploring this issue may be very helpful. Take it to the extreme in your mind, imagining for just a moment what may seem like really absurd or highly unlikely outcomes. "Will somebody kill me if I do a bad talk?" Well, no. "If I don't do well on this talk, will I be sent to prison?" Of course not. "Will my career be completely ruined if I do poorly in a twenty-minute talk?" And so forth. Continue to question yourself until you reach what you consider to be realistic, possible consequences. For example, "Is it possible that some people may in fact smirk, laugh, or look like they're disinterested?" And the answer may be "Yes, that is a possibility."

Finally, ask yourself, "Ok, this may happen, so *can I live through this?* If it does hurt, if I feel embarrassed or humiliated, *how much* is it going to hurt and *how long* will the hurt last?" For example, you may ask yourself, "Is it possible that later in that day I will feel some degree of uneasiness?" And maybe the answer is "Yes, I would." How about the next day? And the answer may be "probably." How about a week from now or a month from now? "Probably not, by then." In all likelihood, as you go through the process of asking yourself these questions, you will discover that *even if the worst outcome were to occur, the distress will be rather short-term* in most instances, although there is some degree of unpleasantness. The process of asking these questions is an active way to help you realistically evaluate the danger in a particular situation.

### Remember: "Possible" Doesn't Mean "Probable"

Besides assuming the worst possible outcome, a second common problem that increases the perception of danger is a tendency to believe that a bad outcome absolutely will happen, i.e., to see bad outcomes in terms of *probabilities* rather than *possibilities*. When I was in high school, I took a Latin class in which there were only ten students. I remember worrying if the teacher would call on me in class when I was not well prepared. The chances of being called on in class were very great. Besides being called on frequently and hating every minute, I hated Latin generally and learned virtually nothing. In contrast, in a big psychology class of 400 students, my chances of being called upon were much lower, especially since I was hidden in the audience about two-thirds of the way back in the room.

(Maybe this explains why I became a psychologist and not a Latin teacher?)

Let's take a look at how probabilities rather than possibilities can be operating in common anxiety provoking-situations.

Many people are afraid to fly. When Bea says, "I'm not really so much afraid to fly, it's the crashing that scares me," she is probably thinking, "Oh my God! I'm going to crash, I just *know* it." In reality, however, the probability of a plane crash is extremely low given the thousands and thousands of flights each year. In fact, someone has calculated that, if the only way a person could die would be to in a plane crash, the average life expectancy would be 3,500 years!

This thinking can be seen in any number of other situations in which a person is perceiving that some terrible outcome is *absolutely* going to result: "I *know* my wife is going to divorce me," "I *know* I'm going to die from this cancer," "I *know* that I'm going to get fired if I screw up." All of these statements reflect an assumption of high probability. The strategy to lessen anxiety is to consciously and realistically remind yourself, "What is the real probability of a bad outcome... What are the *actual* risks?" As you evaluate the actual risks, you may conclude, "I may feel uneasy about this, but the chance — the probability — of extreme catastrophe is quite low. It may be unpleasant, and it may be difficult, but I'm probably not going to die. It's *possible*, but not *probable*, that I will experience overwhelming, unbearable pain that lasts forever." This way of thinking will not completely eliminate emotional distress or anxiety, of course. But it can be a very powerful way to counter the tendency to think in terms of high probability. The result — feeling less worry and a greater sense of competence — will help you hang in there in difficult times.

### *Maintain Your Self-Confidence*

Let's shift the focus now and look at the kind of thinking that under-estimates self-confidence. Again, self-confidence is basically the ability to trust in your coping resources. "Do I have what it takes to cope with this situation?"

There are two main ways people can inadvertently under-cut

self-confidence. The first is a *selective recall* of their track records. Many times people more or less forget how they have functioned in the past, oftentimes remembering and focusing on failures or times of poor performance. It's more helpful for the person giving a talk in front of people at work, to remind himself of past successes and accomplishments: "Ok, I need to remember that I have a good work record, that I'm well liked in this office, that my interactions with my boss have generally been positive. I've given talks before; sometimes I've felt pretty uneasy, but I've never been fired or reprimanded, and I get over the distress within a day or two." The goal is not to try to fool yourself into believing that there are no risks or that you are without fault, but simply to use an active strategy to counter that tendency to under-cut your self-confidence.

The second way to diminish self-confidence is to *think in very self-critical ways.* Often almost in an automatic way, all sorts of negative, scary thoughts — very conscious or just beneath the surface of awareness — can pass through a person's mind. Such thoughts may be self-deprecating: "I know I'm going to make a mistake; I know I'm going to look foolish. This experience is going to be absolutely overwhelming; I can't handle this. I can never do anything right; I'm going to look like a complete idiot. I'm going to completely fall apart emotionally and break down; I'm going to feel absolutely out of control." These statements, in a real sense, represent a flood of danger signals which can evoke strong feelings of uncertainty, worry and anxiety. These thoughts, like the negative self-talk discussed earlier in this chapter, make you believe that you are powerless and extremely vulnerable.

Psychologists have found that a couple of simple techniques can work remarkably well to stop the flood of self-critical thoughts. The first is to recognize that your thoughts are making you feel more anxious, that you are scaring yourself, that you need to stop these negative thoughts. Then actively replace negative thoughts with what some therapists have called *positive coping statements,* such as the following: "I am anxious but I'll just stay with the situation... stay focused on what I'm doing. I'm going to make it through this... Anxiety and stress are time-limited. I may feel nervous now but I will feel better later... Anxiety and stress are uncomfortable but not dangerous, the situation will pass... I've faced tough situations before, I can face this... My job right now is to put my feet flat on the ground, feel as solid as I can and do my best" (Adapted from Beck and Emery, 1985).

### Overcome the "Shoulds"

Certainly some very stressful situations place people in overwhelmingly helpless and vulnerable positions. As we have seen, however, the *perception* of helplessness, powerlessness and victimhood are often set in motion by certain inner negative thoughts. One common example of this process is thinking with "shoulds." You can recognize this type of thinking by noticing inner thoughts that include *should, shouldn't, have to, must,* or *ought to.*

These statements may take several forms: "It shouldn't be happening!", "He shouldn't do this to me!", "She ought to know better!", "I can't believe this is happening! (and it shouldn't be happening)." As people are blasted by painful experiences, they naturally think such thoughts. But doing so increases a sense of powerlessness. "Shoulding" is a way of strongly insisting that things must be a certain way. Yet thinking these thoughts never alters painful realities, and it turns up the volume on feelings of helplessness. Thoughts guide and mold perception. In a very real sense, when you think with "shoulds," you are looking through a certain kind of lens that alters perceptions, and casts you in the role of a powerless victim.

A simple but very helpful way to counter this form of negative self-talk is to say to yourself, "Wait a minute... It is not a matter of shoulds or shouldn'ts. The reality is that this painful event *has* occurred. And I don't like it one bit." You have reframed your perception to include a realistic awareness of a painful experience, and in stating "I don't like it!", you have altered the perception from one of helpless victim to one of a human being, understandably in pain, and capable of honestly stating how you feel.

This approach may, at first glance, seem incredibly simplistic. It certainly did to me when I first learned about it. However, in my own life and in the lives of my psychotherapy patients, reframing the perception has proven to be a potent strategy for empowerment which has a direct effect on self-confidence and often results in an immediate sense of decreased stress. If you're skeptical, try out this approach two or three times and judge for yourself. I think you'll find it to be helpful.

Negative self-talk operates like a pain amplifier — intensifying and prolonging misery. The strategies mentioned above actively interfere with negative thinking and can often restore a balance between the demands of life and your self-confidence. These techniques are not magical solutions. They are simple yet effective strategies for increasing the accuracy and clarity of perception, a potent way to reduce distress here and now. One of the worst things about encountering difficult life circumstances is the sense of being overwhelmed and out of control. In my experience, the self-help techniques discussed in this chapter have been extremely useful in rapidly "turning down the volume" of stress-related symptoms. The name of the game is not to *eliminate* distressing feelings and symptoms, but to regain some degree of *control* over them, and thereby to reduce the level of distress.

In the following chapter, we'll look at some ways of dealing with stress even more directly.

## Sixteen

## *Action Plan #7:*
## *Stay Healthy and Reduce Emotional Stress*

$S$ince the 1940's, it has been recognized clearly in psychology and medicine that emotional stress and physical health are related. Physical problems often cause emotional distress, and emotional upsets may produce physical symptoms. While it is beyond the scope of this book to discuss physical conditions in depth, we can take a close look at how you can reduce emotional stress by keeping yourself well physically. That's the subject of this chapter.

Stressful life events often bring on very unpleasant and sometimes painful or dangerous physical symptoms including tension headaches, insomnia, fatigue, restlessness, loss of sex drive, ulcers, high blood pressure and decreased energy, to mention just a few. In addition, more recent evidence suggests that prolonged, significant emotional distress can also have an impact on the functioning of the immune system. Impaired immune functioning can result in increased risk of developing certain kinds of infectious diseases, play a role in retarding recovery from any number of physical illnesses and, in some extreme cases, open the door for the development of cancer. Three primary approaches have been shown to be quite effective in reducing some of the physical symptoms associated with life stress: *changing unhealthy habits, relaxation,* and *appropriate use of medications.*

### Change Unhealthy Habits

This first approach relates to restoring healthy habits and lifestyles. It's been shown over and over again that under the impact of emotional distress, people develop bad habits. When distressed, many people tend to gravitate toward excessive use of alcohol, tobacco, caffeine and junk foods. These poor nutritional and health habits can, in the long run, result in serious physical illnesses, such as cardiac disease and cancer. However, there are also a host of short-term risks associated with the use and over-use of these substances and foods.

*Alcohol:* One of the most used — and abused — drugs in the United States, alcohol can provide a very potent and quick sense of release from physical tension and can promote a feeling of euphoria or relaxation. Obviously, when people are experiencing emotional pain, understandably they might seek the quick relief alcohol provides. I don't intend to become moralistic about the issues of alcohol use; however, the evidence clearly shows that the use of alcohol, especially over a prolonged period of time on a regular basis and in high amounts, can backfire. Alcohol, in and of itself, is responsible for tremendous aggravation of the symptoms of depression and anxiety. However, alcohol is a seductive substance; because the *immediate* result of drinking is relief, the person perceives that the alcohol is helpful. But prolonged use actually results in a change in the neurochemistry of the brain that can result in severe symptoms of depression and anxiety. Avoiding, reducing or eliminating alcohol intake during stressful times is a critical action that you can take. *(Note: If you have been drinking heavily, it is important to know that abrupt discontinuation of alcohol can result in very unpleasant and sometimes dangerous withdrawal symptoms. Such discontinuation should only be done under medical supervision.)*

*Caffeine:* This widely-used drug is found in some unexpected places: in coffee, of course, and in a host of other substances that people consume, including tea, certain soft drinks (especially colas), and — horrors! — *chocolate;* in a number of pain medications (e.g., Excedrin); in a number of diet pills. Caffeine is a seductive drug. For many people, one physical effect of stress is a sense of fatigue and decreased energy. Caffeine is a potent stimulant and can provide, rather quickly, a sense of improved alertness and energy. Some researchers believe that caffeine has mild anti-depressant effects and thus may be used by some chronically depressed people to elevate their mood.

Caffeine also can backfire. The average cup of coffee contains approximately 150 mg of caffeine, and the typical soft drink (e.g., a cola drink) or tea contains around 50 mg of caffeine. Studies of caffeine use and abuse indicate that when people ingest more than 250 mg per day of caffeine, there is a significant likelihood of developing stress-related symptoms which, in particular, include jitteriness, tension, anxiety and insomnia. The risks of symptoms increases dramatically when the amount of caffeine surpasses 500 mg per day.

In addition to the well-known effects of caffeine (e.g., nervousness and insomnia), another often unrecognized but important symptom of caffeine use is the disruption of the *quality* of sleep. It has been shown that even when a person is able to go to sleep, if large amounts of caffeine have been ingested, the quality of sleep often is significantly changed; sleep becomes more restless. As a result, the person fails to receive adequate rest during the night, which leads to excessive day-time fatigue. To combat this fatigue, the person chooses — you guessed it — to drink more caffeine.

In the midst of difficult times, it may seem rather silly to consider that the amount of coffee you're drinking can have a dramatic effect on how you feel. Many people "pooh-pooh" the notion of caffeine contributing to emotional problems. Yet clinical research has indicated that caffeine plays an important role either in causing or exacerbating stress-related symptoms.

The bottom line here: *One decisive action you can take during times of stress is to reduce or eliminate caffeine.* Note that if you are accustomed to drinking large amounts of caffeine, and you quit "cold turkey," you will likely experience significant caffeine withdrawal symptoms: anxiety, restlessness, tension and headaches. Thus, if you have become accustomed to ingesting large amounts of caffeine, you'll want to *gradually* decrease your intake of caffeine over the period of two to three weeks, progressively replacing caffeinated beverages with decaffeinated beverages.

*Exercise:* At times of great emotional distress, you may experience a tremendous sense of decreased energy and fatigue. And during such times, motivating yourself to engage in normal physical exercise becomes even more difficult. You'll probably feel like stopping your normal exercise program, perhaps reducing your normal daily activity level as well. There are a number of negative consequences to reducing activity levels over a period of time. The first is that fatigue feeds on itself. The more tired you feel, the more you're inclined to be inactive, to sit on the couch or lie in bed. However, increased inactivity almost always leads to a progressive cycle of increasing fatigue. Another common outcome of emotional distress is a significant weight gain because of decreased activity coupled with increased appetite for inappropriate foods. This weight gain can have negative consequences for both physical functioning and emotional well-being; for most people, this tends to result in feelings of inadequacy and low self-esteem. In addition, weight gain can contribute to significant physical difficulties, such as obesity, hypertension and diabetes.

An important decision you can make during difficult times of emotional distress is to take care of yourself as best you can, focusing on proper nutrition, exercise and a reduction in and an avoidance of alcohol and caffeine. Again, these are not magical solutions; no one has ever survived emotionally traumatic times simply by ceasing to drink coffee. But such actions can be simple ways to take control of part of your life, to reduce some amount of stress-related symptoms, and to promote a sense of physical well-being.

### Learn to Relax

In the early days of psychosomatic medicine, it was commonplace for people to go to their family physicians and complain of noticeable physical symptoms, only to be told, "It's just stress" or "It's all in your mind." As a result, many people left the doctor feeling misunderstood or that they were crazy or just imagining these problems. Emotional distress is more than just a state of mind; it's much more than just feeling bad or having negative, unpleasant thoughts. During the past five decades, a tremendous amount of accumulated evidence has shed light on the important connection between emotional distress and certain changes in physical functioning of the body and of the nervous system.

During times of emotional stress, bonafide physical changes and symptoms do occur, some of which are uncomfortable and painful and some of which can actually lead to life-threatening illnesses. There is clear evidence to suggest that significant stress, including anxiety and depression, can lead to profound changes in brain chemistry that then influences or affects the release of many different hormones from the endocrine glands of the body (the pituitary gland, the adrenal gland and the thyroid gland). Hormones are specifically designed to regulate normal metabolic functioning that either control or influence many basic biological rhythms, drives and processes. Without the combined effort of intricately complex hormonal systems, survival would be impossible. However, during times of stress the brain can activate the endocrine system in a certain fashion resulting in the development of a number of stress related physical symptoms such as rapid heart rate, high blood pressure, decreases or increases in metabolic activity. In addition, the hormonal system can profoundly affect the functioning of the immune system, altering the functioning of specific white blood cells.

Although ultimately the solution to reducing stress is somehow to come to terms with painful life events or to alter the course of those events in your life, at the same time, you can employ intervention strategies designed to reduce physiologic distress. Since the 1950's a number of techniques have been developed, modified and refined, enabling people to learn strategies which can directly alter physical functioning. Relaxation exercises (sometimes accompanied by biofeedback) and meditative techniques have found increasing acceptance in the medical profession as treatments or adjunct treatments for many physical illnesses, including migraine headaches, hypertension, ulcers, chronic pain conditions, chronic fatigue syndromes, and others. These approaches are designed to directly affect arousal levels in the body and can be very effective in reducing stress-related physical symptoms.

It is common to give some "good advice" to friends who are under stress: "just relax." Just relaxing is not what I'm talking about here. I'm referring to specific techniques that have been demonstrated to have a profound effect on physical functioning. The sidebar describes two effective proven procedures for learning to relax deeply.

### Relaxation Techniques

Two common and effective techniques have been found to be especially helpful ways to learn to relax completely: progressive muscle relaxation and visualization.

*Progressive Muscle Relaxation.* During times of stress, particular muscles and muscle groups tend automatically to become tense. Such tension is hard to ignore when it results in low-back pain or tension headaches. However, many people experience considerable chronic muscle tension that goes relatively unnoticed. Persistent muscle tension can contribute to fatigue and poor quality sleep and can set the stage for more significant tension-related pain. Progressive muscle relaxation techniques are designed to produce tension-reduction in particular muscle groups. The goal, however, is much more than muscular relaxation per se. When done appropriately, you may experience decreased physical tension/arousal throughout the body (e.g., decreased heart rate, decreased blood pressure, etc.)

To accomplish this, find a period of time when you will not be disturbed. Either sit in a comfortable chair or recline on a couch. Close your eyes and take two slow, deep breaths. As you exhale, notice the gradual release of tension in chest and shoulder muscles. Feel the weight of your body against the chair and the gentle pull of gravity as you settle into the chair. After a few moments, you can begin a series of simple exercises. The technique involves the tensing of particular muscles, holding the tension for a count of "three" and then releasing. Each time you tense and then release, you can enhance the effect by paying particular attention to the experience of relaxation/letting-go that occurs immediately after release.

Allow ten or fifteen seconds between each tensing of muscles before proceeding to the next muscle group. The tensing exercises begin with the feet and are followed by
1. Calves/lower legs

2. Thighs
3. Buttocks (squeeze together)
4. Abdomen
5. Lower back (arch)
6. Chest (hold in a deep breath)
7. Hands (make fists)
8. Upper arms
9. Shoulders (shrug)
10. Face (squeezing eyes and mouth closed)
11. Face (opening eyes and mouth)

Many experts on relaxation techniques recommend that people take fifteen to twenty minutes twice a day to go through this exercise. Although this is undoubtedly helpful, especially when you're first learning the procedure, it's been my experience that few people will make/take time to do this on a regular basis. A realistic alternative, after you've learned how to relax deeply, is to abbreviate the technique (this whole procedure can easily be done in two to three minutes) and repeat it several times a day. When time allows, you can, of course, give yourself permission to expand the procedure and achieve a deeper sense of relaxation.

The immediate results can be a noticeable reduction of muscular tension. However, the more important, beneficial results occur if the exercise is done several times a day (even if done briefly) on a regular basis. For many, this procedure can reduce *chronic* tension levels; what you may notice is less daytime fatigue, more productive energy, and an improved ability to fall asleep.

*Visualization.* Many different visualization techniques have been suggested. Here's a description of one of the most commonly employed:

Begin by finding a quiet time and a comfortable chair or couch. Close your eyes and take two slow, deep breaths. Notice the physical sensations of relaxation as you gently exhale.

After a few moments, imagine yourself standing at the top of a flight of stairs with ten steps. In a moment you can begin to see yourself slowly and gradually walking down the stairs, one at a time. When you begin your descent, you will notice a sense of increasing relaxation as you move downward. With each step, experience the feeling of deeper and deeper relaxation. As you take each step, silently count to yourself: ten... and nine... and eight... lower and lower as you go. Throughout your descent, you feel safe and in control, as you choose to let go of tension. The mental image of downward movement has been found to trigger a relaxation response.

As you reach the bottom of the stairs... and two... and one, then let your mind take you to a particular setting, a place you know that you associate with feelings of comfort, security and well-being. It may be a beautiful meadow, a warm, sunny beach, or a rustic cabin in the forest. The choice is yours as you create an image of serenity. The experience of relaxation is enhanced by taking particular note of all sensory experiences in your image (the sights, sounds, smells, and feelings of the peaceful setting).

After a few minutes, you can then decide to leave the relaxing setting by slowly counting from three to one — three... and two... and one — as your eyes open and you, again, are fully alert, but relaxed.

You'll have to discover for yourself whether the progressive muscle relaxation technique or visualization (or a combination of the two) works best. Please keep in mind that simple relaxation techniques obviously don't solve major life crises. "Just relaxing" or "taking it easy" are not the answers as we go through difficult times. But these particular relaxation approaches clearly do reduce physical tension, and they are ways that you can give yourself some amount of self-nurturing. They are direct ways to exert some control over physiologic tension while taking other actions to promote coping and emotional healing. (For a more complete discussion, please see books by Davis, et. al., and Benson, listed in the References.)

## *Use Medication Appopriately*

In 1954, the first effective psychiatric medication was introduced to the market. The anti-psychotic medication known as Thorazine was greeted with great enthusiasm in the psychiatric community because for the first time ever, researchers and psychiatrists had discovered an effective medical approach to treating a very serious type of mental disorder: schizophrenia. In the years that followed, a number of other psychiatric medications found their way onto the market, including drugs designed to reduce anxiety, anti-depressant medications, mood stabilizing medications, and stimulant medications (used to treat hyper-activity in children).

With the emergence of new medications in psychiatry came both enthusiasm and controversy. Prior to the 1950's, many of the major mental disorders, such as schizophrenia and manic depressive illness, were virtually untreatable. As a result of the development of particular psychotropic medications, many thousands of patients were able to leave state mental hospitals and return to a somewhat more normal lifestyle in the community. At the same time, there were many instances of inappropriate uses of psychiatric medications. Newspaper and magazine articles about the use of medications as "chemical straight-jackets" were not unusual. Along with appropriate use of these medications in many facilities, came a considerable amount of inappropriate use, for the goal of using these drugs was to control behavior or to reduce aggression at all costs. Thus, as psychiatry was making discoveries about the biological basis of mental illnesses and stress-related problems, the public became increasingly skeptical and fearful of psychotropic medications for reasons that are understandable.

Three major events have changed the course of psychiatric medication treatment in recent years. The first is *better understanding of the brain* and the brain functioning. There has been a literal explosion of research on the brain and a number of new technologies which have allowed doctors and researchers to study more precisely and understand the functioning of the central nervous system and the neurochemical problems underlying many psychiatric disorders. A second series of events relates to advances in pharmacology.

Pharmaceutical companies have been highly motivated to develop and refine new drugs that, on the one hand, are more effective and, on the other hand, carry fewer risks and side effects. Within the last few years these newer, "cleaner" medications have found their way into the market and have been used by psychiatrists to treat effectively a host of serious mental and emotional disorders. The final set of events relates more to *changing values* in the fields of psychiatry, psychology and medicine. With widespread abuse or overuse of tranquilizers in the 50's and 60's, the medical profession has become more skeptical and more thoughtful about the use of psychotropic medications. While the inappropriate use of medications continues, more and more psychiatrists and other physicians are learning how to treat mental and emotional disorders appropriately, without unnecesssary medication.

The symptoms of some forms of major mental disorders (for example, psychotic disorders, panic disorder, depression, manic depressive illness, attention deficit disorder) appear to be related to biochemical changes in the central nervous system. As millions of people in the United States can attest, simply gritting your teeth, trying harder or using will power to overcome these incredibly painful symptoms simply doesn't work. In addition to psychotherapy and other forms of psychological or emotional help, many people have benefited tremendously by the appropriate use of certain types of psychotropic medications.

In the words of Dr. Karl Menninger, medications will probably never be developed which can fill empty lives or mend broken hearts. There is no kind of medication that can give a person a sense of connection with other human beings, a feeling of self, or instill the kind of values that make life worth living. At the same time, many newly developed psychotropic medications can dramatically affect the course of a person's life in a positive sense. Figure 16-A summarizes a few symptoms which respond to medication. Appendix A provides a more complete list of the symptoms of major mental disorders and indicates which particular disorders may be helped with psychotropic medications.

The thinking of most psychotherapists these days is that even for those emotional disturbances that do respond well to medications, treatment with medication is only one of a number of actions that people can take in order to heal, survive and recover from major life crises. Certainly at times, the physical malfunction underlying certain psychiatric conditions can become so devastating that people are unable to mobilize their own resources for emotional healing. They may be so incapacitated that they find themselves unable to reach out effectively to others for support and connection. In such cases, treatment with medication may be a critical first step, and as people start to experience some recovery from debilitating symptoms, then they can then begin the process of growth and emotional healing.

---

### Figure 16-A

**Appropriate Targets for Psychiatric Medication Treatment**

**<u>Depression</u>**

Severe insomnia
Daytime fatigue
Loss of sex drive
Poor concentration
 and memory
Pronounced weight loss/gain
Extreme agitation
Profound loss of capacity
 for joy
Severe mood swings

**<u>Anxiety/Panic Attacks</u>**

Trembling, restlessness
Shortness of breath,
 smothering sensations
Rapid heart rate
Light-headedness
Sense of panic or
 impending doom

**<u>Psychosis</u>**
Extreme disorganization
Halllucinations
Very unrealistic thinking

---

---

## Seventeen

# Action Plan 8:
## *Explore Self-Help and "Recovery" Groups*

### *The Recovery Movement: For Better or For Worse*

It is in vogue these days to talk about the "wounded child," "dysfunctional families" and all sorts of human limitations and misery. People are addicted to alcohol, drugs, relationships, gambling, sex and sugar. Self-help revivals abound on public TV; bookstore shelves are stocked with self-help guides and audio cassettes. It is hard to meet someone these days who is not an "Adult Child" of something. Such widespread media attention certainly is changing the way Americans perceive emotional distress.

The "Recovery" movement has helped millions of people to acknowledge openly their emotional problems and to discover some possible solutions. That's the good news. At the same time, however, you should be aware of two common errors self-help gurus make.

The first is their tendency to "pathologize" — i.e., to focus on illness, dysfunctionality, and maladaptive lifestyles. We must not ignore the fact that serious mental illnesses do exist, but the almost-exclusive focus on pathology of many "recovery" programs may result in the failure to appreciate that most of us have tremendous adaptive resources. *Millions of "Adult Children" live satisfying, productive, healthy, functional lives;* they have succeeded in spite of difficult early experiences. This is not "denial" — rather it is a triumph of the human spirit.

If you look closely enough and stretch to really understand the most distressed, disabled, dysfunctional people in the world, you will see their strengths and come to appreciate and admire their attempts to adapt and to survive. Almost any type of neurotic problem, personality disorder, or maladaptive lifestyle begins to make sense once you understand where that person is coming from (e.g., the emotional atmosphere she encountered early in life). You don't help people by branding them "victims" or other labels. You help them by understanding and assisting them to mobilize their inner strengths and resources.

The second error in many self-help programs is to speak of human emotional concerns in ways that are simply too general, talking about cures in a generic, cookbook fashion. (I perhaps risk committing this error by writing this book!) I believe that at the heart of a truly helpful, healing relationship (whether in the context of a friendship or in psychotherapy) is the capacity for one person to genuinely listen and gradually come to understand the unique experience of the other. Pat answers, snazzy stress-management techniques and good advice often don't help in the long run.

Many people can and do find an incredible amount of support from family, friends and colleagues. In this book, we have certainly looked at a host of problems that do occur in an atmosphere of emotional conflict, neglect and abuse. Yet many folks do have caring people in their lives who can provide support. The majority of people in our society do not see psychotherapists or join self-help groups. Rather, they go it on their own or draw strength from other important people in their lives.

### Group Programs for Help With Emotional Problems

One outcome of the "recovery movement" has been the proliferation of self-help and support groups. Such groups vary tremendously and while some can be very helpful, others can create serious emotional problems for those seeking help. I hope this chapter will help you evaluate the possible role of a support or self-help group in your life.

In most communities, there are several different types of groups available. Let's take a look at three basic types: group psychotherapy, support groups and specifically designed recovery programs.

*Group psychotherapies* typically are led by a professional, licensed psychotherapist. The therapists generally have specific training in group processes, psychotherapy and group dynamics. Some groups are largely supportive in nature, while others are considered to be "exploratory" (i.e., the aim of exploratory groups is to share deep personal experiences and to deal either with important current stressors or long-standing emotional and personality difficulties). There are risks in this work. Emotional experiences may be intense in such groups. Yet with a good therapist, such treatment is powerful and can be helpful for many individuals. (More on psychotherapeutic approaches in the next chapter.)

*Support and self-help groups* abound. Many of these are either leaderless or are led by a lay person (not a professional therapist). These groups often center around common concerns such as bereavement, divorce, women's or men's issues. Often these groups provide a considerable amount of support and human connection for the group members. It's generally not advisable for such groups to get into intense exploration of emotional issues since there is an inherent risk in doing so without the appropriate guidance of a trained professional. Support groups have provided solace and support for thousands of people. A risk in such situations is the possibility of psychiatric disasters when extremely intense issues emerge in the group and untrained leaders are at a loss in knowing how to help. If you are experiencing some extremely difficult, intense emotions, be sure to check out potential support groups carefully and be cautious about involvement. Also, remember that most appropriate support groups show a good deal of respect for people's rights to remain silent, i.e., *you do not have to talk or participate in group exercise if you don't want to,* and you can always choose to discontinue attending if the experience does not feel right to you.

Specifically *organized self-help/recovery programs* have enjoyed growing popularity. These programs are often based on an established set of values, philosophies and guidelines. (Most notable are the various twelve-step programs: Alcoholics Anonymous and its dozens of clones.) A part of their popularity can be attributed to their high level of success in helping people overcome chemical addictions. The twelve-step model has expanded beyond the realm of substance abuse and is now applied to an assortment of human problems (e.g., gambling, obesity, "co-dependency," "sexual addiction"). Their traditional commitment to confidentiality may be compromised by their popularity and rapid proliferation. Some of these programs are run by trained professionals, others by lay people.

### How Do I Know if a Self-help Program Is Right for Me?

To address this issue, let's briefly look at an outline of the potential benefits and possible risks associated with self- help/support groups. Please consider the following issues carefully to decide which self-help program, if any, is right for you.

Benefits:
• *Validation.* Sharing feelings and being heard/understood. Feeling acknowledged for the experiences you've encountered.
• *Emotional support.* Contact with others who understand and share your concerns. Resources for support between meetings.
• *Advice.* Sharing strategies and solutions. Learning "what works and what doesn't" for others.
• *Guest speakers.* Many programs invite professionals to speak on various topics.
• *Networking.* Learning about resources in the community. Making connections with others.
• *People helping people.* Often people experience a special sense

of satisfaction in providing support to others, which can promote a sense of involvement and personal connection. We learn much from teaching others.

- *Affordable.* Most self-help groups are free or available for a very low fee.

- *Interaction.* In a group context, people are able to provide honest feedback and to take opportunities for practicing communication skills.

- *Privacy and Confidentiality.* Appropriately-run support groups also provide an atmosphere of privacy and confidentiality. The group can be a place to express emotions without worry about burdening friends or family members.

- *Step-by-step strategies.* Some programs have well-developed, step-by-step strategies that have been shown to be very effective in helping people overcome difficult problems such as alcoholism.

Risks:

- Some groups encourage or promote intense emotional openness which may not be appropriate for all individuals, or may not be dealt with adequately by untrained leaders.

- Some groups may unknowingly re-create maladaptive patterns of relating. For example, in a group for people who are passive and dependent, an authoritarian leader tells members what to do. This experience re-enacts the group members' problems in a new setting rather than encouraging change, growth or autonomy.

- Some groups amount to "cults" that initially provide support, but gradually devolve into destructive forms of persuasion or brainwashing. In some cases, group members are coerced into contributing large sums of money, are influenced to devote their lives solely to the group and/or to begin to adopt values and beliefs that simply mimic those held by the group. (Such groups do not foster autonomy, but instead promote adherence to rigid group norms.)

- Some groups try to fix all or cure all with one model. Pat solutions and rigid guidelines often may reflect helpful advice *in general,* but may not fit the unique needs of *individuals.* In such cases, group leaders and members may come to adopt overly simplistic views about human nature, emotional distress and psychological growth. The individual may get lost in the shuffle.

• Some groups do absolutely no screening for serious mental health problems. Should a group member begin to experience a significant emotional breakdown, sometimes leaders are at a loss to know how to intervene or make referrals. Domineering members may "bully" others or waste group time.

• Some groups offer unrealistic promises. Many desperate, hurting or lonely people may be attracted to groups hoping for answers. Good groups only promise to help, but never offer guarantees of happiness or mental well-being.

• Some groups espouse religious/spiritual beliefs that may not be consistent with the values of all group members.

• Some groups fail to appreciate the value of other mental health treatments (such as psychotherapy and medication treatment) and may shame members who seek out such treatment, or in other ways undermine treatment. There *is* a place for support groups *and* psychotherapy as people tackle difficult life circumstances.

• Some groups do not truly believe in real growth or healing. "Once an addict... always an addict." They may overtly or covertly convey the message that "you don't have what it takes to really grow and thus must replace one addiction for another" (for example, replace drug addiction with addiction to this group).

• Some groups attract members by way of a sort of "conversion" experience, by talking about emotional issues and providing understanding and validation. But the process stops at that point. An important issue to consider is what the group provides in the long-run in terms of on-going involvement and follow-up. True emotional healing doesn't occur only in the emotional excitement of an inspirational lecture, revival or weekend workshop. True healing is often a long-term process, as we know, and the question, "Will a group provide on-going contact and care?" is an important question to ask.

It is important to thoroughly check out groups in your community, getting references and recommendations just as you might as you try to locate a doctor or a dentist. It's very important and appropriate to talk at some length to the group leader prior to the first meeting and also helpful to speak with a group member. And when you do decide to attend a group, it's always ok to view this meeting as a trial visit — check it out and see if it feels right for you. *Ask questions!*

Groups are powerful. Many people have experienced remarkable emotional growth in the context of support groups, but some disasters have occurred, too. As you look into the possibility of support groups, remember that you can feel hopeful at the same time you are exercising caution. (Politicians call this "guarded optimism.")

*Eighteen*

---

*Action Plan #9:*
*Consider Psychotherapy*

*I*n a recent survey funded by the National Institute of Mental Health, 43% of adults polled had sought some form of counseling at one time or another during their lives. Such counseling was not limited to psychotherapy, but included pastoral counseling and visits with a family physician regarding emotional issues. Thankfully, in the past fifteen or twenty years, there has been a significant change in society's attitudes regarding the acceptability of seeking out professional help during times of emotional crisis.

In ancient times, epilepsy was considered to be a sign of possession by evil spirits. Much more recently, people only whispered the word "cancer," and alcohol or other drug abuse has been a human problem about which people feel ashamed. Yet new, effective treatments have been developed for many sources of human suffering, and the negative stigma has slowly dropped away. People in our society are coming to their senses. Now more than ever before, entering psychotherapy is seen as a helpful and healthy response to times of emotional upheaval. Emotional despair, in one form or another, at least during certain times of life, will enter the lives of most people. It makes sense to acknowledge this as a human problem and, when it is indicated, to take advantage of professional help.

In this chapter about psychotherapy, we'll look at what it is, how it can help, under what circumstances it is especially helpful, and how to go about selecting a therapist.

### Therapists as Guides

Professional psychotherapists are trained to provide a special relationship that can be helpful for many people encountering emotionally stressful times. Contrary to some popular beliefs, therapists generally don't give advice. Many folks can benefit from helpful suggestions and good advice from time to time, but such input is readily available from friends and relatives (sometimes even when you don't want it!). Most therapists aren't really any better at giving common sense advice than anyone else. But they can and do provide an important resource that goes beyond advice. They have a number of skills and abilities in dealing with emotions — skills in which your network of friends or family are not trained. Therapists are trained to understand how emotional distress really works and how to facilitate the process of emotional recovery. In a sense, they understand the general terrain of the human landscape and can help guide people through painful times toward growth and healing.

One important way in which therapists are able to go beyond the help of friends and family is their willingness and ability to face very strong emotions. It's hard to be with someone who is experiencing intense feelings of depression, anger, or self-doubt. To have to witness human suffering in itself is difficult. It is also hard for many people to experience another's pain without its affecting their own feelings. Good therapists, owing to their training and their own experience with psychotherapy, are able to stay "in tune" with their psychotherapy clients, to resonate with their pain, yet to avoid being overwhelmed by the client's emotions. Some degree of emotional distance is necessary in order for the therapist to maintain objectivity amid waves of the client's intense emotions. Many psychotherapy clients find it extremely helpful to be able to express strong feelings and to know that the therapist cares, but is not overwhelmed or shocked by the power of the emotions. This balance provides considerable stability and safety for the client.

Good therapists also know that healing often takes a long time and are quite willing to be understanding and patient as their clients go over similar ground, again and again. Many clients are understandably concerned that, because of their need to repeatedly talk about ("work through") their problems, relatives and friends may get burned-out.

Most good therapists operate from a non-judging perspective. They understand that most interpersonal and emotional distress is evidence of attempts to survive emotionally and of problems common to human beings in daily life. The therapist's way of being and interacting with the client, more than what the therapist says, transmits this attitude of respect, understanding, and acceptance. In psychotherapy outcome studies, therapy clients most commonly reported that the factor they judged to have been most helpful was the therapist's ability to care genuinely and to understand the client. Apparently, in an atmosphere of understanding and safety, many (if not most) therapy clients seem to identify with the therapist's compassionate attitude. They adopt this more benign attitude for themselves; they eventually start to reduce excessive self-criticism and to develop an enhanced capacity for self-acceptance.

Good therapists also provide support for self-expression and, thus, enhance the growth of the true self. This kind of support and encouragement of honest self-expression shores up and solidifies the development of the self. To use an analogy, when building a concrete wall, a contractor uses wood forms to provide support for the concrete as it begins to harden. At some point, the wood can be removed; the wall is solid because the concrete has developed its own strength and can stand on its own. Often people entering psychotherapy begin to express true inner feelings, opinions, and thoughts, with a certain amount of caution and uncertainty. But as the therapist encourages self-expression, the client comes closer and closer to noticing and articulating the truth of her inner emotions, and the self starts to feel more solid. She feels more "ok" to talk openly about how she really feels. In proper therapeutic relationships, the therapist makes this process safer and more comfortable for the client. Although certainly the reduction of emotional distress (e.g., decreased depression, anxiety, tension) is a primary goal for most people entering treatment, among the most common results of psychotherapy are increased awareness of self and increased self-esteem.

Going to regular psychotherapy sessions is a way of making a time and a place for self-exploration and healing to occur. Without this structure, true healing may take place in a rather unguided, haphazard manner — or not at all. To decide to enter therapy is to make a decision to give personal growth and healing a priority in your life.

Therapists also encourage people to talk about their life experiences and inner emotions. They actively help the client work through life issues at a pace the client can handle. In helping the client deal with difficult problems, good therapists make sure to avoid over-whelming or out-of-control expression of emotions.

At times of tremendous emotional suffering, people can easily become engulfed in pain or tremendous hopelessness. The therapist's job is to maintain a sense of realistic hope during difficult times (i.e., *not* phony, "Everything will be all right" hope, but instead a realistic perspective and a trust that the process of working through will lead to healing). In the words of psychologist/professor Michael Mahoney, at such times a therapist becomes the "guardian of hope."

Finally, therapists help people by not repeating maladaptive patterns of interaction, a point which deserves some explanation. Many times people's unintentional or unconscious behavior in relationships evokes hurtful reactions from others. Alice is a very dependent woman whose "helpless" style brings out the "caretaker" in others. As a result, she often enters into relationships in which others treat her like a child. This behavior becomes a repetitive "interpersonal dance" between a parent-like man and the child-like woman. This dance feels good at first because it is familiar, but ultimately it keeps Alice stuck in child-like behavior; she never grows up. The pull may be very strong from someone (including a therapist) to rush in and rescue such a "helpless" woman. On the surface, this action seems kind, while on another level, it maintains her position as a child. A good therapist would certainly empathize with Alice's distress, but would resist the urge to treat her like a helpless child. With time, this refusal to perpetuate the dance — perhaps accompanied by support for her development of independence skills — stands a good chance of helping Alice to grow up and experience her own strength. The pull to recreate the dance can be subtle, but incredibly powerful. The therapist may be the first person ever not to repeat this pattern! People have an uncanny ability to unwittingly orchestrate repetitive interpersonal patterns. In psychotherapy, there is a chance to break the pattern.

Let's look at another example. A number of people who have been badly treated by others (especially early in life) develop a potent defense — an outwardly abrasive, harsh interactional style. This style is a bit like being a porcupine: the quills guarantee that no one gets too close. However, beneath the quills often lurks a lonely person. His repeated experiences are that "everyone hates me... I don't know why, but people want nothing to do with me." This defense serves to protect, but also results in increased feelings of aloneness in the world. The good therapist recognizes that this defense is not a good solution. The therapist comes to understand the inner fear, the need for distance and protection, and appreciates the need to respect the client's defenses. Yet the therapist is not driven away or driven into retaliation by the harsh, abrasive style. If with time and repeated experiences the client feels safe with the therapist, this client may slowly drop his guard. The therapist's refusal to join in the dance (i.e., not to back off) can be a new, totally unique experience for this client that might open the door to a more trusting way to relate to the therapist — and eventually to others. And thus the healing begins.

### When To Seek Out Therapy

In years past desperation or very severe symptoms (serious depression, suicidal ideas, psychotic symptoms) drove people into therapy. Clearly, these continue to be important reasons for seeking out psychological treatment. However, many people now enter psychotherapy for less urgent, but very important and legitimate reasons. More and more people are recognizing that simply to survive life isn't enough. Issues such as improving the quality of life and the desire for personal growth are frequently the motive to seek therapy. People do not need to convince themselves (or others, or therapists) that they are in "bad shape" in order to see a therapist. The desires to work through long-standing problems, to heal from old wounds, or to find more fulfillment in life are absolutely legitimate, understandable reasons for seeing a therapist.

### Should I See a Therapist? Issues To Consider

The following are questions to consider in deciding to seek psychotherapy.

• Are there life-threatening issues (strong thoughts about suicide, self-harm, or impulses to hurt/abuse others)? If you honestly answer yes, please call a professional *today*.

• Are there major stress-related physical symptoms causing noticeable discomfort? Examples of such symptoms include:

  • Sleep disturbances
  • Pronounced weight loss or weight gain
  • Severe day-time fatigue
  • Headaches
  • Poor concentration and memory; forgetfulness; an inability to keep focused or to attend
  • Inability to recover normally from physical illnesses (when your physician has determined emotional stress to be a contributing factor)

• Are emotional problems seriously interfering with functioning in daily life? For example: missing work or school, inability to care for the needs of your children, unsafe driving due to poor concentration or extreme anxiety.

• Are emotional problems leading to significant abuse of alcohol or other substances?

• Do you simply not have the social support network to provide help during hard times? A supportive family, close friends, a church or community group — all can contribute to effective healing if they are willing and able to listen; however, such people may not be there for you to turn to.

It is also important to note that friends and family may not be willing to support change and growth. At such times, the other person may genuinely care for or love you, but may also have an investment in maintaining the status quo. Common examples include a husband's difficulty accepting his wife's new-found assertive and out-spoken style, or a wife's discomfort as she starts to see her husband's soft, vulnerable side. Even very positive change and growth are often difficult for others to understand and accept. A therapist may be able to provide support for change when others can't.

• Are there emotional issues that are simply too private to discuss with friends or family members?

• Are you doing all you can to cope and to heal but simply feel overwhelmed or especially stuck?

• Are you wrestling with life problems which are not the direct result of current life stressors? These difficulties, which are rooted in long-term personality characteristics or patterns that may be the result of adapting to pervasively stressful conditions during childhood, can be sources of considerable emotional despair and dissatisfaction, and psychotherapy often can be helpful. Examples of personality disturbances include long term difficulties in the following areas:

- Intimacy problems
- Overly strict or unrealistic standards for yourself
- A pronounced difficulty with procrastination
- Being unable to tolerate times when you must be alone
- Incapacitating phobias or obsessions
- Chronic feelings of emptiness or inferiority
- Extreme sensitivity to criticism and/or rejection
- Repeatedly entering into abusive, hurtful or otherwise maladaptive relationships
- Chronic or pervasive bitterness or pessimism

Should you at this point be thinking that psychotherapy may be helpful but you're still on the fence, consider the following three issues:

• Am I fooling myself by believing "Oh, it's not that big a deal... I can cope with this... I just need to try harder"? Denial is a common human tendency. Many people, if honest with themselves, are suffering tremendously and yet feel compelled to minimize or deny the truth of their own inner feelings. Denial may be a short-term solution (like trying to deny that you have a bad toothache) but won't serve you well for very long. There is a place for honestly confronting yourself to see if you are trying to cover up genuine emotional pain.

• Do I value the quality of my life enough to make emotional healing and growth a priority?

• Have I exhausted all my other resources — including an effort to try the approaches described in this book — to no avail?

### Selecting a Therapist

If you are considering psychotherapy, selecting the right therapist is very important. Here are three main steps to follow in your search:

• Speak with your family doctor, pastor, friends, or others who may have contact with the professional community, and collect the names of two or three therapists in your area. In most towns, there will be a handful of therapists with established reputations. The therapist you choose should be well-recommended — by two or three people you trust — and should have good credentials (graduate degrees, supervised training, licensure, recognition by professional societies).

• Once you have satisfied yourself as to the therapist's recommendations and credentials, the second step is to telephone the therapist to talk about your main reason for seeking therapy now. Obviously, it is impossible to fully explain your life circumstances in a minute or two, but the main reason for doing so on the phone is to see how the therapist responds to you. This initial contact with the therapist is important; it may be possible to get some first impressions. Often people feel anxious about making an appointment. Most therapists understand this anxiety and use this first contact to help put you at ease and tell you something about their practice (e.g., how often they meet with a client, their fees, their specialities, their approach). Two of my main goals in talking to potential patients in advance of the first visit is to help them feel more relaxed about this decision to see me and to express my intent to work together with them.

If you feel reluctant to make an appointment, it is fine simply to call a therapist and talk for a few minutes and possibly share your apprehension about coming in. If you still feel hesitant, remember that when you go to see a therapist, in a real sense, you are hiring him or her to assist you in a professional way. If for any reason you are not comfortable with the person, you don't have to go back. You are in control of that decision at all times.

• The third step in your selection process is to evaluate the therapist and the therapy process in general after the initial session. After talking to the therapist during the initial session, you will very likely be able to judge for yourself if this therapy seems to be a good approach for you. The therapist should provide considerable information about his/her approach and why it is appropriate to your needs. There should be an open discussion of such issues as fees, "informed consent," and any limits of confidentiality. You'll also be getting a "feel" for the therapist's personal style in relating to you. Important things to look for during the first session are: "Does the therapist seem to understand me?" and "Do I have a sense of hopefulness about her kind of treatment?" No type of treatment can resolve emotional issues immediately; it will take some time and effort on your part. But if your answers to the two questions are "yes," then you have reason to believe that working with this particular therapist may be beneficial.

### Types of Mental Health Therapists
• *Psychiatrist (M.D.):* Psychiatrists are medical doctors who have received specialized training in the treatment of emotional problems, including both medication and psychological treatments. (It is possible for a physician to practice psychiatry without specialized training; however, very few do so. Again, it is appropriate to ask about *any* professional's background, training and experience in dealing with conditions like yours.) Most psychiatrists treat emo-

tional disorders with medications. Some psychiatrists also provide psychotherapy, behavior therapy, or cognitive therapy. "Board certification" is an advanced designation granted by the profession to those psychiatrists who are especially well-qualified.

• *Psychologist:* Psychologists hold doctoral degrees in psychology (Ph.D., Psy.D., Ed.D.), have three or four years of postgraduate training in psychological methods, and in most states, are licensed to practice. They also have specialized training in the administration and interpretation of psychological tests. The most advanced designation for a practicing psychologist is that of "Diplomate" of the American Board of Examiners in Professional Psychology.

• *Clinical Social Worker:* Clinical social workers generally hold masters degrees (M.S.W.), have considerable supervised experience and are usually licensed by the state (hence the designation, "L.C.S.W." — Licensed Clinical Social Worker). A nationally recognized certification is "A.C.S.W." — for members of the Academy of Clinical Social Workers.

• *Marriage Family and Child Counselors/Therapists:* Some states grant licenses to Marriage, Family and Child Counselors (or Marriage, Family and Child Therapists). Such therapists generally have at least a masters degree in counseling (M.A. or M.S.), usually with specialization in treatment of marriage and family problems or problems of children and adolescents. "Clinical Member" or "Supervisor" designations by the American Association for Marital and Family Therapy are further evidence of qualifications of MFCC's.

• *Pastoral Counselors:* Some clergy have received training in counseling and may provide supportive therapy to members of their church or to others desiring a therapist who addresses both emotional and spiritual concerns. A few pastoral counselors are also qualified under one of the categories above.

### If At First You Don't Succeed

Not all people experience a positive outcome in psychotherapy. Hundreds of research studies have looked closely at the effectiveness of psychotherapy and have found that most people who enter treatment do benefit. However, a significant minority do not, and this may come as no surprise. Not all people who go to school graduate; not all people who go to doctors are cured. A number of factors certainly influence the eventual outcome of psychotherapy. If you have been in treatment and the experience was not positive or helpful, it may be important to consider the following reasons:

- *The chemistry has to be "good enough."* Not everyone will make a good connection with even very good therapists. However, the client must feel some degree of comfort and compatibility with a therapist. You may not feel 100% comfortable with your therapist, but it is quite important to feel a basic sense of trust; the perception that you and your feelings are being treated with respect; and some degree of confidence that your therapist is competent. First and foremost, good therapists, beyond being well-trained and skilled, need to be basically good, decent people. Unfortunately, there are some in practice who are not.

Although you may not initially hit it off with your therapist, giving the treatment a chance is helpful. Most people feel at least somewhat uncomfortable at the beginning of therapy and simply need a while to settle in. Some therapies fail because people bail out too early. But therapies also fail because there truly is not a good fit between therapist and client. If that's the case for you, start looking for another professional in whom you'll have confidence.

- *The type of treatment must be appropriate.* Not all problems are best approached in the same manner. While individual therapy may be the treatment of choice for some, in other instances, couples' therapy, family therapy or group therapy may be more effective. In addition, the theoretical orientation of the therapist is a factor. Only a small fraction of therapists practice "psychoanalysis"; however, many lay people are aware only of that "talking cure" approach. Other important therapeutic procedures include behavior therapy, cognitive therapy, existential-gestalt therapy, "client-centered" therapy, Adlerian therapy, Jungian therapy and more. Ask lots of questions in your first interview and satisfy yourself that your therapist's recommended (and usual) approach is right for you. A good therapist will evaluate your situation within the first session or two, and talk with you about what kind of treatment he or she recommends.

Some types of emotional problems are due either in part or in full to medical/biochemical disturbances. These problems may simply not be helped adequately by psychotherapy alone. Medical treatment and/or psychiatric medication treatment may be helpful or even necessary (see Appendices A and B).

• *Some therapies/therapists can be destructive.* Any approach powerful enough to help can be powerful enough to cause harm if in the hands of an incompetent or destructive therapist. Most licensed therapists are well-trained and helpful to most of their clients. However, as in any other profession, incompetence and/or unethical behavior does exist.

In the practice of psychotherapy, relating to a patient in non-professional ways is absolutely not appropriate, ethical, or legal. This means that social friendships outside the therapy hour, business deals, or intimate involvement is prohibited by the professional code of ethics. Such "dual relationships" are never helpful and may create extreme distress for clients. Ethical misbehavior on the part of a therapist should be reported to licensing boards (e.g., State Medical Board, Psychology Board or the Ethics Committee of the local professional society; for example, County Medical Association).

Some therapists use approaches intended to be helpful, but the result is extremely negative. These practitioners may not be willfully trying to exploit or hurt patients, but simply may be poorly trained or incompetent. If you sense such a circumstance, don't hesitate to terminate the relationship.

• *Psychotherapy is not a panacea.* In some instances, the very best efforts of well-qualified therapists are simply not enough. Treatment methods help the large majority of patients entering psychotherapy, but for some people, psychotherapy may be ineffective or only partially helpful. In medicine, some grave conditions (e.g., terminal cancer) do not respond to even heroic treatment attempts. In such cases, the doctor's goal is to do his best to reduce suffering and help the patient strive for the best quality of life possible. This limited goal sometimes applies to emotional and mental illness, too.

If you have been in a treatment that failed or are currently in a destructive or unproductive treatment, please do not lose hope. Many people have made the decision to seek out another therapist and go on to achieve very good results. You are hiring a therapist to provide a service, and if it doesn't help, you can fire your therapist. Don't bail out too quickly and try to discuss any feelings of dissatisfaction with your therapist directly. (This often can be extremely helpful.) But if in your heart you know your current therapy is not right for you, find another therapist. It's your right.

## Nineteen

## Pathways To Healing

**D**on't lose sight of our common humanity. Therein lies frailty and limitations and the capacity to experience emotional pain. Yet within most human beings is tremendous potential for survival, resiliency, aliveness and growth.

*My garden **
— by Marian Szczepanski

*My garden grows*
*ever slowly.*
*New shoots bloom, then bend.*
*To the cold, wild wind they often bow.*

*My garden knows*
*the heavy blows*
*of aimless, hurling hailstones,*
*the careless footfalls of friends turned foes.*

*My garden's rows*
*shrink from the glow,*
*undone by an incessant sun,*
*don drought's brown, crackling clothes.*

*My garden's throes*
*crave peace, repose.*
*But, though it cowers from many ills,*
*it sometimes flowers. It, stubborn, grows.*

In this last chapter, we'll meet our four "example" people from the Introduction to see how they decided to approach their own life crises. Each took a different path, but common to all were two elements: finding the courage within to face the truth of their pain and turning to others for support.

---

*Reprinted with permission from the author.*

<u>Sharon</u>

After eight or nine months of deepening despair, Sharon entered psychotherapy. At first she felt uneasy about taking this step. She told her therapist, "I'm not sure if I even need to be here... things aren't *that* bad." However, her therapist encouraged her to talk, and by the end of the first session, she had decided that her choice to enter therapy was right. She saw her therapist once a week for five months.

"I guess I never felt my feelings really counted. They didn't matter to my mom or dad, they didn't matter to Tim, and lots of times, they really didn't even matter to me. I kept thinking I was being too sensitive, that what I wanted was selfish and not realistic. Many times I remember saying to myself, 'You should be thankful for what you have. Stop complaining...' "

"In therapy my counselor really listened to me. Sometimes I'd think my thoughts or emotions were stupid or silly, but he confirmed that they were important and took me seriously."

"I think that two main things happened in my therapy. One was that I really started to believe I have a right to want a happy marriage. I'm not convinced Tim will ever be all I want him to be, but at least *my* needs and feelings are important to me. Another thing is that I learned how to speak my mind. I started to be a lot more direct with Tim. My therapist recommended a book on assertiveness, I read it and in therapy sessions, practiced what I wanted to say to Tim."

"When I did actually talk to Tim directly, he wasn't too wild about the 'new me.' It pissed him off and I think it kind of scared him. But over the last couple of months, I have felt better. I feel good when I come right out with how I truly feel. And overall, Tim seems to be more willing to really listen to me. Things aren't perfect in our marriage and the issue regarding having kids still isn't resolved — but mainly I'm the one who made changes. It's made a big difference in my life."

Many people like Sharon benefit tremendously from short-term counseling. In a few months of therapy very deep wounds may not heal completely, but brief therapy can help people get unstuck and back on track. For Sharon, the therapy experience was very helpful, but the majority of her own healing came from within herself, because she was able to recognize her true inner self and take steps toward growth.

---

### Dale

Dale received a good deal of support from friends during the first six months after Joyce's death. But after this time, the support seemed to drop off. He seemed to think that most people in his life thought he was "over it." On occasion when he did mention Joyce to his friends and felt tearful, he got the strong impression that it was "not ok" to still be grieving.

Dale went to his minister for only two counseling sessions. During the first session, his pastor helped Dale to see that his continued grieving was absolutely normal, appropriate, and probably necessary. He loved Joyce, they had been married for twenty-three years, and his heart ached.

The pastor suggested that Dale go to a local bereavement support group. Although he was a little reluctant, Dale did decide to go; he attended this first meeting three weeks later. The group was lead by a social worker and by a very old woman who was herself a widow. (This lady had organized the group some ten years before.) All sorts of people were at the meeting: several widows and widowers, a brother and sister who had lost their younger sister in a car accident, five or six people who had lost a parent, and one couple whose child had died.

"The first meeting was pretty intense... I only talked for about a minute. The leader said it was fine not to talk if I didn't want to. And it was kind of scary, but it was good. These people seemed to understand about grief. I feel support from the group, but not pity. I feel like we are a bunch of people traveling through a hard part of life together. The group has been a tremendously important support for me."

Dale visited with his pastor a second and last time about six months after the initial session just to touch base with him. Dale clearly was still grieving, but his feelings made sense to him, and he felt hopeful about the future.

"I'll always love Joyce... I'll always miss her... and I've decided that I want more life. But she'll always be in my heart."

## Gary

"The cancer was bad, but the worst part was the worry. I spent several months being scared out of my wits. I couldn't stop worrying about it... I was so scared that my life was over. Looking back on it now, I know that talking with my friend Neal was the single most important thing I did that helped me. Just like when I was a kid and I'd visit my grandfather, I could say anything to him. It was great. I should have known that really opening up to someone would help. But I felt ashamed... I felt like I needed to 'be a man' and tough it out."

"The first time I really opened up to Neal, I started to cry and I felt embarrassed. But he just looked me straight in the eye and didn't seem the least bit uneasy. That reaction meant so much to me. And when he said it was ok to talk again, he really meant it. He periodically called to see how I was doing. Sometimes I would say 'Oh, I'm ok,' then Neal would say 'Oh, really?! Don't bullshit me Gary.' And his response made it easier to talk about how I really felt."

"I often worried that I'd burn Neal out, but actually we only got into 'heavy' talks five or six times during the last few months. He never seemed to mind. He's a good guy, and I love him."

Fortunately, Gary's cancer treatment was successful and the disease did not return. His pathway to emotional healing came from the support he felt from his good friend and his own courage to risk opening up to Neal. It would have been easy to stay locked within the prison of his own mind, to grit his teeth and tough it out alone. But Gary reached out to another, and it made the difference. Who knows? Perhaps it aided his recovery from the cancer as well.

---

### Katherine

Katherine has now been in therapy for two years. Although she still has occasional waves of memories and pain, they are less frequent and intense. She at times is weary of therapy and dealing with the painful past, and sometimes wishes the memories had not returned. However, on a deeper level, she knows that she now feels more solid about herself than she ever has. She has experienced a new sense of acceptance of who she is and the reality of her past. In addition, she feels an increasing sense of inner strength; and the old feelings of shame and self-hatred have diminished.

Katherine is deeply connected to her therapist, whom she has struggled to trust. "After I had been betrayed and hurt so much by people, it was hard to truly trust and be vulnerable with anyone — including my therapist. I kept expecting him to hurt and use me like the neighbor did or not believe me like my mother had, but he didn't. My faith in people has begun to grow as a result. This experience of being very vulnerable in talking to another person about the awful memories and experiencing a caring, appropriate response without shame or manipulation has really helped me to heal. I know I have more work to do in therapy, and I don't know how much longer it will take. But I now can see the light at the end of the tunnel and know I will not only make it through this but will be a stronger, more confident person as a result."

When people sustain very deep hurts either in childhood or in adulthood, the road to healing is difficult. Psychotherapy can often make *the* difference. But quick cures are the real exception and not the rule. Katherine eventually completed therapy after three years of weekly sessions. Her courage and willingness and the sense of safe connection with her therapist allowed her to come to terms with the pain. Like many people who have faced apparently overwhelming despair, Katherine has been helped to reach inside herself, to discover unknown strengths and resources, to face her human pain, to survive, to heal and to grow.

It's sometimes been said that in the wake of hard times, the best revenge is to live life well. How? By giving life your best shot, accepting your human limitations, striving to live the truth of who you really are, and being decent to yourself. People are pretty remarkable. Their courage, strength, tenderness and capacity for love are the human "stuff" that allow most to make it... to survive, to heal and to grow in aliveness.

I sincerely hope that this book has been of help to you as you travel on the journey that is your life.

*APPENDICES:*

# APPENDIX A

## Symptoms of Major Adult Psychiatric Disorders

The following list can serve as a guideline for recognizing the signs and symptoms of major psychological disorders. The list does not include all emotional/mental disorders, however, the most commonly encountered syndromes are highlighted. Please note that these disorders are generally severe enough to warrant psychiatric or psychological treatment. Effective treatments (psychotherapies and medical treatment) are available for most of the disorders listed below.

*If you suffer persistent symptoms of any of these disorders, please strongly consider consulting with a mental health professional.*

**Depression** *(other common names: Major Depression, Clinical Depression)*
- Mood of sadness, despair, emptiness
- Anhedonia (loss of ability to experience pleasure)
- Low self-esteem, feelings of inadequacy
- Apathy, low motivation, and social withdrawal
- Excessive emotional sensitivity
- Negative, pessimistic thinking
- Irritability, anger outbursts
- Suicidal ideas
- Sleep disturbance (early morning awakening, frequent awakenings throughout the night, occasionally hypersomnia: excessive sleeping)
- Appetite disturbance (decreased or increased, with accompanying weight loss or gain)
- Fatigue
- Decreased sex drive
- Restlessness, agitation
- Impaired concentration and forgetfulness

**Manic-Depressive Disorder** *(Bi-polar Disorder)*

Episodes of serious depression (see symptoms above) alternating with periods of mania: Symptoms of mania include:

- A pronounced mood of euphoria (elevated or elated mood) or irritability
- Increased self-esteem
- Decreased need for sleep
- Rapid speech
- Racing thoughts
- Distractibility
- Increased activity
- Behavior that reflects expansiveness (lacking restraint in emotional expression) and poor judgement, such as increased sexual promiscuity, gambling, buying sprees, giving away money, etc. (APA, 1987)

**Dysthymia** *(mild, chronic depression)*

Prolonged (more than two years) mild symptoms of depression characterized mainly by the following:

- Low energy, day-time fatigue
- Decreased capacity for joy, "aliveness"
- Negative, pessimistic thinking
- Low self-esteem, feelings of inadequacy

**Phobic Disorders**

- *Social Phobia* Fearful feelings when in social situations; fears of embarrassment and humiliation
- *Agoraphobia* Fears of being in places from which escape may be difficult; e.g. fears of driving across a bridge, fears of being outside familiar settings, fear of crowds, fears of traveling.

---

*N.B. The notation "(APA, 1987)" is a reference to the* Diagnostic and Statistical Manual of Mental Disorders *of the American Psychiatric Association. See References.*

**Panic Disorder** *(anxiety attacks, anxiety disorder)*
Episodes of intense anxiety (usually lasting from 30 seconds to 10 minutes). Often these symptoms seem to come out of the blue (i.e. not necessarily provoked by stress). Symptoms include:
- Trembling, feeling shaky, restlessness, muscle tension
- Shortness of breath, smothering sensation
- Rapid heartbeat
- Sweating and cold hands and feet
- Lightheadedness and dizziness
- Panicy feelings: fears of death, loss of control or fears of going crazy
- Phobias
- Feelings of unreality

**Post-Traumatic Stress Disorder**
This disorder presents with a rather characteristic group of symptoms in response to exposure to life events that are either extremely dangerous or frightening and/or in which a person encounters a tremendous sense of powerlessness. The event may be a recent trauma or may be an event that occurred many years earlier (in the latter case, a person may massively block out the memory and feelings of the original event(s), which months or years later begin to surface in the form of intrusive memories or dreams). Symptoms include:
- Vivid re-experiencing of the traumatic event in thoughts, recollections or dreams. Extremely vivid recall of events result in an experience of mentally reliving the moment; these episodes are known as flashbacks
- Avoidance of situations which remind one of the traumatic event
- Memory impairment (e.g. amnesia for the event)
- Feelings of numbness, detachment and unreality
- Intense feelings of anxiety, irritability or depression
- Sleep distrubances
- Nightmares
- Stress related physical symptoms, e.g headaches

In extremely severe cases of emotional trauma encountered in childhood, particular types of post-traumatic stress disorder can develop: Dissociative disorders and multiple-personality disorder.

### Anorexia Nervosa *(APA, 1987)*
- Abnormal concern about weight leading to extreme attempts to lose weight (e.g. dieting, exercise, laxatives)
- Body weight that falls below 15% of that expected given the person's age, sex and height
- In women, is often accompanied by the absense of menstrual cycles

### Bulimia *(APA, 1987)*
- Binge eating, followed by:
- Self-induced vomiting, laxatives, strict dieting, or excessive exercise to prevent weight gain

### Neurological Disorders
A host of neurologic disorders may present with psychological and emotional symptoms, in addition to sensory, motor and intellectual impairment. Almost any psychiatric symptom may be seen with neurologic disorders (e.g. anxiety, depression, etc.). In addition to psychological symptoms, the cardinal signs of possible brain dysfunction include the following:
- Confusion, disorientation
- Memory impairment
- Difficulties with: speech, reading, spelling, or hand writing
- Sensory changes (impaired hearing, smell, vision, touch or taste)
- Balance, coordination and gait problems. Slurred speech
- Over-sensitivity to lights or noises
- Muscular weakness
- Unexplained drowsiness or loss of consciousness

If any of the above symptoms are noted, one should immediately seek medical attention.

### Substance Abuse Disorders

This includes the use/abuse of a wide array of substances including alcohol, stimulants, cocaine, heroin, marijuana, hallucinogens and the excessive use of caffeine and nicotine.

### Obsessive-Compulsive Disorder

Recurring, persistent unpleasant or senseless thoughts or impulses which are difficult to prevent or ignore. Behavior includes repetitive actions or rituals carried out in an attempt to reduce obsessive ideas (e.g. repeatedly checking to see if doors and windows are locked; repeatedly washing hands). Such thoughts and actions are not just occasional in obsessive-compulsive disorder. In this disorder these symptoms come to dominate a person's life and can be the source of considerable despair.

### Psychotic Disorders *(including schizophrenia, some forms of bipolar disorder and paranoia)*

- Hallucinations
- Confusion and grossly impaired judgement
- Delusions (extremely unrealistic or bizarre thoughts/beliefs)
- Profound feelings of apathy, emptiness
- Agitation or chaotic behavior

### Severe Personality Disorders *(including borderline personality disorder) (APA, 1987)*

- Long standing pattern of very intense, unstable relationships with others
- Marked emotional instability
- Impulse control problems including: self-mutilation, suicide attempts, violence toward others, substance abuse, sexual promiscuity
- Bouts of severe anxiety and/or depression
- Intense fears of abandonment or being alone
- Chronic feelings of emptiness

## How Common Are Major Emotional Disorders?

| | Life-Time Prevalence Rate |
|---|---|
| **Anxiety Disorders** | |
| Panic Disorder | 2-4% |
| Phobias | 3-5% |
| Generalized Anxiety | 2-4% |
| Post-Traumatic Stress Disorder | 1% |
| Obsessive-Compulsive | 1-3% |
| **Depressive Disorders** | |
| Major Despression | 2-3% (men) |
| | 5-10% (women) |
| Dysthymia | 3% |
| Bi-Polar Disorder | 1% |
| **Schizophrenia** (and other Psychotic Disorders) | 1% |
| **Anorexia Nervosa** | 1-2% (adolescent girls) |
| **Bulimia** | 4-15% (adolescent girls) |
| | 1-2% (adolescent boys) |
| **Substance Abuse** | |
| Alcoholism | 14% |
| Other Substances* | 6% |
| **Severe Personality Disorders** | 4-5% |

*Excluding caffeine and tobacco

# APPENDIX B

## Medical Disorders and Drugs
## That May Cause Psychiatric Symptoms

If you are experiencing emotional symptoms it is very important to first determine if the symptoms are being caused by a medical condition and/or drugs. If this is suspected, consult a physician.

## Depression

*Common **medical conditions** that may cause symptoms of depression:*

- AIDS
- Alcoholism
- Anemia
- Chronic infection (e.g., mononucleosis, TB chronic fatigue syndrome)
- Chronic pain syndromes (e.g., fibromyalgia)
- Head injury
- Hormonal changes associated with premenstrual syndrome, childbirth and menopause
- Hypothyroidism
- Infectious Hepatitis
- Influenza
- Malignancies (cancer)
- Strokes

*Widely-used **drugs** that may cause depression:*

- *Antihypertensives* (for high blood pressure and migraine headaches) — e.g., reserpine, propranolol, methyldopa
- *Steroids* — e.g., cortisone
- *Hormones* — e.g., estrogen, progesterone
- *Antiparkinson Drugs* — e.g., levodopa, carbidopa, amantadine
- *Tranquilizers* — e.g., diazepam, Valium, Librium
- *Birth Control Pills*
- *Alcohol* — wine, beer, spirits

## Anxiety

*Common **medical conditions** that may cause anxiety:*

- Alcoholism
- Delirium*
- Head injury
- Hypoglycemia
- Hyperthyroidism
- Mitral valve prolapse**
- Premenstrual syndrome


\* Delirium can occur as a result of many toxic/metabolic conditions and often produces anxiety and agitation.

\*\* The mitral valve prolapse probably does not cause anxiety, but it has been found that MVP and anxiety disorders often coexist. This may be due to some underlying common genetic factor.


*Widely-used **drugs** that may cause anxiety:*

- Alcohol (withdrawal)
- Amphetamines
- Asthma medications
- Caffeine
- Cocaine
- Nasal decongestant sprays
- Tranquilizers (withdrawal)
- Steroids

## REFERENCES

Alberti, R., & Emmons, M. (1990). *Your Perfect Right* (sixth edition). San Luis Obispo, CA: Impact Publishers, Inc.

American Psychiatric Association (1987). *Diagnostic and Statistical Manual of Mental Disorders - III*. Washington, DC: A.P.A.

Andreason, N. (1984). *The Broken Brain*. New York: Harper & Row.

Bass, E. and Davis, L. (1988). *The Courage to Heal*. New York: Harper and Row.

Beck, A. T. and Emery, G. (1985). *Anxiety Disorders and Phobias*. New York: Basic Books.

Beck, A. (1967). *Depression: Causes and Treatments*. Philadelphia, PA: University of Pennsylvania Press.

Benson, H. (1975). *The Relaxation Response*. New York: Avon.

Blank, G. and Blank, R. (1975). *Ego Psychology*. New York: Psychotherapy Tape Library.

Bly, R. (1990). *Iron John*. Reading, MA: Addison-Wesley Publishing Co.

Bower, S. A. and Bower, G. H., (1976). *Asserting Your Self*. Reading, MA: Addison-Wesley Publishing Co.

Bradshaw, J. (1989). *The Family*. Deerfield Beach, FL: Health Communications, Inc.

Budman, S. and Gurman, A. (1988). *Theory and Practice of Brief Therapy*. New York: The Guilford Press.

Buntman, P. H. and Saris, E. M. (1980). *How to Live with Your Teenager*. Waco, TX: Success Motivation, Inc.

Burns, D. D. (1980). *Feeling Good*. New York: Signet.

Cohler, B. J. and Boxer, A. M. (1984). Middle Adulthood. In D. Offer and M. Sabshin (Eds.). *Normality and the Life Cycle*. New York: Basic Books.

Coleman, J. C., Butcher, J. N. and Carson, R. C. (1980). *Abnormal Psychology and Modern Life*. Glenview, IL: Scott, Foresman & Co.

Colgrove, M., Bloomfield, H., & McWilliams, P. (1976). *How to Survive the Loss of a Love*. New York: Bantam.

Daro, D. (1989). *The Most Frequently "Asked About" Issues Regarding Child Abuse and Neglect*. Toledo, OH: N.C.E. Foundation for the Prevention of Child Abuse.

Davis, M., Eshelman, E. R., & McKay, M. (1982). *The Relaxation and Stress Reduction Workbook.* Oakland, CA: New Harbinger.

Doak, J. L. (1987). *Coming to Life.* Nevada City, CA: Blue Dolphin Publishing.

Duveneck, M. J., Portwood, M. M., Wicks, J. J., and Lieberman, J. S. (1986). Depression in Myotonic Muscular Dystrophy. *Archives of Physical Medicine and Rehabilitation.* Vol. 67, pages 875-877.

Emmons, M. L. and Alberti, R. E. (1991). *Accepting Each Other: Individuality and Intimacy in Your Loving Relationship.* San Luis Obispo, CA: Impact Publishers, Inc.

Fieve, R. (1975). *Mood Swings.* New York: Bantam Books.

Fisher, B. (1981). *Rebuilding: When Your Relationship Ends.* San Luis Obispo, CA: Impact Publishers, Inc.

Fiske, D. W. and Maddi, S. R. (Eds.) (1961). *Functions of Varied Experience.* Homewood, IL: Dorsey.

Garbarino, J., Guttman, E. and Seeley, J. W. (1986). *The Psychologically Battered Child.* San Francisco: Jossey-Bass Publishers.

Garmezy, N. (1983). "Resilience to the Development of Psychological Disorders." Talk presented at Pennsylvania State University.

Gil, E. (1983). *Outgrowing the Pain.* Walnut Creek, CA: Launch Press.

Helmlinger, T. (1982). *After You've Said Good-bye.* Sacramento: Brooks Publishing.

Horney, K. (1950). *Neurosis and Human Growth. New York: W.W. Norton & Co.*

Horowitz, M. J. (1976). *Stress Response Syndromes.* New York: Jason Aronson.

Isaacs, K. S. (1990). *A Psychoanalytic Re-examination of Affect.* Paper presented at the 1990 American Psychological Association Annual Conference.

Janoff-Bulman, R. (1992). *Shattered Assumptions.* New York: Free Press.

Johnson, S. M. (1985). *Characterological Transformation.* New York: W. W. Norton and Co.

Johnson, S. M. (1987). *Humanizing the Narcissistic Style.* New York: W. W. Norton and Co.

Konner, M. (1982). *The Tangled Wing: Biological Constraints on the Human Spirit*. New York: Henry Holt and Co..

Kushner, H. S. (1981). *When Bad Things Happen To Good People*. New York: Avon.

Kushner, H. S. (1986). *When All You've Ever Wanted Isn't Enough*. New York: Pocket Books.

Lerner, H. G. (1989). *The Dance of Intimacy*. New York: Harper and Row.

Mahler, M. S. (1975). *The Psychological Birth of the Human Infant*. New York: Basic Books.

Mahoney, M. J. (1983). "Constructive Psychotherapy." Talk presented at Monterey, California.

Mahoney, M. J. (1991). *Human Change Processes*. New York: Basic Books.

Mantell, M. R. (1988). *Don't Sweat the Small Stuff: P.S. It's All Small Stuff!* San Luis Obispo, CA: Impact Publishers, Inc.

Marmar, C. R. (1991). "Grief and Bereavement After Traumatic Loss." *Audio Digest Psychiatry*, Vol. 20, Number 5.

Maslow, A. H. (Ed.) (1970). *Motivation and Personality*. New York: Harper and Row.

Masterson, J. F. (1986). *The Real Self*. New York: Masterson Group, P.C..

Millon, T. (1981). *Disorders of Personality*. New York: John Wiley and Sons.

Moyers, B. (1993). *Healing And The Mind*. New York: Doubleday.

Ornstein, R.E., & Thompson, R.F. (1986). *The Amazing Brain*. Boston, MA: Houghton Mifflin.

Osterweis, M., Solomon, F. and Green, M. (1984). *Bereavement: Reactions, Consequences and Care*. Washington, DC: National Academy Press.

Peck, M. S. (1990). *Growing Up Painfully, Consciousness and the Problem of Pain*. New York: Simon and Schuster.

Peck, M. S. (1983). *People of the Lie: The Encounter with Evil in Everyday Life*. New York: Simon and Schuster.

Peck, M. S. (1978). *The Road Less Traveled*. New York: Simon and Schuster, Inc..

Peebles, M. J. (1987). *Diagnosis of Post-Traumatic Stress Disorder*. Topeka, KS: Menninger Video Productions.

Preston, J. (1989). *You Can Beat Depression: A Guide To Recovery.* San Luis Obispo, CA: Impact Publishers, Inc.

Preston, J. D., & Johnson, J. (1991). *Clinical Psychopharmacology Made Ridiculously Simple.* Miami, FL: MedMaster.

Quackenbush, R. L. (1991). "The prescription of self-help books by psychologists: A bibliography of selected bibliotherapy resources." *Psychotherapy,* Vol. 28, Number 4. 1991. Pages 671- 677.

Rakos, R. F. and Schroeder, H. E. (1980). *Self-Directed Assertiveness Training* (audiotape). New York: Guilford Publications, Inc..

Seligman, M. E. P. (1975). *Helplessness.* San Francisco: W.H. Freeman.

Stephen, F. J. (1974). *Liberty, Equality and Fraternity.* 2nd edition. London: Smith Elder.

Straehley, C. J. (1990). *Expanding Your Ability to Love Yourself.* Sacramento, CA: Unpublished manuscript.

Straehley, C. J. (1991). Personal Communication.

Szczepanski, M. (1992). *My Garden.* Sacramento, CA: Unpublished manuscript.

Terr, L. C. (1991). "Childhood Traumas: An Outline and Overview." *American Journal of Psychiatry,* Vol. 148, Number 1. 1991. Pages 10-20.

Viscott, D. (1978). *The Language of Feelings.* Waco, TX: Success Motivation, Inc.

Winnicott, D. W. (1965). *Maturational Precesses and the Facilitating Environment.* New York: International Universities Press.

Young, J. E. (1990). *Cognitive Therapy for Personality Disorders.* Sarasota, FL: Professional Resource Press.

# INDEX